Developing Around Transit

Strategies and Solutions That Work

Robert T. Dunphy
Robert Cervero
Frederick C. Dock
Maureen McAvey
Douglas R. Porter
Carol J. Swenson

**Urban Land
Institute**

ABOUT ULI–THE URBAN LAND INSTITUTE

ULI–the Urban Land Institute is a nonprofit education and research institute that is supported by its members. Its mission is to provide responsible leadership in the use of land in order to enhance the total environment.

ULI sponsors education programs and forums to encourage an open international exchange of ideas and sharing of experiences; initiates research that anticipates emerging land use trends and issues and proposes creative solutions based on that research; provides advisory services; and publishes a wide variety of materials to disseminate information on land use and development. Established in 1936, the Institute today has more than 23,000 members and associates from more than 80 countries representing the entire spectrum of the land use and development disciplines.

Richard M. Rosan
President

For more information about ULI and the resources that it offers related to development around transit and a variety of other real estate and urban development issues, visit ULI's Web site at www.uli.org.

Recommended bibliographic listing:

Dunphy, Robert T., et al. *Developing Around Transit: Strategies and Solutions That Work*. Washington, D.C.: ULI–the Urban Land Institute, 2004.

ULI Catalog Number: D106
International Standard Book Number: 0-87420-917-X
Library of Congress Control Number: 2004115049

Cover photo: Canary Wharf, London, England
© Luis Veiga/Photographer's Choice/Getty Images

ULI PROJECT STAFF

Rachelle L. Levitt
Executive Vice President, Policy and Practice
Publisher

Gayle Berens
Vice President, Real Estate Development Practice

Robert T. Dunphy
Senior Resident Fellow for Transportation and
    Infrastructure
Project Director

Nicole E. Witenstein
Research Assistant

Nancy H. Stewart
Director, Book Program

James A. Mulligan
Managing Editor

Libby Howland
Manuscript Editor

Betsy VanBuskirk
Art Director/Book Design

Helene Y. Redmond/HYR Graphics
Layout

Kim Rusch
Graphics

Diann Stanley-Austin
Director, Publishing Operations

Ronnie Van Alstyne
Senior Administrative Assistant

ACKNOWLEDGMENTS

Many individuals contributed their time and talents to this effort. I would like to thank especially my coauthors—Doug Porter, Maureen McAvey, Robert Cervero, Fred Dock, and Carol Swenson. Together they represent a breadth of knowledge, experience, and insight that has made it possible for *Developing Around Transit: Strategies and Solutions That Work* to thoroughly examine the transit, design, development, regulatory, market, and quality-of-life issues involved in development around transit. In a number of cases their work on this project meant putting off more remunerative work and they all graciously responded to my many requests for clarification, additional information, and photos, maps, and drawings.

I would also like to thank the people who diligently located and provided hard-to-obtain information for many of the project and program examples illustrating and expanding upon the points made by the contributing authors and for letting us adapt their work for this book—especially Katherine Gray Still, G.B. Arrington, and John Boroski of Parsons Brinckerhoff (Portland, Oregon), and Mike Mehaffy of Pacific Realty Associates (Portland, Oregon).

Developers, transit officials, designers, architects, planners, and local public officials too numerous to list provided written materials and photographs that are used in the book's examples of developing around transit—examples that are, perhaps, the key contribution of *Developing Around Transit* to actually promoting such development. These various individuals also answered my frequent questions on the details of their projects, programs, or policies, and reviewed drafts of the chapters, often on very short notice. I would like to thank especially Art Cueto of LandTran (Los Angeles), Alice Steiner of the Utah Transit Authority, Rosemary Siciliano of Goody Clancy & Associates (Boston), and David Leland of the Leland Consulting Group (Portland, Oregon) for their generosity in sharing photos.

ULI and I also appreciate the work performed by the reviewers of the manuscript, which helped assure that the overall direction and conclusions of this book are useful to the development and transit communities. These reviewers are listed following these acknowledgments. In 2002, a task force of 17 planning, development, and transit experts convened by ULI devised ten principles for successful development around transit, which form the core of this book's final chapter. The members of this task force are also listed following the acknowledgments.

Finally, I would like to thank the numerous ULI staff members who helped me bring this book together. Nicole Witenstein, who jumped into this project in midstream, assisted with research and the often tortuous task of tracking down photos and data. Ronnie Van Alstyne diligently kept the project on track and enthusiastically helped me dig out unknown resources. Rachelle Levitt provided inspiration, leadership, support, and the resources needed to develop and publish a ULI book on the important subject of developing around transit. Many of the research directors in ULI's policy and practice department shared important ideas during a brown-bag lunch that kicked off work on the book, and they continued to provide me with insights, tidbits, news, and good contacts throughout the writing process. Libby Howland edited the manuscript, Betsy VanBuskirk designed the book and provided artwork, Helene Redmond laid out the book, Jim Mulligan managed the editing and production process, and Diann Stanley-Austin coordinated the book's publication.

To all who had a hand in this work, I extend my sincere appreciation and thanks.

Robert T. Dunphy
Project Director

AUTHORS AND REVIEWERS

PRINCIPAL AUTHOR

Robert T. Dunphy

Dunphy is senior resident fellow for transportation and infrastructure at the Urban Land Institute. He has more than 30 years of experience in the areas of traffic congestion, transit, transportation solutions, and parking—and the relationship of these issues to land use and development. His ULI work involves studies, speaking, and hands-on advice to communities throughout North America. He has contributed to numerous books and articles on traffic, transit, parking, and street design. He is an active member of the Transportation Research Board, the Institute of Transportation Engineers, and other national transportation committees. He has been a consultant, metropolitan transportation planner, and teacher.

CONTRIBUTING AUTHORS

Robert Cervero

Cervero is a professor of urban planning at the University of California, Berkeley, and has served as a visiting professor and researcher at several universities abroad. He has worked as a planner, consultant, legal expert, and speaker on land use and transportation issues throughout the world. His most recent books—*Transit-Oriented Development in the United States: Experiences, Challenges, and Prospects; The Transit Metropolis;* and *Transit Villages in the 21st Century*—focus on the role of public transit within metropolitan land use structures.

Frederick C. Dock

Dock is a traffic engineer and transportation planner with more than 25 years of experience. He is a principal with Meyer, Mohaddes Associates in Minneapolis. Educated at the University of California, Berkeley, his areas of expertise include livable communities and transit-oriented planning and design. His work with mixed-use centers, suburban transit-oriented development, context-based street design, and analytical tools to address connectivity and transit readiness is nationally recognized. He is an appointed member of the Metropolitan Council's Livable Communities Advisory Committee and is a director for the nonprofit Transit for Livable Communities.

Maureen L. McAvey

McAvey is a senior resident fellow and ULI/Klingbeil Family Chair for Urban Development at the Urban Land Institute. She has more than 25 years of experience in real estate development, consulting, and the creation of public/private financial structures. As senior fellow, she is a frequent speaker on changes in metropolitan growth patterns at meetings of real estate professionals and at major universities. Prior to joining ULI, she was director of business development for Federal Realty Investment Trust, director of development for the city of St. Louis, manager of the real estate consulting practices in Boston for Deloitte & Touche and for Coopers & Lybrand, and director of the West Coast operations of a national development firm.

Douglas R. Porter

Porter is president of the Growth Management Institute in Chevy Chase, Maryland. Well known as an authority on all forms of growth management, he conducts research and writes extensively about many aspects of community development, including transit-related development, and transportation and land use relationships. He wrote the books *Inclusionary Zoning for Affordable Housing* in 2004 and *Making Smart Growth Work* in 2003, both published by the Urban Land Institute. He is a fellow of the American Institute of Certified Planners and has urban and regional planning degrees from Michigan State University and the University of Illinois. He served for two years as chair of the Maryland Transportation Commission.

Carol J. Swenson

Swenson is a consultant with the Center for Policy, Planning, and Performance, a nonprofit organization in Minneapolis, Minnesota. She has more than ten years of experience working with communities and neighborhoods on issues of urban design and planning livable communities at the subregional and neighborhood scales. She has investigated transit-oriented development in suburban settings, the relationship between urban design and the design of central-city and suburban arterials, and the diversification of older suburban housing stock through transit-oriented development. Her work currently focuses on citizen engagement in the development of affordable housing on central-city transportation corridors.

REVIEWERS

Kenneth H. Hughes
President
Kenneth H. Hughes Inc.
Dallas, Texas

James Van Zee
Director, Regional Planning Services
Northern Virginia Regional Commission
Annandale, Virginia

Jack Wierzenski
Assistant Vice President, Economic Development and
    Planning
Dallas Area Rapid Transit
Dallas, Texas

ULI TASK FORCE ON DEVELOPMENT AROUND TRANSIT

TASK FORCE CHAIR

Marilyn J. Taylor
Skidmore, Owings & Merrill LLP
New York, New York

TASK FORCE MEMBERS

Anne P. Canby
Surface Transportation Planning Project
Washington, D.C.

Robert Cervero
University of California at Berkeley
Department of City and Regional Planning
Berkeley, California

Richard J. Dishnica
The Dishnica Company LLC
Point Richmond, California

Michael Dobbins
Georgia Institute of Technology
Atlanta, Georgia

Robert T. Dunphy
Urban Land Institute
Washington, D.C.

John Gosling
RTKL Associates
Washington, D.C.

Oscar L. Harris Jr.
Turner Associates/Architects and Planners
Atlanta, Georgia

Kenneth H. Hughes
Kenneth H. Hughes Inc.
Dallas, Texas

Steven R. Kellenberg
EDAW Inc.
Irvine, California

Sandra Kulli
Kulli Marketing
Malibu, California

Chris Luz
Lansing Melbourne Group, L.L.C.
East Lansing, Michigan

Maureen McAvey
Urban Land Institute
Washington, D.C.

John R. Shumway
The Concord Group
Newport Beach, California

Belinda M. Sward
Newland Communities
La Jolla, California

Marilee A. Utter
Citiventure Associates LLC
Denver, Colorado

Jack Wierzenski
Dallas Area Rapid Transit
Dallas, Texas

CONTENTS

DEVELOPING AROUND TRANSIT

CHAPTER ONE

ROBERT T. DUNPHY

WHO, WHAT, WHERE, WHY

In the 1990s, many planners and environmentalists began advocating transit-oriented development as a means of organizing suburban development near new light-rail systems. Transit orientation as a means of organizing development in urban areas, on the other hand, is both a more recent idea and an old idea that has been revived. After all, for older U.S. cities that grew up around transit systems—like New York, Chicago, Boston—the idea of transit-oriented development as a planning scheme seems obvious, if not redundant. While transit-oriented development as a concept has gained new currency lately in both Chicago and Boston, neither city can be viewed as a "Johnny come lately" to the concept.

Nor is the concept really new in the New York region, where New York City and its suburbs developed around transit during the first half of the 20th century. But since World War II, growth has largely followed highway corridors, ignoring the region's transit heritage. In 1997, New York's Regional Plan Association established a transit-friendly communities program by which it hopes to transform existing rail communities into truly transit-friendly places.[1]

But transit-oriented development requires transit. In many U.S. regions, waning or nonexistent transit service precludes development that is oriented to transit. As of

New York City exemplifies the potential symbiosis of transit and development. Because much of the city's growth occurred before the use of private automobiles became widespread, the street grid as well as the design of buildings are pedestrian and transit friendly. Of all commuting trips made by public transit in the United States, one-third occur within the New York City region.

2000, transit's market share among various modes of commuting reached 5 percent in only 13 large metropolitan areas. (All of Canada's six large metropolitan areas exceeded this share easily.)

A variety of terms have been applied to the concept of development near transit. The most widely used is "transit-oriented development" or "TOD," coined in the early 1990s by Peter Calthorpe, an urban designer and one of the founders of the new urbanism movement. Calthorpe has been a consultant on many regional TOD plans (including those for Portland, Oregon, and Salt Lake City), local TOD ordinances (including San Diego's 1992 TOD ordinance, the first such ordinance adopted in the United States), and transit-oriented project plans. When San Diego incorporated TOD in its development guidelines in 1992, the term was so well established that Michael Stepner, the planner who led the effort, acknowledged: "We bought a brand name."[2]

"Transit villages" is another term that has been widely used. It was popularized by Michael Bernick and Robert Cervero in their 1966 book, *Transit Villages for the 21st Century*. The term "transit villages" has been used in California state legislation. The state of New Jersey has designated 14 transit villages, which qualify for priority access to state urban renewal and transportation grants and coordinated technical assistance from ten state agencies.

A synthesis of practice published by the Transportation Research Board uses the term "transit-focused development."[3] The Puget Sound Regional Council in Seattle has adopted the term "transit station communities." Legislation in Minnesota refers to "transit-

supportive urban design." Other frequently used terms include "transit-related development" and "transit-friendly development."

This book is about "developing around transit." Its principal topic is the special considerations involved in developing in a transit district and it takes a broad view of the theme, well beyond the scripted and formulaic notion that the only kind of development that qualifies as TOD is a master-planned mix of retail uses, office uses, and different types of housing. While a range of uses and central planning is desirable for projects around transit, such development represents a small part of the potential. There are many undeveloped or underdeveloped areas near transit stations where some development is possible. Any development —small scale or large scale—in such locations is likely to enhance the urban qualities of the transit district, including the availability of transit. This book focuses on the relationship of development to transit, a relationship that is shaped largely by the project's location—whether it is downtown or in a suburban area.

Well-planned development around transit can benefit both transit and communities. It can help transit advocates counter what is known as the "1 percent argument," which says that because transit captures only a 1 percent share of personal travel in the United States, investment in transit is inefficient. (Actually, the most current survey puts transit's share at almost 2 percent, but the point is the same.) By taking advantage of prime locations served by transit as sites for land uses that are likely to provide customers for transit, developing around transit works to expand the transit market and justify investment in transit resources.

The community benefits of developing around transit are discernible in the goal statements of advocates of transit-oriented development: to create better communities and reduce driving by making walking and transit more realistic travel options. The so-called "four Ds" of transit-related development are distance, density, diversity, and design—which add up essentially to a concentration of development of different types oriented toward the street and within walking distance of a transit station. Transit-related development typically includes

• a variety of services within walking distance of the transit station;

• good pedestrian connections to transit and between buildings; and

• buildings that are outwardly oriented toward the street rather than inwardly oriented toward parking.

Developing around transit involves elements of community building that can help improve deteriorating neighborhoods—the kinds of neighborhoods that characterize many old transit districts. Furthermore, developing around transit requires more than individual transit-oriented development projects if it is to succeed as a community-building strategy. For individual transit stations, the challenge is to create an entire transit-oriented district. For metropolitan areas, developing around transit requires an underlying regional strategy focused on clustering housing and employment and on linking development nodes with transit.

On the community and regional levels, developing around transit requires planning that makes transit considerations a centerpiece of development strategies. Arlington County, Virginia, for example, took the opportunity provided by the construction of Washington's Metrorail system to encourage the development of station districts. (See page 75 in Chapter Three for a discussion of Arlington's station district policies.) Another example is provided by the development of central Contra Costa County, California, around the Pleasant Hill BART (Bay Area Rapid Transit) station. On the regional level, Toronto, Portland (Oregon), and Vancouver exemplify metropolitan areas in which transit is considered a key element in regional development strategies that encourage growth in some areas, including areas served by transit, and discourage it in others. Among the many other examples of places that emphasize transit as part of development are San Mateo County and other jurisdictions in the San Francisco Bay Area; San Diego County; Montgomery County, Maryland, in the Washington metropolitan area; Pasadena, California; and the cities of Plano and Richardson outside Dallas.

Dallas Area Rapid Transit

Some critics of the strategy of encouraging development around transit fault it for failing to solve the problems of sprawl. Economist Anthony Downs, for example, contends that even considerable improvements in transit are unlikely to contain the trend of outward expansion in growing metropolitan areas.[4] But transit-oriented development has never been put forth as a cure-all for the deep-rooted problems of sprawl. Solving sprawl would require a consensus on the benefits of the alternatives to sprawl and a willingness to say "no" to inappropriate development. While such a consensus is not in sight in most places, the simultaneous development of communities that support transit and of transit services that offer people acceptable travel options, which is eminently possible in many regions, would be a giant step in the right direction.

TOD has an evil brother, however, that might be named TAD—transit-adjacent development. Although located near transit, TAD is "evil" to the extent that it fails to provide good links to transit and incorporates land uses and development patterns that do not support transit. Clustering development near transit is not beneficial if the development and the transit are not functionally related. The transit accessibility

In the Sunbelt suburbs, much of the development adjacent to transit corridors is not particularly oriented to available transit. This picture shows the DART rail line heading toward downtown Dallas.

must add value to the location; and the development must generate transit riders. Development adjacent to a transit station that does not promote the use of transit burdens the community with the costs of higher-density development without offsetting transportation benefits. In fact, it can also make access to the transit station harder for transit users.

FACTORS FAVORING DEVELOPMENT AROUND TRANSIT

In the last few years, the appeal of developing around transit has benefited from numerous trends, including

- growing transit ridership;

- increased funding of transit;

- the emergence of a variety of new concepts and new kinds of investment in transit;

- strengthening of the market for intown living; and

- the growing popularity of smart growth and place making as development concepts.

Transit benefits from the resurgence of intown living in cities like Philadelphia, which are losing population overall, but gaining in the central area.

Bob Krist

With 9.5 billion trips in 2001, transit ridership in the United States reached a 40-year high. Between 1995 and 2001, ridership grew by 22 percent. Ridership has since dropped by 1 percent because of economic recession. Gains in ridership in New York, Boston, and Philadelphia—all primary transit markets—over the past decade are of particular note. The American Public Transportation Association credits a strong economy, improved customer service, and higher levels of public and private investment in public transportation. Transit ridership in Canada also is growing. According to the Canadian Urban Transit Association, transit trips in 2002 exceeded 1.5 billion for the first time in 12 years.

Funding for public transportation by all levels of government in the United States jumped 63 percent between 1990 and 2000, from $19 billion to almost $31 billion, with the implementation of the Intermodal Surface Transportation Efficiency Act of 1991 (ISTEA) and the Transportation Equity Act for the 21st Century (TEA-21, passed in 1998). Existing services have been expanded and major new transit services added.

Since 1990, light-rail service has made a first-time appearance in Baltimore, St. Louis, Dallas, Denver, Salt Lake City, Jersey City (New Jersey), and Houston. In the past decade, San Jose, Portland, San Diego, and Los Angeles expanded their light-rail networks and Los Angeles added heavy-rail and commuter-rail lines as well. Five new-start projects out of nine submitted were recommended for federal funding in 2004, at a cost of $8.4 billion. Another 28 projects, with a price tag of $35.4 billion, were approved for preliminary engineering.

Among the emerging new concepts in transit investment are bus rapid transit and people movers. Bus rapid transit (BRT) is a transit solution that is gaining interest. Transit aficionados who have studied the development of the pioneering bus rapid-transit system in Curitiba, Brazil, now can point to a number of North American examples—in Ottawa, Vancouver, Boston, and Los Angeles—and a growing list of U.S. BRT projects, including a federally sponsored program involving ten jurisdictions. People movers are a transit technology that has proved workable in airports and downtowns but that has yet to be put into more general use. However, a four-mile monorail serving the Las Vegas resort corridor opened in 2004, and its extension to downtown by 2007 is planned.

Census data confirm a stronger market for intown living in general. In the 1990s, a number of major cities experienced significant increases in both downtown and citywide populations, as shown in figure 1-1. These cities include Boston and Chicago, which are primary transit markets; urbanized cities, like Seattle, Denver, and Portland; and even some low-density Sunbelt cities like Atlanta and Houston. Other major cities that experienced population decline citywide

Figure 1-1

DOWNTOWN GROWTH, SELECTED CITIES, 1990–2000

	Change in Population			Change in Population	
	Downtown	Citywide		Downtown	Citywide
GROWING DOWNTOWNS, GROWING CITIES			**GROWING DOWNTOWNS, DECLINING CITIES**		
Houston	69.0%	19.8%	Cleveland	32.2%	−5.4%
Seattle	67.4	9.1	Norfolk	20.5	−10.3
Chicago	51.4	4.0	Baltimore	5.1	−11.5
Denver	51.4	18.6	Philadelphia	4.9	−4.3
Portland, Oregon	35.4	21.0	Detroit	2.9	−7.5
Atlanta	25.1	5.7	Milwaukee	2.5	−5.0
Memphis	18.2	6.5	**DECLINING DOWNTOWNS, GROWING CITIES**		
San Diego	16.1	10.2	Charlotte	−0.7%	36.6%
Colorado Springs	7.2	28.4	San Antonio	−5.9	22.3
Los Angeles	5.7	6.0	Lexington	−6.1	15.6
Boston	4.5	2.6	Phoenix	−9.1	34.3
Des Moines	0.3	2.8	**DECLINING DOWNTOWNS, DECLINING CITIES**		
			Cincinnati	−16.9%	−9.0%
			St. Louis	−17.5	−12.2

Source: Rebecca Sohmer and Robert Lang, "Downtown Rebound," *Census Notes* (Fannie Mae Foundation and Brookings Institution Center on Urban and Metropolitan Policy), 2001, p. 5.

saw an increase in their downtown populations, which represents the best transit market in most cities. Among these cities are Philadelphia, Baltimore, and Cleveland, all of which are good transit markets. Other cities—including San Antonio and Phoenix—have experienced citywide growth but a decline in their downtown populations.

Developers and local public officials increasingly are embracing the concepts of smart growth and place making, which emphasize compact growth and infill development. These forms of growth and development support transit services and seek locations that are well served by public transportation. They tend to favor developing around transit.

Also contributing to the appeal of developing around transit are the harmful effects of car travel on air quality and the traffic problems arising from the inability of growing regions to add sufficient road capacity to keep pace with development.

FACTORS HINDERING DEVELOPMENT AROUND TRANSIT

The trends favoring more development around transit operate in a context of prevailing development patterns and regional politics that discourage or at least fail to encourage transit-related development. Furthermore, most growth in the United States is occurring outside the places where transit works best.

Transit is something of a conundrum. It works best serving high-density, generally low-income communities located close to a major downtown, like New York—communities that developed before automobile travel was an option. It works worst serving low-density, auto-oriented Sunbelt suburbs, like Dallas.

Overall metropolitan growth trends in the United States—particularly, the fact that more growth is occurring in suburbs than in cities and the fact that more growth is occurring in metropolitan regions

Figure 1-2

TRANSIT'S COMMUTE SHARE IN FASTEST-GROWING LARGE METROPOLITAN AREAS,[1] 2000

	2000 Population	1990–2000 Growth		Transit's Commute Share
		Number	Percent	
Las Vegas	1,563,282	710,545	83%	4.1%
Austin	1,249,763	403,536	48	2.6
Phoenix	3,251,876	1,013,396	45	2.0
Atlanta	4,112,198	1,152,248	39	3.7
Raleigh/Durham	1,187,941	332,396	39	1.7
Orlando	1,644,561	419,709	34	1.7
West Palm Beach	1,131,184	267,666	31	1.4
Denver	2,581,506	601,366	30	4.3
Dallas/Fort Worth	5,221,801	1,184,519	29	1.8
Charlotte	1,499,293	337,200	29	1.4
Portland	2,265,223	471,747	26	5.7
Houston	4,669,571	938,440	25	3.3

1. Metropolitan statistical areas with more than 1 million people that grew by more than 25 percent between 1990 and 2000.

Source: U.S. Bureau of the Census.

in the 1990s, transit's share of commuting trips in 2000 exceeded 5 percent only in Portland (see figure 1-2) and transit's share of travel for other purposes—not reported in the U.S. Census—was even less.

Metropolitan Atlanta grew by more than 1 million residents in the 1990s, but the city of Atlanta, in which transit use is at a relatively high level, captured only 2 percent of this regional growth. Most of the region's growth took place in counties unserved by public transportation. (Until recently, only the region's two central counties were served by public transportation.) The continuation of this kind of dispersed growth pattern in metropolitan areas will limit transit use and, even more importantly, make it difficult to maintain transit's current share of travel within relatively strong transit regions.

Dispersed growth also affects the politics of transit investment. Many transit operations are regional agencies with a broad perspective on service delivery to travel markets that know no jurisdictional boundaries. However, their increasingly suburban constitu-

Prevailing development patterns in much of the United States are part of the transit conundrum. Low-density, single-use communities are poorly served by transit.

without a strong transit orientation than in primary transit markets—do not generally support transit use.

The six largest regional transit markets in the United States are New York, Chicago, San Francisco, Washington, Boston, and Philadelphia. Between 1990 and 2000, the cities of Boston, San Francisco, and Chicago accounted for only a small share of growth in their regions: Boston, 4 percent; San Francisco, 7 percent; and Chicago, 12 percent. Only two of the six largest transit markets—San Francisco and Washington—enjoyed significant growth in the 1990s, and this growth occurred primarily in the suburbs. Among the primary regional transit markets, New York was the only one in which the central city's share of growth was significant. In the 1990s, New York City accounted for 42 percent of the growth in the region. This was a significant factor in the region's transit growth.

Growth of the transit market is limited because the fastest-growing regions generally are not strong transit markets. Among the fastest-growing large regions

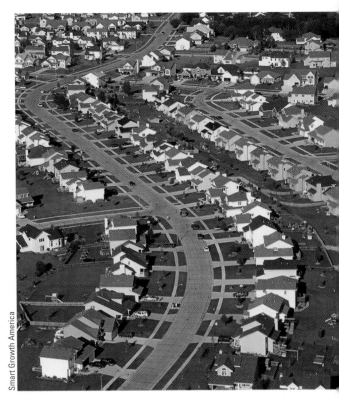

Smart Growth America

encies are increasingly less inclined to support traditional transit operations serving core area residents. Their interests lie more in suburban extensions of transit routes going into the central business district or in cross-suburban routes.

Within metropolitan regions, competition among jurisdictions is more common than cooperation. It can be difficult to convince suburbs that are not part of a regional transit district to join the district. The creation of effective suburban transit services has been a challenge for many major new transit systems.

Investment in new transit systems requires reaching out to a broad suburban constituency for funding. However, to obtain suburban financial support transit agencies often must create a system that is much larger than can be justified by conventional measures of transit effectiveness. San Francisco's 95-mile Bay Area Rapid Transit (BART) system is being expanded to ring the San Francisco Bay in order to bring suburban counties into the transit district. A 22-mile, $3.8 billion extension from Fremont to San Jose is planned, but it was put on hold in early 2004 because of stalled transit ridership and California's financial problems.

A number of communities in which new transit systems have been developed or are under consideration have little or no experience with transit on which they can base their investment decisions. A recent tongue-in-cheek article in the *Onion* suggested that the support most Americans express for transit is based on their desire to drive on less congested roads. A study by the American Public Transportation Association (APTA), the *Onion* reported, "reveals that 98 percent of Americans support the use of mass transit by others." APTA, the article claimed, has kicked off a "use transit" campaign with the slogan: "Take the Bus . . . I'll Be Glad You Did."[5] It is true that one of the best ways to make the case for public transportation improvements in a new transit market—where most voters will not be transit riders—is to emphasize their role in relieving traffic congestion.

Poor people and minorities make up a disproportionate share of daily transit riders (see "Who Uses Transit?" section on page 12), which presents a

Growing frustration with traffic congestion helps support transit investments.

Hugh Broadus, ULI

problem to advocates pitching transit investments to a broader community that is not always sympathetic to the problems of the poor and disadvantaged. The appeal of transit to voters in many new transit markets is that its riders will not be adding to road congestion. The Federal Transit Administration surveyed a cross section of public transit agencies to classify transit use into the extent to which it provides either

• basic mobility (to jobs or nonwork destinations) for people who would not otherwise travel by car, or

• an alternative to driving for people who would otherwise travel by car.[6]

The survey concluded that 20 percent of all transit trips represent congestion relief—in that they would have been made by car had a suitable transit alternative not been available—and that only about 8 percent of transit trips would not otherwise be made in the absence of transit. (The remaining transit trips represent riders without cars and others traveling for nonwork purposes who were unlikely to be on the roads during peak travel periods.) Generally, only half or less of the new riders on expanded transit systems are commuters who formerly drove, but the proponents of new transit systems tend to emphasize the ability of such systems to get drivers off the roads, because this is the benefit of transit that appeals most to suburban constituencies.

THE MANY MODES OF TRANSIT

Regional transit systems comprise various combinations of buses and trains (and occasionally ferries) that may be operated as local or express vehicles. The characteristics and relevance to transit-oriented development of major modes of transit available in the United States—local-bus service, express buses and bus rapid transit, light rail, rapid rail, and commuter rail—are described in the following sections.

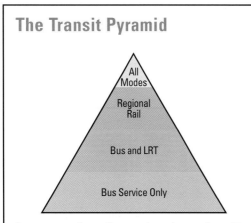

The Transit Pyramid

All
Modes

Regional
Rail

Bus and LRT

Bus Service Only

In many, mostly southern and western metropolitan regions that grew up in the post–World War II era of the automobile, transit alternatives are limited. Most urban areas offer at least minimal bus services and a growing number of cities offer light-rail service as well. However, only a relatively small number of cities offer rapid-rail or commuter-rail services or a full range of transit modes.

Local Buses

The bus is the workhorse of public transit, making up in flexibility what it lacks in razzmatazz. Buses carry two-thirds of the transit trips in the United States. Frequent stops make local service slow—local-bus service averages about 13 mph. Frequent stops also make local service convenient. It offers many riders short walks to and from bus stops.

Transit planners stress the flexibility of bus service, which can add buses or change routes to adjust to new or changed demand (although experience shows that opposition from a few riders can easily kill a proposed change in a bus route).

Even though buses provide the lion's share of public transport, bus routes rarely figure in planning for transit-oriented development. Bus stops do not generally cause an accessibility-related increase in the value of property in their vicinity because the accessibility advantages provided by bus service to closely spaced points along a route are slight.

Express Buses and Bus Rapid Transit

Express-bus service typically involves routes with limited or no intermediate stops between trip origins and destinations. It can achieve high average speeds. Bus rapid transit (BRT) is a variation of express-bus service that operates on dedicated roadways or lanes from which other traffic is excluded or nearly excluded and

Buses are an efficient and flexible form of public transportation that can accommodate changing development patterns by route changes and station additions. Two-thirds of transit trips in the United States are made by bus.

Bus rapid transit offers many of the features of a rail system and achieves average speeds that can be comparable to light rail. BRT can be added to already developed areas in a cost-efficient manner.

typically offers some of the same features as rail-transit systems, such as stations, fast and efficient service, and special quick-loading vehicles.

In Houston and Seattle, for example, many freeway-oriented express-bus routes currently operate. Passengers bound for downtown board buses in park-and-ride lots near freeway exits. Drives to the pickup point are generally short and the buses provide non-stop freeway service to downtown, sometimes on express lanes.

The list of cities from around the world that offer bus rapid transit (BRT) as a transit option is growing. It includes Ottawa, Adelaide, and Curitiba, a fast-growing city of 2.3 million in southern Brazil, which operates a widely publicized BRT system. In the United States, Pittsburgh and Seattle pioneered the concept of busways, but their approaches did not attract many followers until Los Angeles successfully implemented a modified version—Metro Rapid—that operates in mixed traffic on the high-density Wilshire/Whittier and Ventura Boulevards. (See Los Angeles County

Dallas Area Rapid Transit

Regional Transportation Commission of Southern Nevada

visplan.com

section in Chapter Two.) Having gained a significant ridership, the Metro Rapid service is being rapidly expanded. Las Vegas opened the first phase of a BRT system in 2004; other cities planning BRT services include Boston, Houston, Cleveland, and Phoenix.

Because express-bus services offer few points of access and relatively fast access to destinations, property values around the stops may realize an accessibility premium. Property around BRT stations may achieve accessibility values similar to those achieved by property around rail stations.

Few U.S. cities with the exception of Pittsburgh have had much experience in developing around express-bus services. In Pittsburgh, growth has occurred along the East Busway route, which was recently extended from Wilkinsburg to Swissvale. However, experience in Ottawa, Adelaide, Brisbane, and Curitiba has demonstrated that BRT can achieve land use and economic development benefits similar to those produced by rail transit.

Light Rail

Light rail is a high-tech version of streetcars, and it is also known as "trolleys"—or as "trams" in Europe. Its tracks may be located on streets or on dedicated rights-of-way. Sharing the street avoids the cost of securing separate rights-of-way, but also subjects light-rail service to traffic delays, increases the potential for crashes, and lowers speeds. The average speed for new light-rail systems in the United States is 20 mph, compared with only 12 mph for some of the older streetcar lines in New Orleans, Boston, and Philadelphia.

Virtually all current proposals for rail transit in the United States are for light rail because of its cost and flexibility advantages. Among cities with new light-rail operations are Dallas, Portland, and San Diego. A number of cities—such as Philadelphia,

San Francisco, and Toronto—continue to operate older light-rail routes.

Many public officials and transit planners think that light rail has a cachet that buses lack—at least for potential transit users in the Sunbelt. Light rail, it is felt, is needed to attract "by-choice" riders, that is, riders who are not dependent on transit for their travel needs. As a former county supervisor mused during the debate over the rail system in Los Angeles: "The opportunity for riding from Chatsworth to Disneyland on a train far exceeds in excitement and popularity the dismalness of getting on an RTD bus."[7]

Because light rail generally operates at higher speeds than buses, stops less frequently, and offers a more reliable trip, it can offer an accessibility advantage to nearby properties that can result in higher real estate values. Most new and proposed TOD projects are adjacent to light-rail stations.

Rapid Rail

Rapid rail is known also as "heavy rail" or "subways" —or as "metros" in Europe. It operates on exclusive rights-of-way without grade crossings. Its tracks often are located underground. Rapid-rail transit is operated at faster speeds than light-rail transit, and the distances between stations are generally greater, especially on the outer segments of lines. Because of its

Metropolitan Council, St. Paul, Minnesota

People movers have a smaller passenger capacity than traditional rail cars and are used to serve relatively constant crowds in places like airports and downtowns.

Light-rail vehicles are faster than buses but slower than heavy rail, and may travel either on existing streets or on separate rights-of-way. With street-level access, they can deliver riders close to their destinations.

Rapid-rail transit involves high-capacity, relatively high-speed trains operating on separate rights-of-way or in tunnels. Stations are generally spaced farther apart than light-rail stops, especially on the outer segments of lines.

In many metropolitan areas, commuter-rail lines provide high-speed service to downtowns. Unlike rapid-rail lines, these lines typically operate with schedules that serve only those people going in the dominant direction of travel during peak periods.

Chicago Transit Authority/Peter J. Schulz

Dallas Area Rapid Transit

high cost, rapid rail requires high population densities in order to achieve a reasonable cost per rider.

The long distances between rapid-rail stations impart a high accessibility advantage to nearby properties. Thus rapid rail tends to produce higher real estate premiums than does light rail. Stations serving rapid-rail lines in the Washington, Atlanta, and San Francisco regions have attracted large development projects.

Commuter Rail

Commuter-rail lines provide service to downtowns over long distances. Because of long distances between stations—station spacing typically is 3.5 miles—commuter-rail service is relatively speedy, although if tracks are shared with other uses its speed advantage may be diminished. Traditional commuter-rail operations are exemplified by the Long Island Rail Road, which connects Long Island with Penn Station in Manhattan, and by Metra, a rail operation serving downtown Chicago from its suburbs. Newer commuter-rail operations serve Dallas, Seattle, San Diego, and Washington, D.C. (from northern Virginia).

Riders on commuter rail come from a wide area around stations, and when parking is provided they generally arrive by car. While commuter-rail stations would be expected to offer a real estate premium, many are surrounded by land uses that limit the potential property value advantages—including commuter parking or industrial operations served by freight services that share the commuter-rail tracks.

TRANSIT USERS AND TRANSIT USE

Who Uses Transit?

Transit provides mobility for people with no other transportation options. According to the U.S. Department of Transportation's 2001 National Personal Travel Survey (NPTS), two out of three bus riders and half of all rail passengers did not have access to a car at the times that they were traveling.[8] In Atlanta, 41 percent of rail passengers in 2001–2002 did not have access to a vehicle, in contrast to 78 percent of bus riders.[9]

Figure 1-3
TRANSPORTATION MODES COMPARED

	Average Speed (mph)	Distance Between Stops (miles)	Capital Cost (dollars per passenger mile)	Operating Cost (dollars per passenger mile)
Local Bus	13	1/8	$0.16	$0.60
Express Bus	14–21[1]	1–5	–	–
Light Rail	16	1/4–1/2	1.00[2]	0.47
Heavy Rail	20	3/4	0.25	0.29
Commuter Rail	32	3	0.24	0.30
Private Auto[3]	32	–	0.20	0.17

1. Average speed for bus rapid transit demonstration projects in Pittsburgh, San Diego, and San Jose.

2. Capital costs may be exaggerated because of many new projects under construction.

3. Author's estimates based on AAA of Northern California estimates of driving costs and an average of 1.5 occupants per auto trip.

Sources: Federal Transit Administration (transit modes); and 2001 National Personal Transportation Survey (private auto).

Measuring the Costs of Transit

Transit is expensive to build and operate, just as cars and roads are. In choosing modes—heavy rail, light rail, or bus rapid transit in order of most to least expensive—the real question for consumers is not the total cost, but what the money buys. A bottom-line measure of the effectiveness of transit investments is the cost of gaining a regular rider. This measure is conceptually akin to one used by cable companies: the cost of gaining a subscriber. As shown in the table "Recent Transit Projects," the cost of gaining a regular rider by expanding transit can be quite high.

The table shows the range of costs for a sample of recent projects. The two projects in the middle of the cost range—Dallas's first two lines, and Portland's Westside MAX extension—cost $90 million and $54 million per mile to build. Based on current ridership, these two projects involved a total investment of $67,000 and $95,000 respectively per regular weekday rider. Dallas's lower capital costs when calculated as investment per rider reflect the higher ridership levels achieved (although Portland's ridership will likely grow over time). Compared with the high cost of expanding ridership through the extension of transit systems, smaller investments in development around transit to promote ridership appear to be fiscally prudent for transit agencies.

RECENT TRANSIT PROJECTS

	Opening Year	Miles	Daily Trips (000s)	Regular Riders[1] (000s)	Cost (000s) Total	Cost (000s) Per Mile	Cost (000s) Per Regular Rider
Denver Light-Rail C Line, SW Corridor	1994	15.8	28.5	12.8	$277,000	$18,000	$22
Dallas Light Rail, Red and Blue Lines	1996	20.0	60.0	27.0	1,800,000	90,000	67
Portland (Oregon) Westside MAX	1998	18.0	22.5	10.1	963,000	54,000	95
Los Angeles MTA Gold Line (Pasadena)	2003	13.7	14.6	6.6	859,000	62,000	131
Central Phoenix, East Valley Light Rail[2]	2007	20.3	26–50	12–22	1,377,000	68,000	61–117
Orange County (California) CentreLine[2]	2009	8.5	17–25	8–11	966,000	114,000	87–123

1. Regular riders are estimated at 45 percent of average daily trips, meaning that the average rider makes about two trips daily.

2. Projects currently under development; ridership ranges shown are from opening day to 20 years.

Sources: Construction costs and miles reported by transit agencies.

Poor people and minorities make up a disproportionate share of daily riders. On a per capita basis, African Americans were six times as likely to travel by transit as whites in 2001, and Hispanics were three times as likely to use transit as non-Hispanics. People from low-income households, African Americans, and Hispanics combined account for 73 percent of bus riders, 35 percent of urban-rail riders, and 31 percent of commuter-rail passengers.

According to the 2001 NPTS, the work trip is the most common travel purpose of transit users, but—at 38 percent—people going to or from work do not constitute a majority of transit riders. Other major travel purposes are shopping and errands (23 percent), visits or social (18 percent), and travel to school or church (12 percent).

Who uses transit can depend on the type of transit services provided. As has been noted, commuter-rail lines like the Long Island Rail Road or Philadelphia's SEPTA (Southeastern Pennsylvania Transportation Authority) tend to serve people living in upper-income suburbs. Local buses and express buses or light rail often serve different markets. Even in Portland, Oregon, a city which seems an exemption to the rule that only those without options ride transit—nearly seven out of ten transit customers claim to be by-choice riders with cars available—sharp differences are found between bus and rail customers. While the overwhelming majority of transit users who ride only the light-rail MAX service (93 percent) are by-choice riders, only slightly more than half of bus riders fall into this category. The most common trip purpose of MAX customers is recreation, while for bus-only riders it is work.[10]

A regional transit system offering a variety of connected travel modes can provide access to employment centers, shopping, and residential areas for people of all incomes.

In general, new transit projects in the United States have been designed to attract mostly by-choice riders rather than to provide basic service to riders who have limited transportation options. These projects try to attract valuable peak-hour trips and to provide an attractive market to developers. By their emphasis on relatively high quality transit services, these projects attract a demographically mixed ridership.

In their preference for briefcase-carrying, by-choice riders, developers and retailers tend to ignore (and even avoid) the bus-transit market, with some seeking to exclude bus stops—and thus access for stereotypically impoverished, troublemaking bus riders—from their vicinity. Deeper market insight would show potential not only for upscale housing and retail for by-choice transit users, but also for affordable housing and associated services for less affluent transit riders.

Regional Transit Markets

The availability and use of transit services vary immensely among metropolitan areas.

The New York Metropolitan Transit Authority serves one out of every three mass transit riders in the United States. When it comes to transit use, as Hertz might put it, there is New York, and there is "not exactly" (see figure 1-4). Transit ridership in New York exceeds that of the next six largest transit markets combined. At the other extreme are many small communities with no public transportation or with only basic services for people with no transportation alternatives.

In between are a variety of urban areas in which transit use is moderate. Some of these are once strong

transit markets that have lost share to urban decay and suburban sprawl and others are emerging transit markets in which efforts are being made to create serious travel alternatives to driving. Between 1980 and 2000, for example, St. Louis, Chicago, Philadelphia, and Buffalo lost at least one-fifth of their transit ridership. In contrast, San Diego, San Jose, Houston, and Phoenix at least doubled theirs in that period, while Portland almost doubled its ridership and has gained another 9 percent since 2000.

Transit markets are classified here as either primary, secondary, or new, as discussed in the following sections. These classifications have been derived based on commuting estimates from the U.S. Census rather than on counts of transit riders. While the Census data provide an incomplete measure of transit use, they offer consistent data for each region over time.

Primary Transit Markets

In the United States there are six regions that dominate the U.S. transit market—in order of current ridership, New York, Chicago, San Francisco, Washington, Boston, and Philadelphia. These regions offer the best transit access in the country. Their high-density central cities and suburbs developed around transit.

Boston's dense, concentrated urban core facilitates transit use. Fifty-five percent of daily work trips into the center city are by transit. The region's well-established transit system provides a variety of transportation options (bus, BRT, heavy rail, and light rail) serving the urban core and suburban locations.

Figure 1-4
TRANSIT RIDERSHIP IN SELECTED METROPOLITAN AREAS, 1980, 1990, AND 2000

Thousands of boardings; black indicates primary transit markets; dark gray indicates secondary transit markets

| | 1980 | | | 1990 | | | 2000 | | | Percent Change | |
| | | | | | | | | | | 1980–2000 | 1990–2000 |
	Total	Bus	Rail	Total	Bus	Rail	Total	Bus	Rail		
New York	1,488,917	412,426	1,076,491	2,533,454	903,314	1,630,140	2,847,810	1,012,844	1,834,966	91%	12%
Chicago	712,620	562,599	150,021	562,421	414,867	147,554	482,245	335,051	147,194	–32	–14
San Francisco	441,694	400,896	40,798	412,027	330,915	81,112	440,223	328,565	111,658	0	7
Los Angeles	345,793	345,793	0	437,029	433,979	3,050	428,759	379,379	49,380	24	–2
Washington	261,392	179,037	82,876	385,223	200,654	184,569	392,295	165,662	226,633	50	2
Boston	249,497	120,458	129,039	300,843	97,726	203,117	313,829	102,020	211,809	26	4
Philadelphia	333,905	235,035	98,870	257,938	167,425	90,513	271,312	160,420	110,892	–19	5
Atlanta	120,160	108,027	12,133	147,845	78,898	68,947	166,755	82,763	83,992	39	13
Seattle	75,795	75,795	0	78,803	78,803	0	96,539	96,539	0	27	23
Baltimore	115,430	115,430	0	99,341	86,025	13,316	92,582	70,560	22,022	–20	–7
Houston	41,757	41,757	0	82,973	82,973	0	87,267	87,267	0	109	5
Portland	44,629	44,629	0	56,066	48,956	7,110	82,980	61,088	21,892	86	48
Miami	76,446	76,446	0	78,984	63,548	15,436	79,712	65,689	14,023	4	1
San Diego	30,193	30,193	0	51,137	33,625	17,512	78,187	48,152	30,035	159	53
Dallas/Fort Worth	37,697	37,697	0	50,618	50,618	0	64,507	53,088	11,419	71	27
San Jose	23,976	23,976	0	43,855	40,955	2,900	56,692	47,446	9,246	136	29
St. Louis	75,609	75,609	0	44,110	44,110	0	50,274	36,186	14,088	–34	14
Las Vegas[1]	–	–	–	–	–	–	51,800	51,800	0	–	–
Denver	38,127	38,127	0	41,311	41,311	0	48,789	42,114	6,675	28	18
Sacramento	17,900	17,900	0	19,606	14,104	5,501	27,041	18,517	8,524	58	38
Phoenix	12,804	12,804	0	28,909	28,909	0	26,672	26,672	0	108	–10
Buffalo	45,250	45,250	0	31,896	23,789	8,107	26,053	19,506	6,547	–42	–18
Orlando	3,115	3,115	0	7,875	7,875	0	20,476	20,476	0	557	167

1. Public transportation services by the Regional Transportation Commission began in 1993.

Source: American Public Transportation Association.

Georgia Department of Economic Development

Atlanta is a secondary market for transit commuting. Transit use is high among city residents but low among suburbanites. Approximately 60 percent of transit riders in the region access buses or rail stations by foot.

Secondary Transit Markets

Regions in which transit accounts for from 4 percent to 8 percent of regional work trips and generally for at least 10 percent of the work trips of central city residents are classified here as secondary transit markets. In these regions—Atlanta, Miami, and New Orleans in the South; Seattle, Portland, Los Angeles, Denver, and Las Vegas in the West; and Baltimore, Pittsburgh, Buffalo, Minneapolis, and Milwaukee in the Northeast and Midwest—transit is the third most common commuting mode after driving and carpooling.

A number of these secondary transit markets have lost population and transit share, at least in the central city. A smaller share of the residents of the cities of Baltimore and Atlanta, for example, commute by transit now than in 1990, when transit accounted for more than one in five work trips in both cities. In New Orleans, transit's share of regional commuting declined from 29 percent in 1960 to 5 percent in 2000, and in Milwaukee it went from 19 percent to 4 percent over the same period. Other secondary markets—such as Seattle, Portland, Denver, Las Vegas, and Atlanta—are growing and looking to transit as one way of easing their growing pains.

Most of these markets have seen significant transit investments since 1980, including new heavy-rail systems in Miami and Atlanta, new heavy-rail and light-rail systems in Los Angeles and Baltimore, expansions of rail systems in Pittsburgh and New Orleans, and new light-rail systems in Portland, Denver, Buffalo, and Minneapolis. Seattle and Las Vegas are planning for the construction of new light-rail systems, while Milwaukee is planning but not yet committed to light rail.

Transit share is growing in the two northwestern secondary transit markets—Portland and Seattle. Seattle currently has a higher transit share for commuting— 7 percent regionally and 18 percent among central city residents. But Portland is gaining transit riders faster, having experienced a 48 percent jump in transit riders between 1990 and 2000 compared with Seattle's gain of 23 percent. Transit share is growing also in Las Vegas, where transit's regional commute

In New York, Chicago, Boston, and the six largest Canadian metropolitan areas—all of which fit the definition of primary transit market—transit is second only to driving for commuting. In primary markets, transit's share of commuting trips ranges from 25 percent (New York) to 9 percent (Washington, Boston, and Philadelphia). Transit's share of commuting by central city residents is 53 percent in New York City and ranges from 26 percent to 35 percent in the other primary U.S. transit markets. Annual transit ridership (2000) in primary U.S. transit markets ranges from 270 million (Philadelphia) to more than 2.8 billion (New York).

Among primary transit markets, transit's share of commuting gained between 1990 and 2000 in San Francisco, Toronto, Montreal, and Ottawa. Losses in transit's regional commute share were experienced in Vancouver, Chicago, Washington, and Philadelphia.

The extensive transit services available in primary transit markets as well as the depth of the transit habit (people's willingness to consider transit an everyday travel option) create many and wide-ranging possibilities for development around transit.

Figure 1-5
TRANSIT SHARE OF WORK TRIPS BY METROPOLITAN AREA AND CENTRAL CITY, 1990 AND 2000

Black indicates primary transit markets; dark gray indicates secondary transit markets

	1990[1]		2000[2]				1990		2000		
	Region	Central City	Region	Central City	Transit's Rank among Commute Modes[3]		Region	Central City	Region	Central City	Transit's Rank among Commute Modes[3]
New York	25%	53%	25%	53%	2	San Jose	3%	4%	3%	4%	3
Toronto	22	33	23	38	2	Cleveland	4	14	3	12	3
Montreal	20	37	22	38	2	San Diego	3	4	3	4	3
Ottawa	17	20	19	21	2	Houston	4	7	3	6	3
Calgary	13	13	13	14	2	Salt Lake City	3	6	3	6	4
Vancouver	14	24	12	17	2	Cincinnati	4	11	3	10	3
Chicago	13	30	12	26	2	San Antonio	4	5	3	4	3
San Francisco	9	34	10	31	3	Sacramento	2	4	3	5	4
Washington	11	37	9	33	3	Austin	3	5	3	5	4
Edmonton	9	12	9	12	2	Providence	3	7	3	7	4
Boston	9	32	9	32	2	St. Louis	3	12	2	11	4
Philadelphia	10	29	9	25	3	Louisville	3	9	2	7	4
Seattle	6	16	7	18	3	Columbus	3	5	2	4	4
Baltimore	8	22	6	20	3	Rochester	3	11	2	8	4
Pittsburgh	8	22	6	21	3	Phoenix	2	3	2	3	5
Portland, Oregon	5	11	6	12	3	Norfolk	2	5	2	5	5
New Orleans	7	17	6	14	3	Detroit	2	11	2	9	4
Los Angeles	5	11	5	10	3	Dallas/Fort Worth	2	7	2	6	4
Minneapolis	5	16	5	15	3	Orlando	1	4	2	4	4
Denver	4	8	4	8	3	Raleigh/Durham	2	3	2	2	5
Las Vegas	2	3	4	5	3	Charlotte	2	5	1	3	4
Milwaukee	5	11	4	10	3	Tampa	1	3	1	3	5
Miami	4	13	4	11	3	Indianapolis	2	3	1	2	5
Atlanta	5	20	4	15	3	Kansas City	2	6	1	4	5
Buffalo	5	13	4	12	3	West Palm Beach	1	3	1	3	4
						Nashville	2	3	1	2	5

1. Canadian data are for 1996.
2. Canadian data are for 2001.
3. Other travel modes ranked in Census commute data include driving alone, carpooling, walking, and working at home.

Sources: U.S. Census 1990 and 2000; and Canada Census 1996 and 2001.

San Diego Convention & Visitors Bureau, California

San Diego has experienced enormous gains in transit ridership, a consequence of strong regional growth and significant transit investment.

share doubled between 1990 and 2000 to 4 percent, close behind Denver. Los Angeles, despite a relatively low transit share (5 percent regionally and 10 percent in the central city) compared with San Francisco's (10 percent and 31 percent, respectively) and despite a slight loss in transit share in the last decade, is still an important transit market because of its sheer size. Other secondary markets losing transit market share between 1990 and 2000 include Baltimore, Pittsburgh, New Orleans, Milwaukee, and Atlanta.

New Transit Markets

The remaining U.S. metropolitan areas listed in figure 1-5—Houston, San Antonio, Austin, Louisville, Norfolk, Dallas/Fort Worth, Orlando, Raleigh/Durham, Charlotte, Tampa, West Palm Beach, and Nashville in the South; Las Vegas, San Jose, San Diego, Salt Lake City, Sacramento, and Phoenix in the West; and, Cleveland, Cincinnati, Providence, St. Louis, Columbus, Rochester, Detroit, Indianapolis, and Kansas City in the Northeast and Midwest—can all be considered "new" transit markets.

Some of them have only just discovered transit in the last two decades. San Diego, which fits this category, has built one of the best new transit systems in the United States. Dallas, Houston, Salt Lake City, Sacramento, and San Jose have invested in new light-rail transit. Increases in transit's commute share were registered in San Jose, Sacramento, and Orlando.

Other "new" transit markets are actually rediscovering transit after having lost transit share in recent decades. In St. Louis, where a new rail line opened in 1993, five out of every six transit commuters were lost between 1960 and 1990. Cleveland and St. Louis, are making investments intended to help transit regain a stronger travel share and Cincinnati and Kansas City have proposed projects that are as yet unbuilt.

In most of these regions, transit is the fourth, or even fifth most common commuting mode behind even working at home and walking. The transit share for commuting regionwide is under 4 percent, and for the central city it is at 10 percent or above in only Cleveland, Cincinnati, and St. Louis. Most of these regions have major transit projects in the works or planned.

TRANSIT-SUPPORTIVE DEVELOPMENT

The prevalence in America of growth patterns that fail to support transit use means that investment in transit needs to be reinforced with development strategies aimed at building a compelling market for transit. Seminal research on the transit friendliness of various forms of development was conducted in 1987 under the auspices of New York's Regional Plan Association.[11] This research determined that the likelihood that people will use transit will increase

- the higher the density of the community;

- the larger the size of the downtown;

- the closer people live to downtown; and

- the better the transit service.

The success of transit in primary U.S. transit markets is based on a number of important characteristics of the downtowns: They are important commuter destinations, they are well served by radial transit lines, they are densely built, they contain a mix of uses, and they are pedestrian friendly. Furthermore, parking in these downtowns is expensive and transit fares are relatively cheap.

Transit clearly plays an important role in primary markets and many secondary transit markets. Its potential role in places without a history of transit— in places like Dallas, Salt Lake City, Houston, and Phoenix—where growth has created a need to expand transportation choices is uncertain. Is it possible to retrofit transit in places where it never existed before? The answer depends in part on ridership levels and

Figure 1-6

RECOMMENDED RESIDENTIAL AND OFFICE DENSITIES AROUND TRANSIT IN SANTA CLARA COUNTY

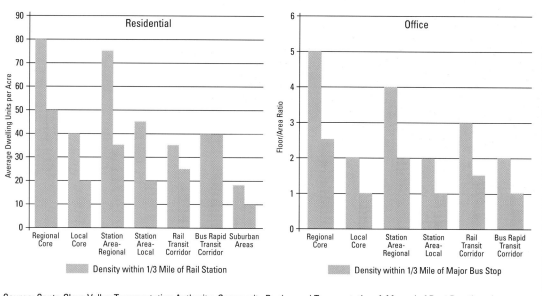

Source: Santa Clara Valley Transportation Authority, *Community Design and Transportation: A Manual of Best Practices for Integrating Transportation and Land Use,* 2003.

in part on community support for public subsidies for transit.

The number of riders is a key factor because more riders mean higher transit revenues. However, transit systems need not attain ridership on a par with New York City's crush loads to be successful. Buses in the United States carry an average of three passengers per mile of service operated. Buses in New York City carry eight passengers per mile of operation while those in Seattle, which has one of the best-run bus operations in the country, carry 2.3 passengers per mile. Rapid rail averages 4.6 persons per mile in the United States.

A second critical factor in the feasibility of transit is public subsidies. Transit service is feasible at minimum levels of population density if the cost of providing it need not be covered by transit revenues. Where there is sufficient public support, public subsidies can be used to help fund high-quality transit services that are not justified by development densities. However, gaining sufficient public support is a special problem in new transit communities where the general public is not initially convinced about the value of transit. Demonstrating the value of transit with the introduction of limited services can help. In Dallas, for example, the widespread skepticism about transit's ability to get Texans out of their cars disappeared after the

first segment of the DART (Dallas Area Rapid Transit) light-rail system opened. Suburbanites discovered that transit worked for them and suburban communities agreed to financially support service extensions. Similarly, ridership on the first light-rail line in St. Louis was high enough to win over enough formerly opposed voters to win approval of a sales tax to pay for the transit system.

Based on research performed in the 1980s, the Regional Plan Association's standards for minimum residential densities most feasible for supporting transit—seven to 15 dwelling units per acre for bus transit depending on its frequency, nine units per acre along a 40- to 150-square-mile corridor for light rail, and 12 units per acre along a 150- to 200-square-mile corridor for heavy rail—have become widely used rules of thumb among transit planners.[12] One of the more aggressive recommendations is that of the Valley Transit Agency in Santa Clara County, California, which encourages local governments to develop at the highest possible densities around regional rail stations and major downtowns, such as San Jose. Within one-third mile of a rail station in the regional core, VTA recommends a residential density of 80 units per acre and a floor/area ratio of 5 for office space, as shown in figure 1-6. These density standards suggest that most suburban areas cannot support transit with today's development patterns. Outside of areas like New York in which the transit habit is strong, density thresholds may be even higher.

In a 1997 review of 11 studies examining the connection between transit and land use, planner Reid Ewing concluded that the rule-of-thumb minimum density thresholds for bus service suggested by the Regional Plan Association research—seven dwelling units per acre for basic bus service and 15 units per acre for "premium" bus service—are workable. However, he suggested that transit-oriented developments designed to support investments in light rail should be built at 20 to 30 units per acre—a considerably higher density than the rule-of-thumb density of nine units per acre.[13]

In practice, new rail service is being provided at lower densities, according to a 2002 review of applications to the Federal Transit Administration for funding rail projects.[14] Two-thirds of these applications estimated that the average residential density in station areas would be fewer than 6,666 persons per square mile, which translates to about four housing units per acre.

As noted earlier, the four Ds of transit-supportive development include not only distance and density, but also design and diversity. A district that supports transit has to be not only sufficiently dense but also enough of a destination—containing a mix of uses with good pedestrian and transit connections—to entice commuters, shoppers, and visitors to arrive by transit rather than by car and to permit residents to satisfy many daily travel needs without driving.

In downtown Bethesda, Maryland, a transit-served, primary suburban business district in the Washington metropolitan area, two-thirds of all midday trips by workers are made on foot.[15] This district's diverse and ample attractions—restaurants, stores, parks—within walking distance of workplaces add immeasurably to the attractiveness of transit as a commuting option. Broadly stated, what is critical for transit support is the creation of *places,* especially in the suburbs.

Place making involves the composition of streets, open spaces, and a mix of land uses into a setting that people enjoy using and in which they want to spend time. Early examples of suburban great places include Country Club Plaza in Kansas City and Highland Park Shopping Village in Dallas, and contemporary examples include Reston Town Center in Virginia (Washington metropolitan area) and Mizner Park in Boca Raton (Florida).[16] The one thing missing from many post–World War II great suburban places is transit, an oversight that is now being addressed.

Great places have a pedestrian orientation, and it is this that not only creates the sense of place, but also makes walking to transit an attractive option. Great places provide civic value as well as a real estate premium. They are in a position to maintain their standing in a competitive regional market. The creation of great places brings broad community benefits, of which transit support is only one.

Park-and-ride facilities are a particular—and often problematical—form of station area development. Park-and-ride delivers transit riders because it offers the convenience of accessing direct rapid-transit connections (rail or bus) by car rather than by bus. But parking, which typically is provided in surface lots, does nothing to enhance the station or terminal neighborhood. The conflict between transit-supportive development and park-and-ride as sources of transit ridership is ongoing. Many transit operators have become the largest operators of parking in their regions. Washington, D.C.'s WMATA (Washington Metropolitan Area Transit Authority) operates 55,000 parking spaces and the demand, especially at end-of-the-line (terminal) stations, seems endless. This issue is discussed in detail in Chapter Six.

A fine-grained mix of uses and convenient transit access make downtown Bethesda, Maryland—a major suburban center outside Washington, D.C.—an attractive transit destination. Currently, 27 percent of business district employees arrive by transit, and most midday trips are by foot.

Bethesda Urban Partnership

DEVELOPMENT-ORIENTED TRANSIT

To succeed, transit-oriented development needs a quid pro quo from transit in the form of development-oriented transit. Transit advocates and managers need to work to improve transit's image and to plan new transit lines to maximize their development potential. Transit managers also must adopt a broad view of place making around stops, stations, and other transit facilities.

Transit's reputation for the places it goes as well as the people it serves is often negative. Developers, retailers, and households often view locations accessible to transit lines serving low-income neighborhoods as undesirable—as being, so to speak, on the wrong side of the tracks.

The development potential of new transit lines often is limited by locational decisions that minimize construction costs but reduce upside potential for maximizing ridership and transit-oriented development. Metropolitan Washington's heavy-rail system bypassed Tysons Corner, Virginia, the region's premier edge city. An extension to serve Tysons Corner is now in planning. Even though Charlotte, North Carolina, is implementing aggressive transit plans, it has proved impractical to provide direct transit service to the tony South Park commercial district because, while it is close to downtown, it is located too far off the main route. In Los Angeles, the rail system goes near but not to the airport. The costs of new transit projects are so high that the pressures to minimize them are understandable. However, planners must think ahead, and pay the additional costs if needed to enhance the long-term contribution of the transit project to the community.

Development-oriented transit requires the operators of transit systems to expand their focus, to stop thinking that their responsibility ends at the bus stop or the station entrance. The creation of great places with good transit requires a broad view of place making in which many parties participate in the development and maintenance of the places served by transit. Transit agency participation in joint efforts to clean and maintain streets and sidewalks, to create a seamless

transition from transit vehicles to destinations, and to brand the transit experience can help promote development around transit.

Development-oriented transit encourages development adjacent to transit properties that is transit oriented. To provide workable incentives and enter into agreements and partnerships with developers, transit agencies must understand the development process. Many transit agencies have established and staffed departments for these purposes, thus helping to advance strategic transit and community goals for development with transit.

FINDING THE PROPER NICHE FOR TRANSIT INVESTMENT

Transit may capture only 1 to 2 percent of personal trips nationally—the 1 percent argument used to oppose transit investments—but a transit option is not reasonably available to most people in the United States. Some locations are more "transit competitive" than others, as conservative commentators Paul M. Weyrich and William S. Lind noted in a 1999 paper that received widespread attention within the transit community.[17] Instead of looking at transit use nationally, said Weyrich and Lind, analysts should look at transit's record in places where transit is a reasonable option. They cited, for example, transit's capture of 50 to 60 percent of the more than 1 million trips a day into downtown Chicago and its capture of 20 to 25 percent of game-day trips to the St. Louis Rams' Edward Jones stadium, which is accessible to the region's MetroLink light-rail service.

Throughout the United States, there are many places that by virtue of their geography or demographics could support transit. These transit niches may be found even in regions where transit's share of travel is still low. As discussed in the following sections, development in four kinds of transit-served locations

The Denver Tech Center, a premier commercial center southeast of downtown Denver, was developed entirely around the freeway. It is now being retrofitted for transit.

Figure 1-7

TRANSIT SHARE OF COMMUTING BY REGIONAL TRANSIT NICHE, SELECTED EXAMPLES

Regional Transit Niche	In Primary Transit Markets		In Secondary Transit Markets		In New Transit Markets	
	Transit Share (percent)	Examples	Transit Share (percent)	Examples	Transit Share (percent)	Examples
CBDs	37–75%	Washington	20–31%	Miami	7–32%	San Jose
		Manhattan		Portland		Houston
Central Cities	26–33	Chicago	8–18	Denver	3–12	Phoenix
		Washington		Seattle		Cleveland
Suburban Business Districts	14–28	Pleasant Hill CA	3–9	South Coast Plaza CA	4–7	Otay Ranch CA
		Bethesda MD		Bellevue WA		Uptown Houston
Transit Suburbs	31–59	Brookline MA	18–32	College Park GA	2–17	Irving TX
		Hoboken NJ		Bainbridge Island WA		Falcon Heights MN

Sources: U.S. Census 2000 journey-to-work data reported by metropolitan planning organizations; Portland Metro, *Portland Region Transportation Facts 2003–2004;* and WestGroup Research, unpublished report on Central Houston 2002 Downtown Commuter Study (CBDs); U.S. Census 2000 (central cities); Calthorpe Associates, *Design for Efficient Activity Centers* (U.S. Department of Transportation, 1996); San Diego Association of Governments, Regional Transportation Vision 2002; and Montgomery County Commuter Services, *Bethesda Urban Partnership Survey 2003* (suburban business districts); and U.S. Census 2000 journey-to-work data reported by place of residence (transit suburbs).

—central business districts, central cities outside the CBD, suburban business districts, and high-transit-share suburbs—is most likely to provide support for transit. Figure 1-7 shows current transit commuting shares within specific places that exemplify each of these four regional transit niches in primary, secondary, and new transit markets.

Central Business Districts

Downtowns typically offer their region's most extensive transportation options—including well-distributed transit, pedestrian connections, and often taxis. The high cost and scarcity of long-term parking in most downtowns makes transit compared with driving a less expensive and more convenient option for commuters. Transit serves 75 percent of commuters to Manhattan and smaller but still substantial shares of commuters to other major downtowns. Even in secondary and new transit markets, the transit share of commuting to downtowns can be high, as shown in figure 1-7. Portland is a secondary transit market with a new light-rail system that has benefited from a strong tradition of transit use to downtown; it carried 31 percent of downtown workers in 2000. Houston is a new transit market where transit captures a substantial share of commuter travel. Only 6 percent of its central city residents commute by transit, but in 2001 three out of every ten people entering downtown during the morning rush hour traveled by transit, even before the Houston region's light-rail line opened in 2004. In San Jose, another new transit market, in contrast, transit's share of commuting travel to downtown was only 7 percent in 2000.

Transit's strength in CBDs means that downtown development represents the best potential source of growth in transit ridership in any region. Office buildings tend to be the CBD land use that is most supportive of transit ridership. Downtown residential development

Bringing light rail to Houston's downtown was a key strategy in the revitalization of downtown's Main Street corridor and is expected to produce $1.5 billion in additional city revenue over the next 20 years, largely from higher real estate values. Transit carries a relatively low share of travel in the Houston region, but even before the new rail line opened almost one-third of workers in downtown commuted by transit.

Hugh Broadus, ULI

also creates a reliable market for transit (as well for downtown businesses).

Central Cities

Central cities' residents are the second strongest regional transit niches, after the CBD, particularly in primary transit markets. Among primary transit markets in 2000, transit captured 26 percent of commuting trips made by the residents of the city of Chicago and 33 percent of those made by Washington, D.C., residents. With a transit share of 21 percent and 20 percent respectively, the cities of Pittsburgh and Baltimore represent the strongest central city transit niches among secondary transit markets. They are closely followed by the city of Seattle, with an 18 percent transit share. Central city transit niches in new transit markets are considerably weaker: In 2000, only 5 percent of Sacramento's residents and 3 percent of Phoenix's residents commuted by transit. (Note: a light-rail line is in operation in Sacramento and one is in planning in Phoenix.)

Central city locations offer many opportunities for residential infill development with good access to transit. Residential development in central cities supports transit to the degree that it appeals to households who are inclined toward transit and willing to

Transit for Recreational Trips

Commuting remains the backbone of urban transit systems, but the growing entertainment market in urban areas offers some upside potential for transit revenue and some built-in political support for transit investment. The use of transit for recreational trips is not generally revealed in available data on transit trends, which concentrate on the commuting market, but the recreational transit market should grow as transit-served city locations become urban fun markets with the development and expansion of sports, cultural, educational, and convention facilities and entertainment zones.

In many cities—including Baltimore, Dallas, Portland, St. Louis, and San Francisco—new stadiums and arenas for professional sports teams have been located in areas close to restaurants, bars, and shops that add to the appeal of attending games and extend the fun. A central location also offers greater choices for transportation, including transit, as well as dispersed parking and access routes. The advantage to the transit operator is extra revenue on existing routes often without the cost of additional service. The MetroLink light-rail system in St. Louis carries a significant share of trips to football games played by the Rams in downtown's Edward Jones Dome. Forecasts issued by the regional transportation authority for the planned light-rail system in Phoenix estimate that six sports and entertainment venues in downtown Phoenix, including the America West Arena and the BankOne Ballpark, and three such venues in Tempe would attract more than 600,000 riders annually, or about 4 percent of the ridership projected.

Transit use for recreational purposes gains not only ridership and revenue, but also visibility for transit, which may be its most important contribution in the long run. For example, many parents living in suburban Dallas who would not normally use transit for commuting have taken their kids to basketball or hockey games by light rail in order to make the trip more of an outing. This good transit experience is likely to gain the support of people living along the lines of future rail extensions for the speedy completion of these routes, as well as to gain the support of people who may never live near transit to vote for the local taxes to fund the system.

John Linden Photography

The Las Vegas Monorail was developed by a private consortium to serve the thriving resort corridor.

Transit use for a variety of travel purposes has been high in the San Francisco region, where approximately one-half of work trips to downtown are made by transit.

limit their car ownership. In new transit markets, central cities with aggressive transit plans, such as Phoenix, face challenges in attracting riders from a residential population unused to traveling by transit.

Suburban Business Districts

Many older suburban business districts have a significant transit presence. In contrast, many new suburban business districts developed around major freeways and little attention was paid to transit in their development. A 1989 survey of some of the most prominent so-called "edge cities"—the Parkway Center (Dallas region), Bellevue (Seattle region), Perimeter Mall (Atlanta region), Southdale Mall (Twin Cities region), South Coast Plaza (Orange County, California), and Tysons Corner (Washington region)—found that transit accounted for not more than 1 percent of commute trips in all but Bellevue, where it accounted for 7 percent. Transit's share of trips made for shopping purposes was similarly low.[18] The latest efforts in regional planning—often under the rubric of "smart growth"—call for integrating transit into developing suburban activity centers and linking them by transit with the central city downtown

Many suburban districts that developed around trolley or other rail lines—especially in primary transit markets like Boston, Chicago, and Washington, as well as in Los Angeles—retain a relatively fine street grid, unobtrusive parking, good pedestrian connections, and existing transit services (or transit potential) that make them strong transit niches. Among such districts are downtown Bethesda and Silver Spring in

Bellevue, a major suburban activity center located three miles from downtown Seattle, is expected to experience continued growth within its downtown. Eight percent of work trips into the downtown are by transit.

Maryland, which now are served by the Washington region's Metrorail system; downtown Berkeley in the San Francisco region; downtown Pasadena in the Los Angeles region; and downtown Oak Park in the Chicago region.

Among newer suburban business districts with significant transit potential are Bellevue, a suburb of Seattle, and Pleasant Hill, a BART station area in Contra Costa County in the San Francisco Bay Area. Significant planning for transit and associated development has taken place in both of these districts.

Among currently auto-dominated suburban edge cities with the potential for a significant transit presence is the Cumberland Galleria outside Atlanta. Here concerns over traffic and livability have convinced the community to devise a development strategy that calls for more walkable destinations, a better mix of housing, and a connection to Atlanta's transit system.[19] While many of the edge cities of the 1980s grew up—in some cases deliberately—without transit service, those that hope to continue to prosper are likely to seriously consider transit options.

Transit Suburbs

Outside of suburban business districts, some pockets of relatively high transit use in the suburbs—typically older, first-tier suburbs—represent transit niches in which further development can provide support for transit. Also, in suburbs with transit routes in place

Figure 1-8
TRANSIT'S COMMUTE SHARE IN SUBURBS WITH HIGHEST TRANSIT USE, 2000

Suburban City or Census Place (and Central City)	Residents Commuting by Transit (percent)	
	Suburb	Central City
Hoboken NJ (New York)	58.8%	52.8%
Bainbridge Island WA (Seattle)	31.7	17.6
Brookline MA (Boston)	30.8	32.3
Mount Rainier MD (Washington)	30.5	33.1
Winnetka IL (Chicago)	28.8	26.1
Darby PA (Philadelphia)	25.0	25.4
Dormont PA (Pittsburgh)	22.4	21.0
El Cerrito CA (San Francisco)	21.6	31.1
College Park GA (Atlanta)	18.1	15.0
Falcon Heights MN (Minneapolis)	16.8	14.6
Florence/Graham CA (Los Angeles)	16.6	10.2
Miami Beach FL (Miami)	12.1	11.4
Imperial Beach CA (San Diego)	11.0	4.2
Beaverton OR (Portland)	8.7	12.3
Winchester NV (Las Vegas)	8.7	4.8
Boulder CO (Denver)	8.3	8.4
Irving TX (Dallas)	2.4	5.5
The Woodlands TX (Houston)	3.1	5.9

Source: U.S. Census 2000 journey-to-work data reported by place of residence.

or planned, opportunities exist for planning new development around transit.

Among suburban pockets of high transit use are many communities in the New York metropolitan area, including Hoboken (New Jersey); a number of suburbs in the Washington metropolitan area, including Mount Rainier (Maryland); several communities in Chicago's suburbs; and Miami Beach (Florida), which has a slightly higher transit share of commuting than its central city (see figure 1-8). Some new transit regions contain transit suburbs, like Imperial Beach outside San Diego, while others offer a special challenge because of the lack of transit suburbs. In Dallas, for example, the municipalities of Richardson and Plano strongly supported the extension of the DART light-rail line, although their pre-DART transit commute shares stood at under 2 percent. The experience of these two communities with encouraging development around their new stations is discussed in Chapter Five.

Developing greenfield areas with good transit access offer another key opportunity for developing around transit. Many of the larger transit-oriented projects that have been developed in recent years have taken advantage of this transit niche, including Orenco Station in Hillsboro, Oregon (Portland region); Otay Ranch outside San Diego; King Farm in Rockville, Maryland (Washington region); and Galatyn Park in Richardson, Texas (Dallas/Fort Worth region). Many such projects are large master-planned communities that face the challenge of appealing to a market that is attracted by transit as an amenity but also seeks a suburban, automobile-oriented lifestyle.

MAKING THE CASE FOR DEVELOPMENT AROUND TRANSIT

Although development around transit seems an obvious winner—it limits the adverse environmental and fiscal impacts of development, supports transit investment, and meets market needs—seeing projects through can be exceedingly difficult. In the urban and suburban transit niches that support transit best, new development or redevelopment faces numerous hurdles.

In built-up areas, the infrastructure—even including the transportation facilities—may need extensive upgrading to support development. Transit stations may be located in untested markets into which developers and lenders are reluctant to go. Projects in transit-served urban and suburban locations compared with conventional suburban locations may be more expensive to build and take longer to be approved. Projects in urban areas are more likely to encounter organized opposition from neighbors and litigation that can force changes in the development program. In short, whereas gaining approval and financing for a conventional suburban development may require little more than a permit application, a transit-related development is likely to need a pioneering spirit, extra planning diligence, negotiating skills, deep pockets, and patience.

For transit districts to take hold as a regional development strategy, developing around transit will need to find support among various constituencies—including developers, transit agencies, public interest groups, local governments, state and federal agencies, financial institutions, and the general public—as discussed in the following sections.

Developers

While developing around transit is still an uncommon form of development in America, enough willing and appropriately talented developers would be drawn to it if the development community were convinced that it offered the potential for some real successes, not just for the community but for developers as well. Currently, too many developers make a business decision to pass on transit-oriented projects because of approval and market issues, while others report that their efforts to develop such projects are rebuffed by the local government.

Transit Agencies

Although transit agencies would seem to be the most obvious ally of developing around transit, their preoccupation with the day-to-day problems of operating complex transit systems often keeps them from focusing on land development issues. Nonetheless, recognizing that supportive development is critical to the success of transit, a number of transit agencies have become involved in development issues.

The Washington Metropolitan Area Transit Authority (WMATA) has a longstanding and successful program of encouraging joint development on land that it controls. San Francisco's BART, in its recent decision to participate in the joint planning of development in a broad area around rail stations, has moved beyond joint development on land adjacent to stations to focus on entire transit districts. In some communities such as Dallas and Denver, transit agencies have engaged real estate professionals in order to become more active in development.

In San Diego, the Metropolitan Transit Development Board puts preliminary ideas and proposals for development near stations on its meeting agendas, so that local officials on the board will better understand the development proposals when they reach the public docket in their home jurisdictions.

Seeking to provide the best opportunities for transit-supportive development, a few transit agencies have taken steps to engage the development community early in the planning stages for new transit investments. Charlotte's Metropolitan Transit Commission, for example, has commissioned panels of experts to examine development options for each of five proposed light-rail transit corridors in the Charlotte Area Transit System (CATS).

Public Interest Groups

Support for transit and transit-supportive development is a natural position for environmental, smart growth, housing advocacy, and other public interest groups that oppose sprawl development and promote

housing opportunities. However, groups whose membership includes people adamantly opposed to new development and to added street traffic sometimes have trouble supporting development around transit because it is still development, generally requires parking, and generates street traffic.

Transit-oriented projects proposed for transit districts should be rendered relatively immune from conflicts over traffic and parking impacts. The bottom line, however, is that transit-oriented development is development and that it generates traffic. Managing parking to keep it from taking over is a challenge in transit districts. Smart growth advocates may prefer little or no accommodations for parking in such districts, but realists understand that the viability of new development depends on the availability of parking—even if transit accessibility reduces parking requirements below what is required in conventional zoning codes.

Even a project with a fairly high transit share among trips generated adds traffic to the surrounding roads. For example, in terms of its local traffic impact, the development of a ten-story office building with a 10 percent transit share is equivalent to the development of a nine-story building with a zero transit share. Thus, the development of transit-supportive districts depends on the existence of broad, regional planning efforts to address traffic issues and remove traffic considerations from the debates over desired projects in transit districts. Success in the creation of transit districts also depends on reasonable planning for the density of development. Although higher densities improve transit ridership, planning density to meet transit thresholds is a mistake. The density of proposed transit districts should be geared to the context of what is appropriate to the community and the market.

Environmental and other public interest organizations need to define good development practices and then spend as much effort supporting projects they like as opposing those they do not. If powerful environmental watchdogs become strong supporters of good development around transit, their standing with their members can help create a favorable approval climate for developing around transit. On the local level, groups formed to garner public support for transit investment, such as the Citizens for Mass Transit—which was formed to help win support for St. Louis's MetroLink light-rail line—can also be enlisted to garner support for proposed land uses that support transit. Housing advocacy groups can help make the case for affordable housing in transit districts, as has the Santa Clara Manufacturing Group in that California county's high-price housing market. Support from such groups for projects seeking approval could carry much weight with local governments.

Local Governments

Developing around transit requires a regional collaboration among local governments. Local governments must lead the process of determining what types of development should be sought for particular station areas, adopt appropriate regulations and incentives for private development, implement the timely completion of supporting public facilities, assure that all parties remain in continuous communication, and maintain a long-term commitment to transit district development.

In areas well served by transit, local governments ordinarily should be disposed to favor transit-related development, but the natural alliance of local governments and the developers of community-sensitive projects often is undermined by the negative reactions to projects from neighborhood groups and by the application of antiquated zoning codes. Local public officials are potentially some of the most effective advocates of developing around transit. They should be encouraged to take a leadership role in identifying development options near transit.

State and Federal Agencies

The programs that states can bring to bear on the promotion of development around transit are wide ranging. They may make financial contributions, sup-

Many constituencies are natural supporters of development around transit. Gaining their support can expedite project and plan approvals.

port or mandate the adoption by local governments of relevant planning and zoning provisions, and even locate their offices and other employment centers in transit districts. Eleven states have adopted laws, programs, funding initiatives, or policies that promote transit-oriented development by providing financial incentives, technical assistance, or planning assistance to localities. Some states seek to assure that the actions and programs of state agencies are coordinated—sometimes through metropolitan planning organizations (MPOs, agencies that meet federal requirements for the regional coordination of transportation planning) and sometimes directly through local entities—to support transit-oriented development. At least eight state governors have proactively championed policies, funding, or legislative initiatives on transit-oriented development.

At the federal level, transportation agencies understand that their funding decisions and regulations can exert a strong influence on development—however loath they may be to get involved in local planning processes. The Federal Transit Administration includes land use criteria in its rating of transit projects seeking federal funding.

Financial Institutions

Developers are learning how to finance urban projects with good transit connections and with a mix of uses, and the list of lenders with experience in financing such projects is growing. Developers know that pitching the special transit and environmental benefits of developments around transit is not likely to appeal to hard-hearted lenders, so they focus on the special market opportunities afforded by these projects. Many developers try to obtain some local financial support, because this communicates the idea that a transit connection counts for something in the community and makes the financing package look better to major lenders.

The General Public

In that neighbors are often the biggest impediment to new development, it is important to involve them early and try to gain their support for overall transit district plans. It is also advisable to take into consideration the likelihood of effective neighborhood-based opposition to development around transit in planning the location of transit stations. For example, transit planners might bypass communities desiring access to transit but judged to be unwilling to seek and approve transit-supportive development.

THIS BOOK

The foregoing introduction to the issues and opportunities relating to developing around transit is followed by chapters covering specific aspects of developing in a transit district. Chapter Two, which was written by University of California planning professor and consultant Robert Cervero, discusses the financial value of transit to adjacent properties. It includes some original research commissioned by ULI for this book. Chapter Three, by traffic engineer and transit planning consultant Fred Dock and geographer Carol Swenson, describes planning for development around transit and the key elements of a successful transit district. The next two chapters—Chapter Four by ULI fellow Maureen McAvey and Chapter Five by urban planning consultant Douglas Porter—focus on the specific issues in and successful approaches to developing around transit in urban areas and suburban areas. In Chapter Six, Fred Dock discusses the particular issues involved in developing around terminal stations and provides examples of how the design of terminal stations can encourage or discourage supporting development in adjacent areas. The final chapter, which is based on the conclusions of a special workshop of experts held in 2002, summarizes key principles for developing around transit.

Notes

1. Regional Plan Association, *Building Transit-Friendly Communities: A Design and Development Strategy for the Tri-State Metropolitan Region* (New York: RPA, July 1997).

2. Robert T. Dunphy, Deborah L. Brett, Sandra Rosenbloom, and Andre Bald, *Moving beyond Gridlock* (Washington, D.C.: ULI–the Urban Land Institute, 1997), p. 137.

3. Douglas R. Porter, *Transit-Focused Development* (Washington, D.C.: Transportation Research Board, 1997).

4. Anthony Downs, "Can Transit Tame Sprawl?" *Governing,* January 2002.

5. "98 Percent of U.S. Commuters Favor Public Transportation for Others," *Onion,* November 29, 2000.

6. Federal Transit Administration, *2002 Status of the Nation's Highways, Bridges, and Transit: Conditions and Performance,* (Washington, D.C.: U.S. Department of Transportation, 2002), p. 14-8.

7. Quoted in Jonathan Richmond, "Theories of Symbolism, Metaphor, and Myth and the Development of Western Rail Passenger Systems" (paper presented at a meeting of the Association of Collegiate Schools of Planning, Portland, Oregon, 1989).

8. John Pucher and John Renne, "Socioeconomics of Urban Travel: Evidence from the 2001 NPTS," *Transportation Quarterly,* summer 2003, p. 67.

9. Atlanta Regional Commission, "Regional On-Board Transit Survey, 2001–2002"; available on ARC's Website: www.atlantaregional.com/transportationair/OnBoardTransit.pdf.

10. *Tri-Met Customer Profile 2002* (Portland, Oregon: Tri-County Metropolitan Transportation District, 2002), p.3.

11. Boris Pushkarev and Jeffrey Zupan, *Public Transportation and Land Use Policy* (Bloomington, Indiana: Indiana University Press, 1987).

12. Ibid.

13. Reid Ewing, *Transportation and Land Use Innovations* (Chicago: Planners Press, 1997).

14. Cambridge Systematics and Booz Allen Hamilton, *Summary Analysis of Transit Supportive Land Use for New Starts Projects* (Washington, D.C.: Federal Transit Administration, July 2002), pp. 4–19

15. Geoffrey Booth, et al., *Transforming Suburban Business Districts* (Washington, D.C.: ULI–the Urban Land Institute, 2001), p. 37.

16. Ibid., pp. 154–155.

17. Paul M. Weyrich and William S. Lind, "Does Transit Work? A Conservative Reappraisal" (paper issued by the Free Congress Research and Education Foundation, Washington, D.C., 1999); available on American Public Transportation Association Web site: www.apta.com.

18. Kevin Cooper, *Travel Characteristics at Large-Scale Activity Centers,* National Cooperative Highway Research Program Report 323 (Washington, D.C.: Transportation Research Board, 1989), pp. 34–36.

19. Booth et al., *Transforming Suburban Business Districts,* pp. 212–214.

CHAPTER TWO

ROBERT CERVERO

THE PROPERTY VALUE CASE FOR TRANSIT

REAL ESTATE MARKETS REVEAL THE BENEFITS OF TRANSIT in dollars and cents. Transit investments create value because the benefits of being well connected to the rest of the region—that is, of being accessible—are capitalized into the market value of land. In theory, transit-served properties in desirable areas are ideal real estate locations— for living, because residents are within easy reach of jobs and shops; for retailing, because stores are within the reach of many potential shoppers; and for office employers because transit access enlarges their laborshed (the area from which workers commute). Thus, access-sensitive households, retailers, employers, and employees bid up land prices near transit stations.

This, of course, is theory. In reality, for every two studies showing that land prices increase when transit stations open, at least one study shows that land values go down. Some property owners or tenants view transit in negative terms. At a conference on joint development sponsored by the American Public Transportation Association a few years ago, a developer told the audience that he would not allow prospective tenants to lease retail space in his mixed-use project near a San Diego Trolley stop if they were mainly interested in being near transit. The developer confided that he did not want transit-dependent people coming to his project because their presence

Downtown Washington, D.C. Many of the Washington region's Metrorail stations have attracted place-making development that has contributed to local tax coffers as well. In the view of communities bypassed by Metrorail's initial phases: "Where the Metro goes, the money flows."

District of Columbia Office of Planning

might discourage more affluent shoppers and increase the costs for on-site security. To him, being near transit was a potential liability.

This chapter reviews the growing body of research on transit and property values, and presents original research on three California regions conducted by the author and Michael Duncan, the author's graduate assistant. The California research was sponsored by the National Association of Realtors and the Urban Land Institute.

Most evidence suggests that being near transit enhances property values and rents. Next to the Mockingbird light-rail station in Dallas, for example, office and retail space rented for $40 per square foot in mid-2002, which was about 60 percent above market rates. Even higher premiums have been recorded in the Washington metropolitan area for office and retail space near Metrorail stations in Arlington, Virginia, and Bethesda, Maryland.[1] Transitional inner-city neighborhoods in the District of Columbia with Metrorail access have also experienced rising land values. For example, land prices near the U and 14th Streets station, a predominantly minority neighborhood known for its jazz clubs and other nighttime entertainment, have nearly doubled in the past three years.

Is the presence of transit responsible for observed jumps in prices and rents? In many U.S. cities with rail-transit systems, land prices are going up everywhere—not only around transit nodes. In fact, while sale prices and rents might be increasing three blocks from a station, they might be rising even faster along a busy highway several miles away. Analytically, the challenge is to isolate the influence of transit from everything else that affects property values.

One way to proceed is to compare transit-served parcels with "comps"—parcels that are nearly identical in all respects except they are not near transit. A study of rental housing in suburban San Francisco revealed that new two-bedroom/two-bathroom apartments located near a Bay Area Rapid Transit (BART) station fetched rents that were, on average, 15 percent higher than rents for nearly identical units in the same cities that were located beyond a half-mile walk of a BART station.[2]

In truth, however, it is often difficult to find good matches. Differences observed may be due to transit's presence or they may be due to imperfect comps. Thus, researchers seeking to estimate the impacts of being near transit are turning increasingly to statistical models that assign a price to each component of a parcel's so-called "bundle of goods." These are called hedonic price models.[3]

Clarifying how transit affects land values can help inform both private and public sector investment decisions. Transit boards that believe that property holdings in station areas not only can leverage transit-supportive projects, but also can be financially profitable are likely to become more entrepreneurial in acquiring vacant parcels near planned rail stations early in the development process. In the Washington region, the transit authority (WMATA) banked land around Metrorail stations and entered into joint development agreements when the time was ripe—thus helping to ensure the development of numerous mid- and high-rise buildings around its stations.

Throwing light on the land value impacts of transit is important as well for settling legal disputes involving transit investments. Across the United States, transit authorities are being sued by landowners who claim that transit's incursions—noise, vibration, and increased traffic—diminish the value of their property. In its 1997 ruling in *Los Angeles County Metropolitan Transportation Authority* v. *Continental Development Corporation,* the California supreme court overturned 100 years of legal precedents in this area by allowing a broader interpretation of offsetting benefit in a condemnation case.[4] This ruling points to a more critical need for evidence that can be used to assess the degree to which any negative consequences or severance damages associated with transit investments are offset by accessibility benefits.

TRANSIT MODE

Transit's land value impacts are partly governed by the design and type of transit system involved. Rapid-rail and commuter-rail systems operating on exclusive rights-of-way achieve the highest speeds and confer the greatest saving in travel times. Thus, they offer the greatest accessibility benefits. Light-rail systems, which sometimes share the streets with other traffic and are therefore subject to traffic delays, usually operate at much slower speeds and cover a smaller geographic area. Accordingly, their land value impacts tend to be more modest. Fixed-route buses that operate in stop-and-go conditions provide the least accessibility benefits. Their impacts on land prices are often so small as to be nonmeasurable.

The land value benefits of fixed-guideway systems generally accrue only to parcels near access points (stations). Being near a rail track but not near a station, in fact, usually diminishes a property's value. For U.S. transit systems, the impact zone—the area wherein appreciable gains in land value occur—generally extends one-quarter mile (and sometimes as far as one-half mile) from a station. This radius of up to a half mile is widely considered to be an acceptable walking distance to transit in suburban settings.[5]

EVIDENCE OF TRANSIT'S IMPACTS

Residential Properties

Most, though not all, hedonic price studies of transit's impact on residential properties have found premiums. Rapid-rail and commuter-rail systems in large metropolitan areas have been found to provide the largest value benefits.

In San Francisco, for example, a study found that for every meter a single-family house was closer to a BART station, its 1990 sale price increased by $2.29, all else being equal.[6] In Alameda County, houses located several blocks from a BART station sold, on average,

for 39 percent more than otherwise comparable houses 20 miles from a station.

A 1993 study of residential properties near the 14.5-mile Lindenwold commuter-rail line in the New Jersey suburbs of Philadelphia concluded that access to rail created an average value premium of 6.4 percent.[7]

In contrast, a study from the early 1990s of residential properties in the Miami region concluded that proximity to Metrorail stations induced little or no increase in housing values. This could be a reflection of the rail system's relatively limited coverage—only 21 miles of one-way tracks compared, for example, with BART's 95 miles.[8] A study of the price of houses near Atlanta's 41-mile MARTA rapid-rail system found that transit accessibility increased housing values in lower-income Census tracts but decreased values in upper-income areas.[9]

Even studies that have focused on differences in transit's impact on residential values in areas within a close distance to rail stations—comparing parcels that are adjacent or a few blocks distant with parcels that are farther away (for example, parcels that are beyond an audible distance)—have yielded conflicting results.

One study that looked at Portland, Oregon's light-rail MAX system found that positive land value effects extended only to within a 500-meter walking distance of stations.[10] Another study that looked at suburban areas served by MAX in Portland and by BART in San Francisco found that residential property values were lower within a few blocks of rail stops than five or six blocks away.[11] Yet another study that looked at areas around rapid-rail (BART) and commuter-rail (Caltrain) stations in San Francisco found that single-family houses within 300 meters of BART stations experienced no negative value effects while those within 300 meters of Caltrain stations sold at an average discount of $51,000, a huge effect.[12]

This last study also found different results for residential areas very near light-rail stations in Sacramento, San Diego, and San Jose. In Sacramento and San Diego, the relationship between a location very near stations and housing value was statistically in-

significant. In San Jose, single-family houses within
300 meters of stations were found to be worth around
$31,000 less than equivalent properties beyond
transit's immediate impact zone, controlling for
other factors.

It seems plausible that in suburban settings a location that is "too close" to rail transit can be a market disadvantage, while in fairly dense, mixed-use
environments it is not. This is because the residents
of areas with high ambient noise levels and busy
streets do not generally perceive nearby transit facilities as a nuisance. The alignment of the rail system,
which affects noise levels, is also a factor in residential value. Elevated rail lines, which are the most noisy,
depress residential values the most. Below-ground
systems often exercise negligible effects on value.

Commercial Properties

Most evidence of transit's impact on commercial properties concerns rapid-rail systems. As is the case with
residential properties, it is inconsistent. An early study
(1978) found no evidence that the value of commercial
properties around BART stations—a suburban station
and two inner-city stops—increased over the long
term because of their proximity to rail.[13] Another
early study looked at commercial properties in Washington, D.C., before the inauguration of rail service
and found that values fell by 7 percent for every 10
percent increase in distance from a planned Metrorail
station, up to a radius of 2,500 feet.[14] No follow-up
work was conducted to see if gains held over time,
though subsequent case study work suggests that
Metrorail has increased the value of nearby commercial properties, sometimes substantially.[15]

Two studies that looked at the impact of Atlanta's
MARTA rail system on the value of commercial properties reached opposite conclusions. The first (1998)
found that while office properties within a mile of
freeway interchanges commanded rent premiums, those
within a mile of MARTA stations typically leased for
less than comparable space farther away.[16] The second study (1999), in contrast, found that commercial
properties were "influenced positively by both access
to rail stations and policies that encourage more in-

David Leland, Leland Consulting Group

tensive development around those stations."[17] The
latter study's findings suggest that targeting commercial development around transit stations in combination with the establishment of special transit
districts within which parking and density requirements are relaxed can produce higher-than-normal
land value premiums.

The degree of physical integration of adjacent commercial properties with rail stations, such as through
air-rights development or direct pedestrian connections, also has a bearing on market performance. A
study of commercial properties at five rail stations in
the Washington region and Atlanta over the 1978–
1989 period found that projects developed through
the joint efforts of the transit agency and private
developers—joint development projects—were better
performers than projects that were not jointly developed. Physically integrated projects achieved average
rent premiums of 7 to 9 percent and tended to enjoy
lower vacancy rates and faster absorption of new
leasable space.[18] Joint development projects, the
study found, were generally "better" projects—that
is, they were architecturally integrated with transit
facilities, achieved better on-site circulation of people
and cars, and used space more efficiently through
shared parking and other resource sharing.

A 2001 study of rail-station revitalization in older
neighborhoods and business districts in the northeastern United States found that rehabilitation had
a positive effect on surrounding property values and
tax revenues, with benefits increasing with city size
and urban densities.[19]

Theory suggests that light-rail systems confer smaller
benefits to commercial properties than do heavy-rail
systems. However, some researchers have reported
otherwise. A study of the Dallas Area Rapid Transit
(DART) system looked at matched pairs of compara-

ble retail and office properties—some near DART and others not.[20] Between 1997 and 2001, the average value of office properties near DART stops increased by 25 percent, compared with 12 percent for comparable properties not near DART.

The findings of several California studies of light rail's impact on the value of commercial properties vary. A 2000 study of Santa Clara County's light-rail system found that commercial properties within a half mile of stations commanded rent premiums, with those that were at least a quarter mile away commanding higher premiums.[21] Compared with other properties in the county, the estimated monthly lease premium for properties within one-quarter mile of a station was 3.3 cents per square foot and for properties one-quarter to one-half mile away, it was 6.4 cents per square foot.

RECENT EXPERIENCE IN CALIFORNIA

Suffice it to say, the effects of transit on real estate performance are far from crystal clear. While differences in research findings are attributable, in part, to local contextual factors, such as the design of stations or the softness of the local real estate markets, and to whether the market was on the upswing or the downswing, they also reflect differences in methodologies, measurements, and research designs.

One limitation of some studies has been their focus on rents as opposed to sale prices. Rental data can be problematic in that contract rents do not always capture the full array of concessions received by tenants. Even if contract rents are fairly accurate, they need to be adjusted for occupancy levels to reveal effective contract rents. Data limitations often preclude such adjustments. Focusing on data from sale transactions avoids such problems.

The remainder of this chapter reports on the author's recent research from three California counties—San Diego, Santa Clara, and Los Angeles—that used hedonic price models to estimate transit's influences on residential and commercial sales prices. Sponsored by the National Association of Realtors (NAR) and the Urban Land Institute (ULI), the analyses cover the 1999–2000 period when California's real estate markets were on an upswing and traffic congestion had reached all-time highs. In contrast, previous research in California that had found no evidence of transit-induced benefits covered periods in the mid-1970s and early 1990s when local real estate markets were generally flat.

Also, the new analyses reflect improvements in the specification of hedonic price models that have been made possible by advancements in geographic information systems (GIS). GIS tools allowed the researchers to precisely gauge the distance of the parcels being studied from transit, freeways, jobs, and labor markets. GIS also allowed the researchers to consistently measure the characteristics—such as population densities and household incomes—of neighborhoods within a one-mile radius of the studied properties.

Over the next 20 years, California is expected to add 15 million residents and more than 5 million house-

A VTA light-rail stop in Santa Clara County. Fixed-guideway transit is expected to assume a major role in shaping California's tremendous growth over the next 20 years.

David Leland, Leland Consulting Group

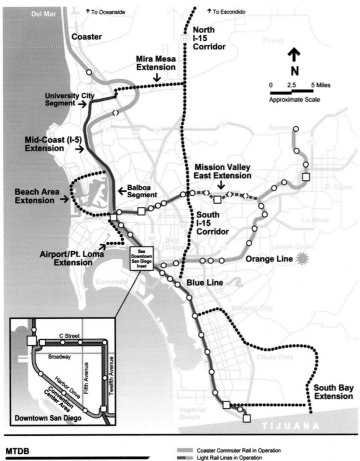

MTDB

San Diego Regional Rail Project Summary

	Coaster Commuter Rail in Operation
	Light Rail Lines in Operation
□	Transfer Stations
○	Rail Stations
( )	Future Rail Stations
▪▪▪▪	LRT Under Development (Final Engineering or Construction)
▬▬▬	Future LRT Extension
●●●●●	Future Transit Extensions Under Study

A plan of rail-transit routes in San Diego County.

holds. Increasingly, fixed-guideway transit is being called upon to guide this growth. Such transit investments are occurring not only in major urban centers, but also along the spine of the state's agricultural belt—the Central Valley between Los Angeles and San Francisco—where a high-speed rail system is proposed.

Over the past decade, more rail tracks were laid in California than in any other state. Between 1990 and 2000, 720 one-way track-miles were added in the state's four largest metropolitan areas and around $20 billion was spent on mass-transit projects.[22] Over this period, San Diego, Sacramento, and Santa Clara Counties ranked first, third, and fourth in transit ridership growth among U.S. counties with light-rail services.[23] Today, California has arguably the richest mix of high-performance transit services in the nation, including rapid rail, commuter rail, light rail, intercity Amtrak services, and bus rapid transit (BRT).

A fair amount of transit-oriented development (TOD) has taken place in California as well, much of it lever-

aged through proactive local initiatives. The state has also played a role, in particular through the California Transit Village Act of 1995, which encourages local jurisdictions to zone and plan for intensive, mixed-use development around rail stations. The state exempts TOD from roadway level-of-service requirements and gives localities that pursue TOD priority access to state transportation funds.

San Diego County

San Diego County, home to 2.6 million residents, boasts 90 directional miles of metropolitan rail services. The planning, construction, and management of transit services in the urbanized southern part of the county are overseen by the Metropolitan Transit Development Board (MTDB). In 1981, San Diego introduced the first modern-day light-rail system in the United States with the opening of a line from downtown to the Mexican border, a distance of 16 miles. Today, the region's Trolley system (known also as "LRT," light-rail transit) includes 47 one-way track-miles and as many track-miles are slated for construction over the next several decades (see transit plan map on this page). A commuter-rail service called the Coaster operates between Oceanside and downtown San Diego, a distance of 43 miles.

Transit-Oriented Development

To date, the San Diego region has been at the forefront in promoting TOD in California. Opting for carrots over sticks, regional and local government authorities have used various incentives to entice private investments near rail stops rather than adopting a regulatory approach.

In 1995, the San Diego Association of Governments (SANDAG) adopted a land use distribution element for its regional growth strategy that promoted growth in "transit-focused areas" along existing and planned high-capacity rail lines. In 1992, the city of San Diego adopted the first TOD ordinance in the United States, which called for compact, infill development near Trolley stops and the creation of "urban village overlay" zones for this purpose. Such zones have been established near most Trolley stations in the city.

Within the region, TOD is occurring around commuter-rail stops and along the Mission Valley light-rail line. In 1999, the county's Air Pollution Control District provided $150,000 in air quality funds (raised by a surcharge on the state motor vehicle registration fee) to the city of Oceanside to support TOD planning around six stations along the Coaster corridor. Over the past few years, the Mission Valley light-rail line has become a model for transit-oriented growth in the region. Designed on the principle of maximizing development potential (rather than on the principle of minimizing construction costs), the Mission Valley LRT line crosses the San Diego River three times in order to promote development on the flat valley floor and preserve the valley's sensitive hillsides.

Among the San Diego region's most notable examples of TOD projects are the following:

• MTS/James R. Mills Office Building at the Imperial Trolley Station just south of downtown;

• the American Plaza luxury hotel/office complex at the main downtown transfer station;

• Grossmont Center, a 103-acre shopping complex, and La Mesa Village Plaza, a mid-rise residential/retail/office development on the Orange (East) LRT line;

• the 41-acre mixed-use Hazard Center, a 41-acre pedestrian-scale residential/office/retail development on the Mission Valley line; and

• Uptown District, a pedestrian-oriented mixed-use retail center and residential development in San Diego's Hillcrest neighborhood, built on a 14-acre site (formerly occupied by a Sears store) and served by bus transit.

Findings of Past Studies

Three years following the 1981 opening of Trolley services from downtown to the Mexican border, SANDAG interviewed developers and retailers about the benefits of being near transit.[24] Most developers stated that proximity to Trolley stops entered into their marketing of lease space. Around 20 percent of merchants felt that the Trolley was an "important

positive factor in the business remaining in its current location." However, nearly 40 percent thought that the Trolley had no impact, positive or negative, on their sales volume.

A 1992 study sought to appraise the value to commercial properties of locations near Trolley stations.[25] In the case of retail businesses, fairly significant benefits were recorded. Monthly rents for retail establishments adjacent to Trolley stations were, on average, 167 percent higher (around $1.35 per square foot higher in 1980 dollars) than rents for control properties that were a half block away. Factors other than adjacency, such as the volume of pedestrian traffic, could have explained such sharp differences.

Using 1990 data for 134 single-family house sales in the city of San Diego, a more rigorous, hedonic price study that controlled for other possible predictors of real estate prices found that locations near transit produced appreciable benefits.[26] For every meter a typical single-family house was closer to a Trolley station, its sale price increased by $2.72. Outside the city limits, the study found no significant premiums for locations near transit stations.

Current Research Findings

The studies just described predate the Trolley's recent expansions and the 1995 inauguration of Coaster services. To provide up-to-date insights, Michael Duncan and I obtained 1999 to 2001 sales data for commercial properties (including offices, retail buildings, restaurants, and hotels) and 2000 sales data for residential properties from *Metroscan*, a proprietary data base available from First American Real Estate Solutions. (Three years of sales were used for commercial properties in order to obtain a database that was sufficiently large to support the analysis; one year of sales for residential properties produced enough data for the analysis.) The share of total sales that were within a half-mile ring of rail stops ranged from 4 percent for single-family houses to 19 percent for commercial properties.

The sales data were combined with information on transportation (for example, highway travel times) and neighborhood characteristics from county sources

Figure 2-1

RESIDENTIAL SALE PRICE PREMIUMS OR DISCOUNTS IN SAN DIEGO COUNTY, BY RAIL LINE, 2000

1. Single-family housing not included, because no single-family houses were sold within one-half mile of downtown Trolley stations.

Source: Author's research (see chapter endnote #27).

Figure 2-2

COMMERCIAL[1] SALE PRICE PREMIUMS OR DISCOUNTS IN SAN DIEGO COUNTY, BY RAIL LINE, 1999–2001

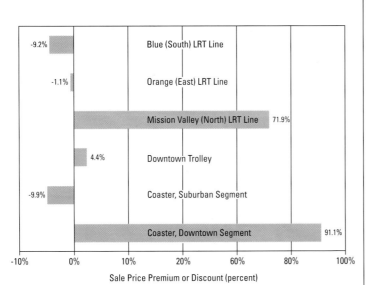

1. Includes office, retail, restaurant, hotel, and other commercial land uses.

Source: Author's research (see chapter endnote #27).

and the Census to estimate hedonic price models for multifamily rental housing, residential condominiums, single-family houses, and commercial properties.[27]

Figure 2-1 summarizes the results of this analysis for residential uses. For "typical" properties, this graph expresses the sale price impact (premium or discount) of a location within a half mile of a Trolley or Coaster stop, holding all other factors constant. "Typical" is determined by the average characteristics of each residential use in the data base. For example, the typical multifamily complex is 5,200 square feet and 1.4 miles from the nearest freeway interchange.

With a few exceptions, residential properties reaped measurable benefits from being near transit. All multifamily and condominium projects near Trolley stops enjoyed premiums, with the largest recorded along the East (Orange) LRT line, where apartment complexes within a half-mile walk of a stop gained, on average, about $100,000 in sale prices. Single-family houses near Trolley stations, on the other hand, generally sold for less than such houses in other locations, suggesting a disamenity effect.

For-sale units—condominiums and single-family houses—near Coaster stations gained the biggest residential premiums. Apparently, many of the professional workers with downtown jobs who live in the North County highly value owning a condominium unit or house within an easy walk of a Coaster station. One reason may be that I-5 north of downtown is the region's most congested freeway. The premium that they are willing to pay for the typical condominium when it is close to a Coaster station is $85,000.

Interestingly, proximity to Coaster stations appears to be a disamenity for multifamily projects, suggesting a different market dynamic for rental units. Association with rail stations could drag down the market prices of apartment buildings in high-income settings like the North County.

Figure 2-2 summarizes the San Diego study's results for commercial uses. The sale prices of office, retail, restaurant, and other commercial properties near Trolley stops on the Mission Valley line and near the downtown stops of the Coaster commuter-rail line enjoyed huge premiums—in the 70 to 90 percent range.

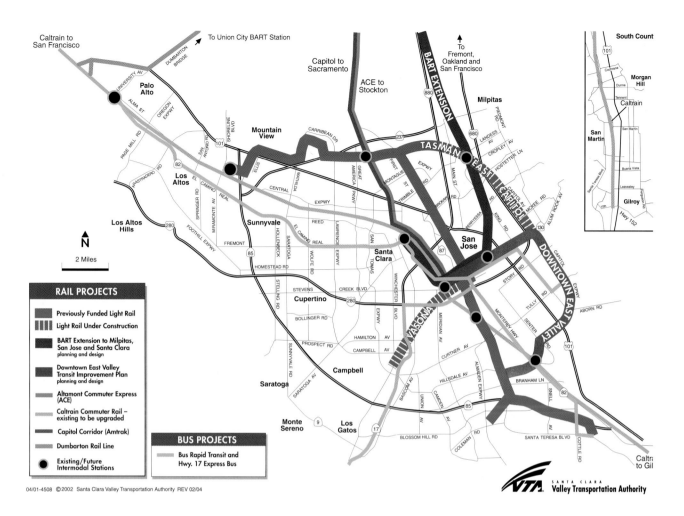

Legend / map labels:

RAIL PROJECTS

- Previously Funded Light Rail
- Light Rail Under Construction
- BART Extension to Milpitas, San Jose and Santa Clara
  planning and design
- Downtown East Valley Transit Improvement Plan
  planning and design
- Altamont Commuter Express (ACE)
- Caltrain Commuter Rail – existing to be upgraded
- Capitol Corridor (Amtrak)
- Dumbarton Rail Line
- Existing/Future Intermodal Stations

BUS PROJECTS

- Bus Rapid Transit and Hwy. 17 Express Bus

04/01-4508 ©2002 Santa Clara Valley Transportation Authority REV 02/04

VTA SANTA CLARA Valley Transportation Authority

These two corridors have been beneficiaries of proactive TOD planning, including targeted public infrastructure improvements (sidewalk upgrades, landscaping of public areas, and so forth), the establishment of overlay zones to encourage a mix of land uses, and streamlined permitting processes. In less vibrant commercial districts, such as those located along the South (Blue) and East (Orange) light-rail lines, the impact of transit locations was found to be muted and sometimes negative.

In sum, our research from San Diego County reveals that rail transit is capable of producing appreciable land value benefits, but not invariably. The relationship between property value and locations near transit vary by the type of land use and character of the transit corridor. Local market characteristics seem to have some bearing on outcomes. In the buoyant North County area, for example, for-sale residential units reap large premiums, and in the economically thriving Mission Valley corridor and downtown's newly refurbished waterfront area, commercial properties seem to flourish in transit's presence. Elsewhere, transit's impacts are modest and, in some cases, negative.

Santa Clara County

In terms of population (1.68 million) and employment (1.08 million), Santa Clara County is the largest county in the San Francisco Bay Area. In addition to being a powerhouse of technological innovation, the county is known for its woeful shortages of affordable housing and for the worst traffic congestion in the Bay Area. From 1995 to 2000, the number of jobs in the Silicon Valley grew by 21 percent while the number of new housing units barely grew by 5 percent.[28] In mid-2000, the median single-family home in the Silicon Valley cost $617,000, an 87 percent jump from five years earlier.

In 2001, the tenth anniversary of VTA (Santa Clara Valley Transit Authority) light-rail services was celebrated. Stagnant ridership along with steadily worsening traffic congestion characterized most of VTA rail's first decade. By the end of the 1990s, the region's transit trends seemed to have turned the tide. New rail lines and services had been added, ridership was up, and transit villages were sprouting in different parts of the county. However, that period coincided

Planned rail and express-bus routes in Santa Clara County.

with the peak of the high-tech boom; with the sub-sequent high-tech bust, sharp declines in transit ridership have occurred.

In 2000, the Tasman West extension to Mountain View was completed, adding 7.6 east/west miles to the 21-mile, north/south Guadalupe Corridor and linking Santa Clara, Sunnyvale, and Mountain View with downtown San Jose and predominantly residential neighborhoods to the south. In 2001, completion of the Tasman East extension brought VTA rail to Milpitas, home of Cisco System's headquarters and other high-tech campuses.

In November 2000, voters approved, by a whopping 81 percent margin, Measure B, which extends for 20 years a half-cent sales tax earmarked for transit. It will finance billions of dollars in new transit investments, including the extension of the BART heavy-rail system to downtown San Jose. Santa Clara County also boasts two commuter-rail services—Caltrain, which runs up the peninsula to San Francisco, and the recently opened Altamont Commuter Express (ACE), a conduit to affordable residential neighborhoods in the Central Valley.

The VTA's service territory is largely sprawling office campuses and car-oriented shopping plazas, which has made building a ridership base a struggle. A number of factors—including extraordinary growth, the beefed-up rail network, and EcoPass, a popular program offering employer-paid annual transit passes—seem to have helped in recent years. Between 1998 and 2000, light-rail ridership rose 11 percent and commuter-rail ridership jumped 25 percent. Transit-oriented development (TOD) has also had a hand in coaxing more motorists into trains.

Transit-Oriented Development

TOD has been seized upon in Santa Clara County as a means to attack housing problems as well as transportation problems. Surveys show that transit's share of commuting trips is five times higher among people living near VTA light-rail stops as it is among residents countywide.[29] This popularity represents self-selection—that is, county residents who are predis-

posed to or receptive to riding a train to work are more likely to seek housing within easy walking distance of a station.

Local governments have adopted various policies and programs to leverage TOD. These include tax-exempt financing, public assistance with land assembly, and overlay zones that permit higher-than-normal densities. So far, these incentives seem to be paying off. Few transit systems in the United States can match the amount of nearby development that has taken place in Santa Clara County in recent years. Between 1997 and 1999, an estimated 4,500 housing units and 9 million square feet of office space were added within walking distance of the Tasman West corridor.

Examples of TOD incentives introduced in the county and the development that resulted include the following:

• In Mountain View, the planning board rezoned 44 acres of industrial land to accommodate more than 600 housing units adjacent to the Whisman light-rail station.

• In Sunnyvale, density bonuses have spurred infill development in the Northside industrial district near the Borregas and Fair Oaks light-rail stations.

• In San Jose, 195 three-story townhouses were recently finished on a former park-and-ride lot adjacent to the Ohlone/Chynoweth light-rail station.

• In Sunnyvale, in return for a 60 percent increase in the allowable floor/area ratio for four office buildings on the new Netscape campus, the developer, Jay Paul Company of San Francisco, helped foot the bill for construction of the Moffett Park light-rail station, a $2.5 million project that opened recently.

• The city of Mountain View created a transit overlay zone at the downtown Caltrain commuter-rail station that allows up to 50 percent higher densities within 2,000 feet of the station. This incentive leveraged the development of a 359-unit complex of townhouses, condominiums, and single-family housing units called The Crossings, which sits on the site of a former shopping center.

Development near a commuter-rail station in Sunnyvale (see Santa Clara Valley transit map on page 11). Research on the land value impacts of transit in Santa Clara County found that locations near commuter rail yielded larger premiums than those near light rail.

David Leland, Leland Consulting Group

• At San Jose's Tamien station, which is a VTA rail transfer point for Caltrain commuter-rail services, the VTA built a daycare center that accommodates 140 children. The idea was to promote light rail as a commuting option by making it convenient for parents to drop off and pick up their kids on workdays.

Not all developers have needed lures to attract them to transit locales. The Irvine Company recently built several thousand luxury apartments within walking distance of light-rail stations in north San Jose without any development incentives. It was the availability of large, undeveloped parcels that happened to be near VTA light rail that attracted the company's interest.

Current Research Findings

Our research on land value impacts in Santa Clara County was similar to that carried out in San Diego County.[30] Sales transaction data were obtained from *Metroscan* for residential parcels that sold in 1999 and for commercial, office, and R&D properties that sold in 1998 and 1999. This time period was used not only because it coincided with a buoyant economic period, but also because sufficient time had elapsed since the introduction of light-rail and commuter-rail services for any benefits to have been reflected in property prices.

Figure 2-4

COMMERCIAL LAND VALUE PREMIUMS IN SANTA CLARA COUNTY, BY RAIL LINE, 1998–1999

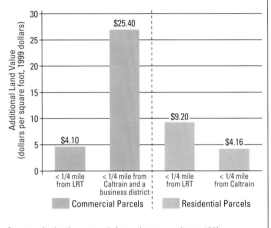

Source: Author's research (see chapter endnote #30).

The hedonic price model used to analyze the Santa Clara data revealed that substantial benefits accrued to residential properties within a quarter mile of a rail station and even more substantial benefits accrued to commercial properties within a quarter-mile radius (see figure 2-4).

Being near a VTA light-rail stop benefited only those residential properties that are zoned and used for five or more apartment units. Large apartment buildings that are within a quarter mile of light-rail stops commanded a premium of around $9 per square foot. Compared with the mean property value of $20.30 per square foot, $9 represents a 45 percent premium. Relative to parcels that are within four miles of a light-rail station, the capitalization premium was 28 percent.

Being near a commuter-rail station, on the other hand, conferred value benefits to all types of residential property—single-family houses as well as small and large apartment properties. The land value premiums for proximity to commuter rail, however, were generally smaller than for light rail.

Being within walking distance of a rail stop conferred value on residential property, as did having good job access via transit. In fact, job access by transit weighed in on residential land values more than did job access by car. The hedonic price model analysis revealed that for every 100,000 additional jobs located within a 15-minute travel time of the county's transit system, residential property values rose by almost $30 per square foot, all else being equal. Apparently, having good transit connectivity to employment opportunities in a highly congested setting like Santa Clara County gets appreciably capitalized into residential property values.

For commercial properties, locations associated with commuter rail yielded larger premiums than those associated with light rail. Relative to the mean square-foot value of the sampled commercial properties, those lying within walking distance of a VTA light-rail stop yielded a $4 per square foot (23 percent) premium and those near a Caltrain station doubled in value, all else being equal. (No premium was associated with being near an ACE station, possibly because there are so few—just three compared with Caltrain's 16.) Why were these premiums larger for commuter rail? Possibly because light-rail trains operate at slower speeds and stop more frequently, thus yielding more modest accessibility benefits.

Only commercial parcels that are within eyeshot of stations enjoyed premiums. In this landscape of office campuses, retail strips, and superblock development, the value added from transit access largely disappeared for locations beyond a five-minute walk.

Los Angeles County

Los Angeles County provides a particularly rich setting for studying the land value impacts of high-performance transit investments, with its four transit modes in addition to traditional fixed-route, fixed-schedule buses:

- subway (Metro Red Line);

- commuter rail (Metrolink);

- light rail (Metro Green Line and Metro Blue Line); and

- bus rapid transit (Wilshire/Whittier Metro Rapid and Ventura Metro Rapid). Unlike the celebrated bus rapid transit (BRT) systems in Ottawa, Curitiba (Brazil), and Nagoya (Japan), the county's BRT services achieve their speed advantage solely through operational and design strategies—signal prioritization, longer bus stops, queue-jumper lanes, far-side bus stops, and low-floor buses for expedited boarding and alighting.

Metropolitan Los Angeles has the dubious distinction of being the nation's most traffic-congested region, according to the Texas Transportation Institute.[31] In 1999, 59 hours per capita were "lost" due to freeway delays and half of the region's freeway lane-miles operated at "extreme" congestion levels (up from 4 percent in 1982). Los Angeles also has the nation's most polluted air, and is the only area classified by the U.S. Environmental Protection Agency as an "extreme non-attainment area" for noncompliance with national clean air standards.

Traffic snarls and air pollution have long been blamed on the region's car-dependent landscape. Curiously, however, Los Angeles ranked second highest among U.S. metropolitan areas in residential density in 2000, just behind Oahu County (Honolulu). From a mobility standpoint, Los Angeles's high density appears to be dysfunctional—uniformly high enough to create widespread traffic congestion but not peaked enough along linear corridors to draw sufficient numbers of people into trains and buses. The region hopes to change this situation through an aggressive program of building rail lines and expanding BRT, and through the pursuit of transit-oriented development.

High-Performance Transit

The Los Angeles County Metropolitan Transportation Authority (MTA) operates 60 miles of rail services that interconnect 50 stations (see map on next page). Its rail services include 42 miles of light rail in the western portion of the county (Blue and Green Lines) and an 18-mile subway from Union Station to North Hollywood (Red Line). With a price tag of $4.5 billion, the Red Line has been the county's most costly rail investment to date.

The Metrolink commuter-rail system, with 416 miles of track and 49 stations, is operated by the Southern California Regional Rail Authority (SCRRA). Five Metrolink routes serve Los Angeles County—the Antelope Valley, Riverside, San Bernardino, Orange County, and Ventura County Lines (see top map on page 45).

Metro Rapid, the county's bus rapid-transit system, presently consists of two demonstration routes: the 26-mile Wilshire/Whittier Boulevards route between Santa Monica and East Los Angeles and the 16-mile Ventura Boulevard route from University City to the edge city of Warner Center (see bottom map on page 45). Current plans call for an ambitious expansion of BRT services to many corners of the county over the next decade.

The county's rapid expansion of transit services in recent years has attracted many riders. Average weekday boardings on the Red Line more than doubled from 63,000 in April 2000 to 137,000 in April 2002. Patronage on light-rail lines exceeds 100,000 per day —the third highest light-rail ridership in the United States after Boston and San Francisco. Metro-

Art Cueto

A new BRT system services L.A.'s Wilshire corridor, with stations located in Los Angeles, Beverly Hills, and Santa Monica.

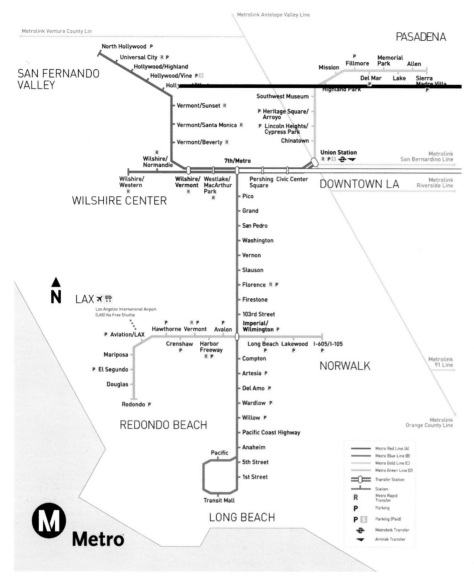

Since the early 1990s, rail corridors—with the help of redevelopment assistance from the public sector and broad-based political support for smart growth—have once again begun to attract considerable amounts of growth. The centerpiece of downtown TOD is the refurbished Union Station—where five Metrolink lines, the subway, and Amtrak intercity services converge.

Among notable examples of TOD in the county are the following:

• MTA's headquarters tower was developed on a parcel next to Union Station through the transportation agency's design/build turnkey arrangement with Catellus Development Corporation.

• Pacific Court, a mixed housing/retail/office project one block from the Blue Line terminus in downtown Long Beach, and Holly Street Village, another mixed-use residential and retail development that was built in anticipation of the extension of light-rail services to downtown Pasadena, exemplify TODs in second-tier downtowns. Both projects were funded by a write-down of land costs and the issuance of tax-exempt bonds under the auspices of redevelopment programs.

• Several recently developed mixed-use projects above Red Line (subway) stations are helping to transform a once stagnant stretch of Hollywood Boulevard. These range from affordable apartments and neighborhood retail at Western Avenue to a 640,000-square-foot entertainment/retail complex and 640-room hotel at Highland Avenue. MTA nets several million dollars annually from these projects through 99-year ground leases.

Metrorail routes, Los Angeles County.

Link serves about 32,000 passengers per weekday, up from around 2,000 a decade earlier. Two-thirds of Metrolink riders previously drove alone to work.[32] The BRT demonstration program has had impressive results: In its first year, ridership on the Wilshire/Whittier Metro Rapid jumped 42 percent and on the Ventura Metro Rapid it rose 27 percent.[33]

Transit-Oriented Development

By the 1920s, Los Angeles County had one of the world's largest intercity rail networks, which channeled growth along its radial spines throughout the first half of the 20th century. After the Second World War, however, passenger rail services were dismantled and an entirely different urban landscape—one governed by cars and freeways—took shape.

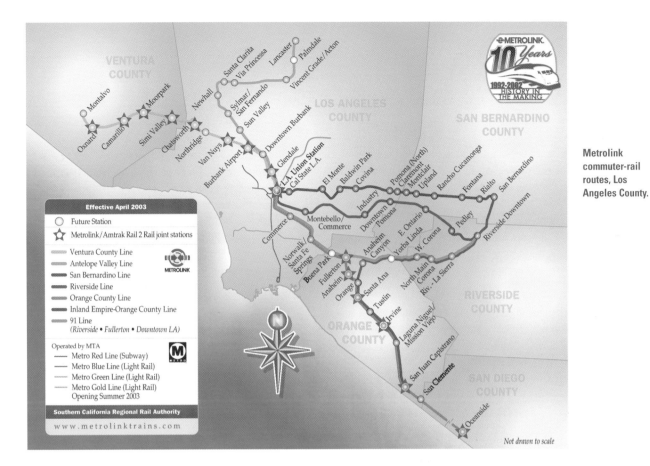

Metrolink commuter-rail routes, Los Angeles County.

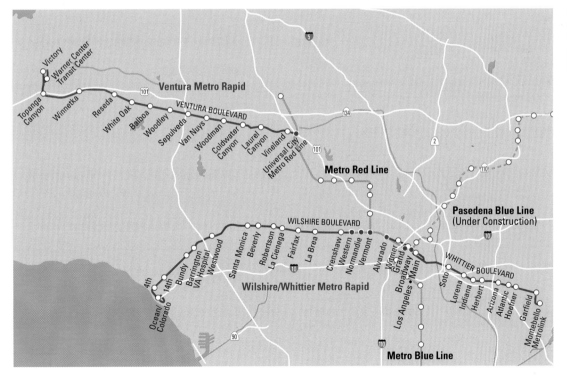

Metro Rapid demonstration bus rapid-transit routes, Los Angeles County.

• NoHo Commons is a mixed-use development located several blocks east of the North Hollywood subway station. It features 220,000 square feet of office space, 228,000 square feet of shops and restaurants, 810 housing units, a community health center, and a child-care center. Recently, MTA approved a second mixed-use project at the North Hollywood station that will occupy a portion of the station's space.

Public policies deserve some of the credit for these changes in land use around rail stops. Most mixed-use projects have been leveraged with redevelopment assistance. All inner-city neighborhoods surrounding stations enjoy a privileged status in terms of development opportunities because of the availability of tax credits, tax-increment financed neighborhood improvements, already assembled land, and other development perks.

The city of Los Angeles, the Southern California Association of Governments, and Countrywide Home Loans, a private lender, cosponsor a location-efficient mortgage (LEM) program that has provided another inducement to TOD. The LEM program makes it easier to qualify for a mortgage on housing units near transit, with the theory being that households near transit stations are likely to own fewer cars and log fewer vehicle-miles traveled and thus can devote more of their income to housing expenses. In fact, research shows that families living in parts of central Los Angeles save, on average, more than $200 a month in vehicle ownership and usage costs compared with the average suburban family.[34] According to LEM proponents, the easing of mortgage qualifications in southern California's high-cost housing market can be effective in luring households to station area locations.

Montage at Village Green, a development of 109 detached, single-family houses across the street from the Sylmar/San Fernando Metrolink train station on SCRRA's Antelope Valley Line, exemplifies projects built under the LEM model. It offers some of the most affordable prices for single-family houses in the San Fernando Valley. The developer, American CityVista,

joined forces with Fannie Mae and the SCRRA to make the project work. Its down-payment requirements are as low as 1 percent, which puts the houses within reach for many low- to moderate-income households. Fannie Mae is an equity investor in Montage at Village Green, providing $1.5 million from its American Communities Fund. Homebuyers at Montage at Village Green receive up to two free Metrolink monthly passes.

Transit-station public art can be an important element in the attractiveness of station environments for development. MTA manages what the *New York Times* described as "one of the most imaginative public art programs in the country," Metro Art, which recently received two coveted national awards.[35] Each subway station features works of art commissioned from local artists and funded by a set-aside from the construction budget. Elements of the artworks in place include recycled film reels, bright murals, cavernous rock sculptures, and archeological artifacts uncovered during station construction. Some critics might write off such add-ons as "frills," but, in truth, studies indicate that transit riders are keenly sensitive to the quality of station environments. Studies of mode choice reveal that transit riders assign a disutility to waiting that is three times longer than the disutility they assign to in-vehicle travel—it is as if the body clock slows down by a factor of three when waiting for a train.[36] What this indicates is that making the transfer and waiting experience more attractive can translate into higher ridership.

Current Research Findings

In Los Angeles, as elsewhere, the expectation is that speedier systems, like the subway and commuter-rail lines, provide the largest land value premiums to nearby properties. BRT, on the other hand, could be expected to produce smaller premiums. After all, buses not only operate in mixed traffic, but also lack the kind of fixed-guideway investments that help guarantee that transit service will continue to be provided in the same locations.

Our research on property values in Los Angeles County obtained *Metroscan* sales transaction data from 1999 to 2001 to examine the influence of Los Angeles County's rich array of rail and BRT services on the performance of real estate markets.[37] Among the land uses studied, the share of total sales that were within a half mile of a rail or BRT stop was largest for residential condominiums—17 percent; for other uses studied, the share of total sales that were near major transit nodes ranged from 13 percent for commercial properties, to 12 percent for multifamily housing, to 6 percent for single-family housing.

The effects of a location near a transit stop on the sale prices of apartment buildings and other multifamily properties were uneven (see figure 2-5). The largest gains accrued to projects within a half mile of a station on the Metro Red subway line, which, all else being equal, sold for $20,000 more (a 6 percent value premium). On other lines, value premiums ranged from 0.5 to 4 percent. A number of near-transit locations were associated with sale price discounts for multifamily properties, with the largest discount (6 percent) occurring along the Metro Rapid Ventura BRT corridor. While it might be posited that this discount was due to the negative impacts of a location near busy roads, this conclusion seems unlikely in that proximity to freeways and highways was used as a control variable in the analysis.

Only along Metrolink commuter-rail lines (excluding the Ventura County line) did for-sale condominium properties receive better premiums than multifamily rental properties—and the discounts that condominium properties near subway, light-rail, and BRT stops sold for were greater than those on multifamily properties (see figure 2-6). Single-family properties followed a nearly identical pattern, enjoying premiums of 2 to 7 percent when located on a Metrolink corridor (excluding the Ventura County line) and selling at slight discounts—suggesting disamenity effects—when associated with subway, light rail, or BRT.

This tendency of condominiums and single-family houses near suburban commuter-rail stops to capitalize accessibility benefits corresponds with experience in San Diego. Because they cater to many nonwork

Figure 2-5

MULTIFAMILY HOUSING SALE PRICE PREMIUMS OR DISCOUNTS IN LOS ANGELES COUNTY, BY RAIL LINE, 2000

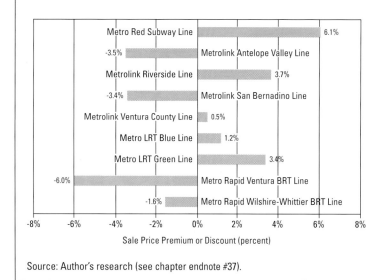

Source: Author's research (see chapter endnote #37).

Figure 2-6

RESIDENTIAL CONDOMINIUM SALE PRICE PREMIUMS OR DISCOUNTS IN LOS ANGELES COUNTY, BY RAIL LINE, 2000

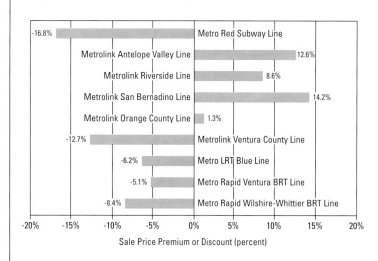

Source: Author's research (see chapter endnote #37).

Figure 2-7
COMMERCIAL SALE PRICE PREMIUMS OR DISCOUNTS IN LOS ANGELES COUNTY, BY RAIL LINE, 2000

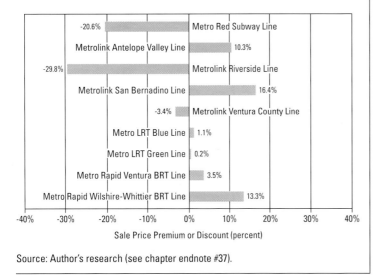

-20.6%	Metro Red Subway Line
Metrolink Antelope Valley Line	10.3%
-29.8%	Metrolink Riverside Line
Metrolink San Bernadino Line	16.4%
-3.4%	Metrolink Ventura County Line
Metro LRT Blue Line	1.1%
Metro LRT Green Line	0.2%
Metro Rapid Ventura BRT Line	3.5%
Metro Rapid Wilshire-Whittier BRT Line	13.3%

Sale Price Premium or Discount (percent)

Source: Author's research (see chapter endnote #37).

trips, Los Angeles's light-rail and subway services may not have produced the same degree of market pressures for transit-served condominiums and detached housing as have commuter-rail lines. Also, the fact that many subway and light-rail stations are located in redevelopment districts is likely to have depressed the prices of nearby condominiums and single-family houses.

A slightly different pattern shows up in the analysis of transit impacts on office, retail, and other commercial properties. Two Metrolink commuter-rail lines, two Metro light-rail lines, and both BRT corridors provided benefits for associated commercial properties, while the subway and two other commuter-rail lines exerted negative price effects (see figure 2-7). Reasons for this particular pattern are difficult to discern. Local contextual factors—for example, zoning policies—could have played a role not accounted for by the many statistical controls introduced in the analysis. The location of subway stations and some commuter-rail stations in distressed inner-city locations appears to have suppressed property values near these stations. Conversely, the attractiveness of locations on the Wilshire/Whittier corridor—a corridor boasting some of the most prestigious office and retail addresses in southern California—could be responsible for a portion of the premiums recorded for commercial properties near Metro Rapid Wilshire/Whittier BRT stops.

CONCLUSIONS

A mixed picture emerges from the research results reported in this chapter. A location near transit seems capable of yielding benefits to property owners. However, it does not do so automatically and profits are by no means guaranteed. For premiums to accrue, it seems important that the transit facilities be located in neighborhoods with a reasonably healthy real estate market and free from signs of stagnation or distress.

In San Diego, our research recorded premiums for commercial properties in the Mission Valley corridor, an area that generally has enjoyed sustained growth over the past decade. Local policies favoring development near transit—such as overlay zoning to encourage a mix of uses and targeted infrastructure investments—seem to have bolstered commercial property values in the Mission Valley corridor and parts of downtown San Diego. In contrast, commercial properties near transit in Los Angeles County seem to have suffered from transit's association with redevelopment districts, despite the recent expansion of rail services.

Perhaps the most consistent finding from our research in California is that for-sale residential properties near suburban commuter-rail stops enjoy premiums. In the face of serious traffic congestion problems, a significant number of households seems willing to bid up prices for condominiums and single-family houses within walking distance of commuter rail. The combination of an overheated housing market and traffic congestion has been particularly favorable to residential property owners in neighborhoods surrounding Santa Clara County's rail stations.

Increasingly, transit authorities are looking to transit-created premiums to finance not only transit construction, but also neighborhood improvements, like sidewalks and public spaces. The Washington Metropolitan Area Transit Authority (WMATA) has pursued value capture as aggressively as any U.S. transit authority. Rather than waiting for developer proposals, WMATA's real estate office actively seeks out joint development opportunities. With financial and institutional support provided by board members, WMATA's real estate office has amassed an impressive portfolio of land holdings, much of it purchased on the open marketplace, and it has undertaken more than 55 development projects with a value of more than $4 billion on land the agency owns.

To the degree that transit creates value premiums that can be shared among public sector and private interests, the future for TOD would seem to be bright. But clearly transit does not always produce appreciable benefits. A benefit assessment that the city of Los Angeles has levied since the early 1990s on commercial properties in built-up, rail-served corridors has generated about $130 million. Our research suggests that not all commercial properties have benefited from transit's presence and underscores the importance of carefully crafting and implementing any value capture program. In Los Angeles's case, redevelopment assistance programs have provided offsetting subsidies to many properties located in rail corridors. Even so, as the evidence suggests, transit has had unanticipated negative effects on property values.

Transit value capture is best accomplished through voluntary, public/private joint development initiatives. Presumably, all parties in joint development deals perceive benefits from investments in development near transit, and transit's value added in such instances is indisputable. New federal legislation allows transit agencies to sell or lease agency land, even if it was purchased with federal dollars, in order to promote TOD. This capability should help rationalize value capture in the United States. Many developers will gladly undertake mixed-use projects on former parking lots when returns on investment seem promising. The prospect of earning income and increasing transit patronage by leasing space in station areas can be expected to spur transit agency interest in value capture. As more deals are negotiated, a better understanding of the land value impacts of transit can help considerably in hammering out fair and mutually beneficial joint development agreements.

Notes

1. Robert Cervero, "Rail Transit and Joint Development: Land Market Impacts in Washington, D.C., and Atlanta," *Journal of the American Planning Association,* winter 1994, pp. 83–94.

2. Robert Cervero, "California's Transit Village Movement," *Journal of Public Transportation,* v. 1, no. 1 (1996), pp. 103–130.

3. Hedonic price models are widely considered to be the most rigorous and accurate basis, in general, for apportioning factors that influence land values. They operate on the principle that consumer goods comprise a bundle of attributes, and that the overall transaction price can be decomposed into the component (or "hedonic") prices of each attribute. The statistical technique of regression analysis is used to estimate hedonic price models. See Sherwin Rosen, "Hedonic Prices and Implicit Markets: Product Differentiation in Pure Competition," *Journal of Political Economics,* v. 82, no. 1 (1974), pp. 34–55.

4. *Los Angeles County Metropolitan Transportation Authority* v. *Continental Development Corporation,* 16 Cal 14th 694 (1997).

5. Peter Calthorpe, *The Next American Metropolis: Ecology, Community and the American Dream* (Princeton: Princeton Architectural Press, 1993).

6. John Landis, Subhrajit Guhathakurta, and Ming Zhang, *Capitalization of Transportation Investments into Single-Family Home Prices,* Working Paper 619 (Berkeley: Institute of Urban and Regional Development, University of California, 1994).

7. Richard Voith, "Changing Capitalization of CBD-Oriented Transportation Systems: Evidence from Philadelphia, 1970–1988," *Journal of Urban Economics,* v. 33, no. 3 (1993), pp. 361–376.

8. Dean Gatzlaff and Marc Smith, "The Impact of the Miami Metrorail on the Value of Residences near Station Locations," *Land Economics,* v. 69, no. 1 (1993), pp. 54–66.

9. Arthur Nelson, "Effects of Elevated Heavy-Rail Transit Stations on House Prices with Respect to Neighborhood Income," *Transportation Research Record 1359,* 1992, pp. 127–132.

10. Musaad Al-Mosaind, Kenneth Dueker, and James Strathman, "Light-Rail Transit Stations and Property Values: A Hedonic Price Approach," *Transportation Research Record 1400,* 1993, pp. 90–94.

11. Steven Workman and Daniel Brod, "Measuring the Neighborhood Benefits of Rail Transit Accessibility," *Transportation Research Record 1576,* 1997, pp. 147–153.

12. Landis et al., *Capitalization of Transportation Investments.*

13. Caj Falcke, *Study of BART's Effects on Property Prices and Rents* (Washington, D.C.: Urban Mass Transportation Administration, U.S. Department of Transportation, 1978).

14. David Damm, Steven Lerman, Eva Lerner-Lam, and Jeffrey Young, "Response of Urban Real Estate Values in Anticipation of the Washington Metro," *Journal of Transport Economics and Policy,* v. 14, no. 3 (1980), pp. 20–30.

15. Robert Dunphy, "Transit-Oriented Development: Making a Difference?" *Urban Land,* July 1995, pp. 32–36, 48; Michael Bernick and Robert Cervero, *Transit Villages for the 21st Century* (New York: McGraw-Hill, 1997); and Alvin McNeal and Rosalyn Doggett, "Metro Makes Its Mark," *Urban Land,* September 1999, pp. 78–81, 118.

16. Christopher Bollinger, Keith Ihlanfeldt, and David Bowes, "Spatial Variation in Office Rents within the Atlanta Region," *Urban Studies,* v. 35, no. 7 (1998), pp. 1097–1117.

17. Arthur Nelson, "Transit Stations and Commercial Property Values: A Case Study with Policy and Land Use Implications," *Journal of Public Transportation,* v. 2, no. 3 (1999), pp. 77–93.

18. Cervero, "Rail Transit and Joint Development."

19. Great American Station Foundation, *Economic Impact of Station Revitalization* (Las Vegas, New Mexico: Great American Station Foundation, 2001).

20. Bernard Weinstein and Terry Clower, *The Initial Economic Impacts of the DART LRT System* (Denton, Texas: Center for Economic Development and Research, University of North Texas, 1999).

21. Rachel Weinberger, "Commercial Property Values and Proximity to Light Rail: Calculating Benefits with a Hedonic Price Model" (paper presented at the 79th annual meeting of the Transportation Research Board, Washington, D.C., 2000).

22. G.B. Arrington and Terry Parker, *Statewide Transit-Oriented Development Study: Factors for Success in California* (Sacramento: California Department of Transportation, 2002).

23. Robert Dunphy, "Transit Trends," *Urban Land,* May 2001, pp. 79–83.

24. San Diego Association of Governments, *San Diego Trolley: The First Three Years* (Washington, D.C.: Urban Mass Transportation Administration, U.S. Department of Transportation, 1984).

25. VNI Rainbow Appraisal Service, *Analysis of the Impact of Light Rail Transit on Real Estate Values* (San Diego: Metropolitan Transit Development Board, 1992).

26. Landis et al., *Capitalization of Transportation Investments.*

27. For more information about these analyses, see Robert Cervero and Michael Duncan, "Land Value Impacts of Rail-Transit Services in San Diego County" (report prepared for National Association of Realtors and Urban Land Institute, June 2002).

28. Association of Bay Area Governments, *Silicon Valley Projections 2000* (Oakland, California: Association of Bay Area Governments, 2001).

29. Gerston & Associates, *Transit-Based Housing* (San Jose, California: Santa Clara County Transportation Agency and Santa Clara Valley Manufacturing Group, 1995).

30. For more information about these analyses, see Robert Cervero and Michael Duncan, "Transit's Value Added: Effects of Light- and Commuter-Rail Services on Commercial Land Values in Santa Clara County" (report prepared for National Association of Realtors and Urban Land Institute, June 2001); and Robert Cervero and Michael Duncan, "Benefits of Proximity to Rail on Housing Markets: Experiences in Santa Clara County," *Journal of Public Transportation,* v. 5, no. 1 (2002), pp. 1–18.

31. Texas Transportation Institute, *2001 Urban Mobility Report* (College Station, Texas: Texas Transportation Institute, A&M University, 2002; available at http://mobility. tamu.edu/ums/study/cities/tables/los_angeles.pdf).

32. Metrolink Web site (http://www.metrolinktrains.com/ about/fastfacts.html).

33. Transportation Management & Design, *Final Report: Los Angeles Metro Rapid Demonstration Program* (Los

Angeles: Los Angeles County Metropolitan Transportation Authority, 2002).

34. John Holtzclaw, Robert Clear, Hank Dittmar, David Goldstein, and Peter Hass, "Location Efficiency: Neighborhood and Socio-Economic Characteristics Determine Auto Ownership and Use," *Transportation Planning and Technology,* v. 25, no. 1 (2002), pp. 1–27.

35. Roger Snoble, "Bringing a Touch of Humanity to the Trip: The Art of Transit in Los Angeles," *Rail* (Community Transportation Association of America) edition 4, 2002, pp. 10–11.

36. Martin Wachs, "Consumer Attitudes Toward Transit Service: An Interpretative Review," *Journal of the American Institute of Planners,* winter 1976, pp. 96–104.

37. For details on this study, see Robert Cervero and Michael Duncan, "Land Value Impacts of Rail-Transit Services in Los Angeles County" (report prepared for National Association of Realtors and Urban Land Institute, June 2002).

CHAPTER THREE

FREDERICK C. DOCK AND CAROL J. SWENSON

PLANNING THE TRANSIT DISTRICT

ENTHUSIASM OVER POST–WORLD WAR II RAIL-TRANSIT SYSTEMS built in the United States—especially BART (Bay Area Rapid Transit) in San Francisco and Metrorail in the Washington region—created a certain irrational exuberance about the salutary impact that rapid transit could have on a community. Planners who looked at how Toronto's Yonge Street subway (opening in 1954, it was Canada's first subway) succeeded in spurring intense apartment and office construction around major intersections in downtown and midtown—in effect, shaping modern Toronto—came up with a pop-up theory of land development: Wherever rapid transit went, development would follow.

This theory has proven wrong. Development does not happen in the absence of good planning. Even in Toronto, subway-oriented development did not happen without planning. Development opportunities around transit that are so compelling that the private market will seize them without the public sector needing to play a role are the exception, not the rule.

Transit stations can exert a key influence on land development over an area—the transit district—that extends at least one-quarter mile from the station. In planning for transit-supportive land uses, the entire transit district should be considered.

New Jersey Transit

Many older transit systems have seen the emergence of transit districts with transit-supporting uses within walking distance of suburban trolley stops and train stations, like at this commuter-train station in South Orange, New Jersey.

The concept of planning for transit districts is not new. In the 1920s and 1930s, mixed-use communities —known as streetcar suburbs— were developed according to (private) plans for linking residential and commercial land uses to transportation services provided by private investors as a means of opening the land for development. Transit district planning and implementation today, however, cannot be achieved by solely private means. All the elements—the provision of transit, the land planning, and the land de-

velopment predicated on access to transit—are part of a complex process that involves the public sector as well as the private sector.

The construction of new transit systems, especially rail systems, has become largely a public function

Making the Case for Transit-Oriented Development in Suburban Minneapolis-St. Paul

In 1995, seven contiguous cities in two counties along the I-35W corridor in the suburban northwest section of the Minneapolis-St. Paul metropolitan area formed a coalition to plan for future growth. The realizations and goals that motivated this collaborative venture were

• a recognition that the individual communities are not "islands unto themselves";

• a wish to draft a vision of what the area should become; and

• a wish to agree on a substantive framework for growth that could guide future decision making.

Metropolitan Design Center, Univ. of Minnesota

As recommended by the I-35W coalition, New Brighton, a coalition member, has transformed its downtown into a mixed-use district through the addition of housing for seniors, office and municipal buildings, and townhouses.

The 83-square-mile area contains 156,000 residents and 85,000 jobs, with more residents and jobs arriving every day, drawn in large part by the accessibility conferred by I-35W and its interchange with I-694. By 2020, the area will have added 60,000 to 70,000 people and 40,000 jobs, according to current projections.

First, the coalition created a demographic database that permitted analyses from the regional level down to the level of individual properties. Analyses indicated that the population was growing older—which could impact schools as well as the character of the community—and that predicted growth would begin to deplete the supply of available land over the next 20 years.

Then the coalition constructed two growth scenarios for the area. The "conventional" growth scenario assumed that growth would follow conventional suburban development patterns. The "coalition" growth scenario assumed that a significant proportion of the area's growth would be directed into about a dozen compact, mixed-use centers accessible to multimodal transportation services. Compared with the conventional scenario, the number of housing units near transit in the coalition scenario would be about 10 percent higher.

primarily because of its cost and complexity. There is an increasing emphasis in public sector transit investment on the productivity of the transit system—measured by such indicators as cost per rider and daily ridership. Thus, new transit investments are focused on areas where ridership is (or is likely to be) present.

To minimize construction costs, transit systems—particularly those constructed since the 1970s—have often been built along freeways or existing rail lines, in some cases using new alignments and in others reusing or sharing transportation corridors. As a result, some new transit stations are at locations—freeway medians, railroad corridors—where private development does not just happen by itself. Other station locations, even though much more attractive to development, often have development issues—like brownfield conditions and incompatible adjacent land uses—attached.

Because such locations are not necessarily the ones that the market would select, especially for housing development, deliberate planning is required to en-

---

Making the Case *continued*

A subregional transportation forecasting model designed to function within the parameters of the regional transportation model was used to analyze the transportation impacts of the two growth scenarios. The first run of the model assumed the following transportation improvements: a moderate amount of new transit services, the widening of segments of I-35W and I-694, and some additions to the county and local roadway network. The second run added bridges over I-35W to better interconnect county and local roads and added $7 million of transit improvements affecting both express and local services.

It was found that traffic congestion on both regional and minor arterial roads would increase under either scenario, which is not surprising given the rapid rate at which congestion is increasing in the region. However, a more efficient pattern of travel showed up under the coalition scenario: Within the coalition area, trip lengths were shorter, more trips were made by foot and transit, fewer vehicle-miles were traveled, and the increase in the number of trips generated per capita was smaller.

Under the coalition scenario, a 25 percent increase in housing generated only 6 percent more auto trips, compared with a 33 percent increase in transit trips and an estimated 23 percent increase in walking trips. (Prediction of walking trips is unusual in traffic modeling.) In addition, because clustering reduces land consumption, the coalition scenario provided capacity for a greater increase in jobs and housing in the area.

The coalition's study concluded with recommendations to

• promote the development of mixed-use centers;

• improve collaboration among the area's cities and counties; and

• work to coordinate regional and state transportation improvements.

Source: Adapted from Douglas R. Porter, "Smart Growth Transportation for Suburban Greenfields" (ULI Land Use Policy Forum paper, October 8, 2002; http://www.uli.org/content/Reports/Papers/PFR_678.pdf).

Land Use and Federal Transit Approvals

The Federal Transit Administration's criteria for funding grants on major capital projects under its New Starts program include land use planning considerations. In making these grants, FTA evaluates the following six aspects of regional land use planning:

- *Existing Land Use.* What is the density of population and employment in the area served by the transit system? How transit friendly is the development pattern? How pedestrian friendly?

- *Containment of Sprawl.* What policies for growth management are in place? How will development trends affect population and employment densities?

- *Corridor Planning.* Are policies in place that encourage transit-supportive development within transit corridors?

- *Station Area Zoning.* Are zoning ordinances in place to support increased development densities near stations?

- *Policy and Plan Implementation Processes.* What processes—including public processes, private processes, and joint public/private processes—are in place to facilitate station area development?

- *Impact of Transit-Oriented Planning.* Have existing transit-oriented policies had demonstrable effects on development in the region?

FTA organizes its evaluation process for these criteria to give the most weight to transit-supportive policies and programs that are in place and operating. The prospect of moving up in the ranking for federal funding creates an incentive for regions and cities to adopt transit-oriented land use planning practices.

---

sure that an appropriate mix of land uses occurs in the right locations to provide for successful development around transit. From the perspective of attracting development, the optimal transit corridor links a region's most desirable destinations—current and future. While transit corridors linking desirable destinations will expand transit's ridership potential, they may cost more to construct than corridors along freeways or existing rail lines.

To address such challenges, many transit planners and advocates recommend that not just the immediate area around stations, but also areas well beyond the station—entire transit districts—be planned. Specifically, they suggest that station areas be planned with a dual intent—to organize land uses to capture value from the accessibility that transit provides and to enhance transit ridership. This chapter focuses on the elements of planning for transit districts and provides examples from a station on Portland, Oregon's Westside MAX light-rail line; a station on the Caltrain commuter-rail line between San Francisco and San Jose; and the Washington region's Rosslyn-Ballston Metrorail corridor in Arlington County, Virginia.

WHAT TRANSIT DISTRICT PLANNING ACCOMPLISHES

Development around station areas should be planned for the same reasons any large-scale land use project—whether it is redevelopment or new development—should be planned. The ability of a location to attract successful development is dependent not only on its attractiveness to the market, but also on the degree of certainty and predictability that is established for the location. Planning establishes a framework of certainty and predictability. In addition to attracting transit-oriented development to transit districts, station area planning should explore ways in which this development can enhance or reinforce the urban fabric surrounding the station.

In transit districts, the planning framework comprises both the public process that identifies a vision for the transit station area and the supporting policies that are implemented by the public entities. Public participation in transit district planning is needed to avoid or overcome local opposition to changes in development patterns and to specific development projects. Supporting policies for transit district planning include the adoption of appropriate zoning, the provision of infrastructure, and the granting of incentives for development.

Station area planning that is intended to catalyze development concurrently with the construction of transit demonstrates a high degree of readiness for transit investments. Thus, it can leverage public investment. As described in the sidebar on the facing page, appropriate levels of planning can figure favorably in the evaluation process for federal funding, on the theory that such planning makes for a better transit system and for a community that is better prepared to use the transit system to its full extent.

THE ELEMENTS OF TRANSIT-ORIENTED PLANNING

Experience has revealed that the appropriate arrangement of transit functions and adjacent development produces mutual benefits—value premiums for property and increased ridership for transit. Adding rooftops that are accessible to transit is the most effective way to increase transit ridership. Improved transit services make locations that are accessible to transit more attractive to households. Fundamental to the

transit/land use relationship is the quality of the pedestrian connections between transit stations and destinations—homes, workplaces, stores and restaurants, and cultural and sports facilities.

Planning around transit involves both the planning of station areas at the regional level and the specific planning of transit districts at the site level. Two concepts are integral to both levels of planning:

• The arrangement of land uses is organized to concentrate activity adjacent to transit and the mix of land uses is organized to generate transit ridership (housing and employment uses) and support transit riders (convenience retail and service uses).

• Within walkable distances of station areas, the design and mix of uses must promote walking. (By the same token, within cycling distances of station areas, street design should be amenable to bicycling.)

A station's pedestrian-influence area typically covers the area within a five- to ten-minute walk, which

Downtown Quincy, Massachusetts, is being redesigned as a traditional neighborhood with pedestrian-oriented, mixed-use streets in hopes of recapturing some of the connectivity and land use variety that have been lost through insensitive development in recent years.

Goody Clancy and Associates

translates to one-quarter to one-half mile. Within the influence area, urban design—block size, building massing and orientation, and circulation—should be oriented to the pedestrian. Obviously, not all transit riders will walk to the station. Riders arriving by car or bus generally come from much longer distances and require parking or transfer facilities in the station area.

While the needs of transit users who arrive by foot, car, bicycle, or bus must be balanced in each station area, planning usually begins in the pedestrian-influence area and focuses on how well the urban environment functions for pedestrians. This pedestrian focus not only enhances transit access and ridership, but also helps create an attractive urban place. Planning the transit district is essentially about creating places rather than about developing projects.

Achieving an appropriate mix of activity that complements the adjacency of transit is just as important as good physical design. A high density of employment uses or housing within walking distance of station areas supports transit. However, transit use tends to focus on peak commute hours, which restricts transit's attractiveness for retail and service uses in transit districts. Sometimes, transit districts can draw on existing concentrations of retail and services to round out their land use mix. Alternatively, they may be able to draw customers from nearby areas to support the development of such uses.

Districts that are compact and walkable, that have a mix of uses, and that are served by transit are not a new form of urban development. In the United States during the first half of the 20th century, most main streets would have fit this description. In the post–World War II rush to develop in suburban areas, however, this form of development lost favor. The kind of development that took its place was typically devoted to a single use (tract housing, shopping mall, office park), unwalkable (low density, blandly designed), accessible only by car, and usually far from the closest transit.

Now, the current generation of planners and developers has adopted the underlying principles for a form

of development termed "new urbanism," or "traditional neighborhood development" (TND), or "place making." Urban designer Peter Calthorpe is credited with refining the TND concept into an urban design strategy that promotes the use of all forms of mass transit—rail as well as bus.

Calthorpe has proposed an urban form of development around transit that is grounded in the traditions of urbanism and place making and he has put forth the following fundamental principles of such development:[1]

• On a regional level, organize growth to be compact and transit-supportive.

• Place commercial, residential, employment, open space, and civic uses within walking distance of transit stops.

• Create pedestrian-friendly street networks that directly connect local destinations.

• Provide a mix of housing types at varying densities and costs.

• Preserve sensitive habitat, riparian zones, and high-quality open space.

• Orient buildings and neighborhood activity to public spaces.

• Encourage infill and redevelopment along transit corridors within existing neighborhoods.

The drawing on the facing page is a schematic diagram by Calthorpe that illustrates spatial organization and density strategies for development around transit. A transit stop located at the center of the transit village is framed by a mixed-use core characterized by relatively high densities and floor/area ratios. Surrounding the core is a secondary area with lower densities and land uses that are oriented to either jobs or housing.

In Calthorpe's transit village, the core occupies a quarter-mile ring from the transit stop and the secondary area occupies the remaining area out to a half mile from the station, yielding an area that can range in size from 60 to 500 acres, depending on whether the location is a one-sided infill site (similar to that shown in the drawing) or a site with developable land in a full circle around the transit stop. The presence of freeways, major streets, large open spaces, or bodies of water at most locations restricts the actual area available for development. Similarly, the presence of dead-end and other disconnected streets reduces the amount of land that is within easy access of the transit stop.

In this scheme, open spaces and public spaces help organize both the mixed-use core and the secondary area. The circulation system for pedestrians and vehicles emphasizes connectivity by maximizing the number of alternative routes to any destination. The provision of a high level of connectivity is intended to encourage people living or working in or near the transit village to conduct their daily errands on foot within the transit stop's influence area.

The transit village diagram is a good visual representation of complex land use relationships, but it is only a framework. Each region and each station area has

its own planning circumstances, which should influence transit district design and the appropriate mix of land uses. The key planning elements that can be made more transit friendly include

- land use mix;

- density;

- connectivity;

- urban design;

- transit access; and

- parking.

These elements can be pulled together in a variety of ways to achieve successful transit districts. Within basically similar patterns of streets and blocks, cultural preferences can (and should) determine densities and types and locations of land uses and thus produce places that differ in character one from another. Every successful transit district will have a sufficiently unique mix of land uses and intensity

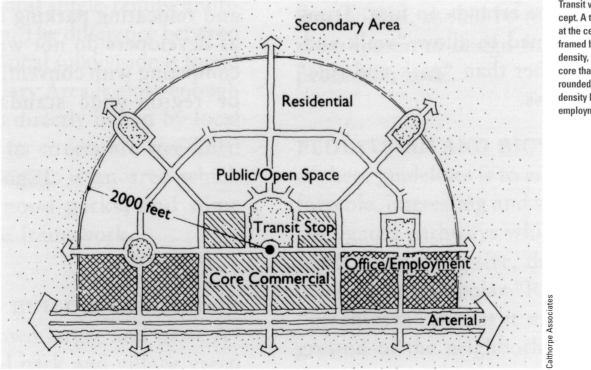

Secondary Area

Residential

Public/Open Space

2000 feet

Transit Stop

Core Commercial

Office/Employment

Arterial

Calthorpe Associates

Transit village concept. A transit stop at the center is framed by a high-density, mixed-use core that is surrounded by lower-density housing or employment areas.

of development to achieve destination quality, to become a place to which people will come.

How to make the six key planning elements for transit districts more transit friendly is discussed in detail in the following sections.

Land Use Mix

An area's land use mix and density levels set the stage for successful synergy between development and transit. Synergy arises from the generation of activity by residential or employment land uses that supports other land uses. Concentrations of housing or employment create demand for transit access, and the arrival of people by transit creates secondary needs for retail and entertainment uses within walking distance of the transit station. A sufficient variety of complementary land uses will help create places in which activity occurs at different times of the day and during different days of the week.

The planning term "mixed use" means different things in different contexts. In transit district planning, it refers not only to a horizontal mix of land uses that, for example, permits residential uses to be located next to light-industrial uses. Mixed use in transit districts refers more frequently to a vertical mix achieved by permitting two or more uses—such as ground-floor retail and upper-story commercial space—in single buildings.

Because it attracts relatively intense and varied activity, vertical mixed use can contribute to two important objectives in transit districts—round-the-clock security and the creation of a sense of place. The inclusion of restaurants and stores in office mixed-use developments makes it convenient and comfortable— and even memorable—for jobholders and business visitors to arrive by transit. And the presence of opportunities for nonwork activity extends the life of the street into the hours between and following commuting hours.

Based on local and regional markets and what is known about transit ridership generated by different kinds of land uses, planners can begin to work out development scenarios for transit districts. An early

indication of the kinds of businesses suitable for and likely to want to locate in the planned transit district can assist the planning by

• providing decision makers—developers, public officials, and residents of the neighborhood—with a range of options for accommodating community and neighborhood needs and market demand;

• allowing planners to estimate the effect of different development scenarios on the volume and pattern of transit ridership; and

• providing the information needed to estimate space needs in the transit district and to formulate a preliminary building program for the station area.

Residential uses can be an important component of strategies for mixing land uses vertically. Housing has the potential to generate more transit riders per resident than employment uses generate per employee. It also contributes a sense of ownership to the neighborhood and adds to street life outside of commuter rush hours and on the weekend. Furthermore, non-work-related travel by households living in transit districts can extend transit use beyond commuting times, which also enlivens the transit district's public spaces, streets, and transit station.

The development of transit-supportive housing in transit districts can encounter neighborhood opposition and be difficult to finance. Neighbors—who are unfamiliar with residential mixed-use development because of its absence from most urban and suburban landscapes—tend to worry that affordable or rental units will attract undesirable residents. They oppose such developments also out of concern that their density (and clientele) will increase demands on public safety departments and strain public budgets. As concerns financing, many financial institutions are also unfamiliar with residential mixed-use development and not used to participating in financial packages that include public subsidies, which many affordable housing projects do. Thus, obtaining financing is usually more difficult than for conventional housing projects.

The development objectives for a transit district must consider its location within the region. If it is in a

jobs-rich area, the most sensible plan might be to add housing and commercial uses in the station area and create links to the nearby jobs. If the station is located in a jobs-poor area, adding employment uses that could tap nearby labor pools might be the best solution. If the station is located in an area from which there is a strong pattern of commuting to regional job centers—like a major CBD or suburban edge city—served by the transit, it may be appropriate to add housing that could capture the commute trip closer to the transit station. In other words, planning for the land use mix in a transit district requires an understanding of the interaction between jobs and housing at the local level and an understanding of commuting patterns at the regional level.

Transit ridership is generated mainly by employment and residential land uses. The main role of retail and service uses in transit districts is not their generation of transit ridership, but their amenity contribution to creating a successful place in which transit riders

will want to live or work. "Retail follows rooftops" is a market mantra, and relatively high densities of housing and, to a lesser extent, employment uses in a station area are likely to create demand for retail development. However, even a relatively high density of housing and employment around a transit station may not be enough to support more than a minimal amount of service retail in the station area. Planners need to focus on the possibility of attracting retail demand to the transit district—or on techniques for "attaching" the station area land uses to nearby retail concentrations if it is determined that retail development in the station area would not be competitive. The transit district examples at the end of this chapter address this issue.

Density

Development at relatively high densities yields many benefits, including more transportation and housing options in suburban settings. As discussed in Chapter

The Market Common Clarendon in the Washington region's Virginia suburbs is a vibrant, round-the-clock, mixed-use retail/residential/office development that offers pedestrian-friendly access to and from a Metrorail station two blocks away.

One, a minimum density of seven dwelling units per net residential acre can support basic bus service with 30- to 60-minute headways (the intervals between vehicles in service). A minimum density of 15 units per acre can support bus service with 15-minute or lower headways. A minimum density of nine units per net residential acre is needed to support light rail, and a density of 12 units per net residential acre is needed to make heavy rail a feasible option.

Employment densities influence people's choice of travel mode more than do residential densities. Thus, the feasibility of different transit options depends as well on minimum employment densities (and on the regional distribution of employment clusters). A minimum density of 20 employees per net employment acre is needed to support intermediate bus service, and a density of 50 to (preferably) 75 employees per acre will support frequent bus service. A minimum of 125 employees per net employment acre around tran-

sit stations is needed to support light rail. The presence of one or more major downtowns or other very high density region-serving employment nodes is required to support heavy rail.

Achieving relatively high levels of mixed-use or employment density typically requires development with high floor/area ratios (FAR), which has important implications for how parking is provided in transit districts. Surface parking is not feasible with FARs above 0.50 to 0.85. (A typical one-story commercial/office building will have an FAR of 0.35 or lower.) To achieve transit-supportive densities in a suburban transit station area, vertical mixed-use development projects should have an FAR in the range of 1.00 to 2.00. Such projects will require structured parking, which, among other advantages, allows more street-fronting buildings to be placed on sites—an important factor in creating streetscapes that are attractive and interesting to pedestrians.

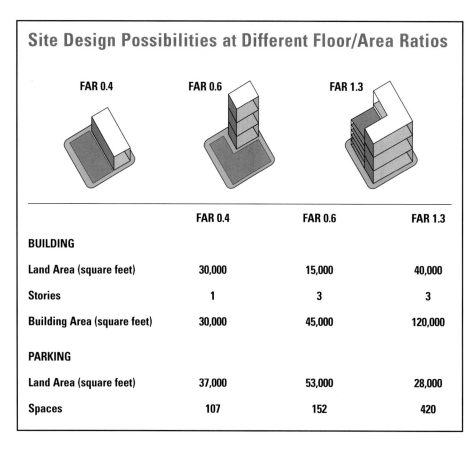

Site Design Possibilities at Different Floor/Area Ratios

FAR 0.4   FAR 0.6   FAR 1.3

	FAR 0.4	FAR 0.6	FAR 1.3
BUILDING			
Land Area (square feet)	30,000	15,000	40,000
Stories	1	3	3
Building Area (square feet)	30,000	45,000	120,000
PARKING			
Land Area (square feet)	37,000	53,000	28,000
Spaces	107	152	420

The illustrations in the box to the left show three different arrangements of buildings and parking on a 300-foot-by-300-foot block with a land use that would require parking to be supplied at 3.5 spaces per 1,000 square feet of building area (a parking requirement that is consistent with retail and office uses in a mixed-use environment). Buildable area on the 90,000-square-foot lot is 75,000 square feet, assuming that a sidewalk occupies the perimeter of the block and that 10 percent of the site will be landscaped.

The left diagram illustrates a typical single-story building design. In this scenario, more than half of the site's buildable square footage is used for surface parking. Thus, long stretches of the block's frontage are occupied by parking rather than by building. When a number of similarly designed blocks are assembled into districts, such interruptions of building frontage by parking break the continuity of interest provided by sidewalk storefronts and building entrances, and thus detract from the pedestrian friendliness of the streetscape.

The middle diagram illustrates a multistory option with surface parking. In order to leave more of the site free for the additional parking required by the larger building, the building footprint has been about halved. The FAR is still relatively low. This scenario represents an extreme condition for surface parking: a building taller than three stories will entail building code–related costs that ordinarily would not be justified for such a low-density project.

The right diagram illustrates a development that includes structured parking. Here, the FAR exceeds 1.00, which allows both a larger building and more parking to be built on the site. With more of the site occupied by buildings, a more continuous building frontage can be provided along the sidewalk. Similarly designed blocks—that is blocks where the sidewalk frontage is uninterrupted by parking, vacant lots, or other visually unappealing land uses—assembled into transit districts have the potential to create a streetscape that will attract people and make the pedestrian experience pleasant. In some cases, permitting structured parking to be shared among complementary uses on adjacent blocks can be used to increase FAR on individual blocks and create longer uninterrupted areas of pedestrian-friendly streetscape.

Connectivity

Planning for circulation systems in transit districts should focus on maximizing connectivity and pedestrian, bicycle, and transit mobility. The propensity of people to walk among uses is based in large part on how well uses are connected one to another.

Connectivity is aided by relatively small block sizes. In 2000, the Minneapolis-St. Paul Metropolitan Council issued block-size guidelines for transit-oriented development: Blocks should be no more than 500 feet long and their total area should not exceed seven acres, and ideally they should be less than three acres

(or approximately 400 feet by 300 feet) in size.[2] If circumstances necessitate larger blocks, pedestrian circulation should be accommodated by a network of pathways that dissect the block and link to public corridors within buildings. In the Seattle area, the Puget Sound Regional Council requires that areas designated as regional growth centers have a plan to break up superblocks for improved pedestrian and bicycle access.[3]

A transit district's circulation system should incorporate human-scale landmarks for the guidance of pedestrians. Pedestrian routes should be direct and well supplied with places for resting or seeking shelter from adverse weather conditions.

A successful circulation system for a district comprising relatively small blocks does not necessarily have to be laid out in a grid or avoid the use of cul-de-sac streets. Within transit districts, however, circulation planning should make liberal and strategic use of the numerous street intersections created by small blocks to achieve a higher level of connectivity than is found in conventional suburban development patterns. Street alignments can be responsive to topographic constraints as long as the number of intersections is maximized. Cul-de-sac streets can work if they are connected to pathways that provide district-wide links.

Transit district planning should be concerned with bicycle connectivity as well as pedestrian and car circulation. Bicycles are used for multiple purposes—including commuting, recreation, and local trips—which has implications for the design of the facilities serving them. Bicycle commuters need routes and facilities that accommodate high speeds and offer some separation from recreational and other slower users of the facility. Bike routes designed for recreational riders and people on household errands do not necessarily need to accommodate high speeds, but they do need to be safe and have excellent connectivity to local destinations.

Urban Design

Buildings that will be situated in the core area of transit districts need to be designed to achieve the

land use mix and development density called for in the transit district plan and also to be appropriate to their context, which in the case of newer transit systems may be more suburban than urban.

Within the pedestrian-oriented core, buildings should be relatively transparent—that is, the ratio of windows and doors to total frontal area should be at least 40 percent. Moreover, it is preferable to have numerous smaller openings rather than a few large ones. The goal of this design element is to provide sufficient variety along building fronts to make walking by them an interesting experience in itself.

Building orientation is important in transit-oriented urban design. In and near transit district cores, the main entrance of buildings should be oriented to the street and setbacks from the property line should range from one foot to ten feet. Such shallow setbacks and direct visual connections to buildings from sidewalks establish a human-scale streetscape, contribute to a sense of place, and promote pedestrian activity.

The massing of multifamily residential buildings to be situated in residential areas adjacent to the transit district core—a location at which relatively high densities are still desirable but where single-family houses are typically the dominant land use—should be compatible with single-family housing. In order to diversify land uses, live/work buildings designed to fit the character of a residential street can be situated in these second-ring locations as well.

Sometimes site conditions or other constraints preclude following best practices for transit-oriented urban design. Under these circumstances, the transit district plan should focus on providing amenity-rich, well-defined, safe, and weather-protected pedestrian passageways throughout the district.

Transit Access

Transit-access planning for transit districts must balance the needs of transit riders arriving or leaving by foot, car, bicycle, and other transit connections. Access considerations include the location and orientation of the stop or station, the design of the stop or station, and the amount and design of arrival/waiting space.

For pedestrians, station areas should provide direct paths with visible landmarks or goals and connectivity to all destinations, protection from cars, protection from inclement weather, sidewalks wide enough to support potential activity (including window shopping and outdoor dining), and occasional resting spots.

For transit riders arriving by bicycle, stations and stops need to provide secured lockers or attended storage. Alternatively, accommodation can be made on buses (bike racks) and trains to transport bikes.

Provision must be made as well for transit riders arriving by car—those being dropped off and those wanting to park. Many of the transit riders accessing stations in emerging transit districts located in relatively low-density areas will arrive by car, which means that park-and-ride facilities (and drop-off/pick-up areas) will be necessary. Planning for park-and-ride facilities for the transit system needs to take account of parking needs and parking issues throughout the transit district. (See next section on planning for parking.) Planning must strive to integrate all the district's parking resources that support the transit system— but without compromising the urban design and place-making aspects of the transit district plan.

For transit riders arriving by bus or other connecting transit service, adequate accommodation of transfer functions is necessary, either through curbside stops or off-street intermodal boarding areas. (See Chapter Six for a discussion of the design of transfer functions.)

Parking

A major goal in specifying a mixed-use, compact, walkable core area for transit districts is to get people out of their cars—and into transit or onto their feet or bicycles. However, the dominant mode of access to land uses developed in transit districts will continue to be the automobile. Automobile storage, both short term and long term, is therefore a primary design concern.

A good supply of on-street parking is critical in mixed-use core areas. On-street parking offers convenient short-term parking for retail customers, buffers pedestrians from traffic, and reduces the land area needed for parking lots. A close grid of streets in the core can maximize the linear footage of curb available for parking.

To maintain a pedestrian-friendly environment, parking-lot street frontage should be kept to a minimum. Doing so may be particularly difficult for park-and-ride facilities. Where appropriate, lots should be buffered from sidewalks by commercial buildings. Parking lots should have a carefully planned and clearly marked pedestrian-circulation system and a landscape plan that aids stormwater management.

In transit districts planned for higher densities, parking structures will be required. They should be designed to include ground-floor retail or office uses on the street-facing sides, in order to promote street life and complement the pedestrian environment.

Parking requirements for the land uses in transit districts—excluding parking for transit riders—can potentially be reduced by shared parking among uses and by increasing the propensity of people arriving by transit, foot, or car to walk to multiple destinations (linked trips). A primary goal of transit district planning is to increase visitors' propensity to make linked trips by assuring a mix of complementary uses and a pedestrian-friendly environment. Another goal related to parking requirements is to provide housing in transit districts with sufficiently good access—by transit or by foot—to jobs and other household destinations to enable households to get by with one fewer vehicle.

The parking ratios for multifamily projects in the core area of transit districts can be reduced from conventional requirements (which call for two or more spaces per unit) by one-half to one space per unit, if adequate visitor parking is provided on the street or in off-street parking areas shared with other land uses. Multifamily projects located near high-density non-residential uses can have parking ratios below one space per unit and parking can be provided in shared-parking facilities.

Retail land uses in transit district core areas also can function well with lower parking ratios than the four to five spaces per 1,000 square feet of leasable area that is standard for typical suburban retail projects. Depending on the mix of uses and the design of the core area, retail parking demand can be reduced to 3.5 to 3.8 spaces per 1,000 square feet. To successfully reduce parking requirements, mixed-use retail cores must be designed to facilitate park-and-walk shopping, meaning that shoppers arriving by car can access multiple shopping destinations on foot from a single parking spot.

Employment land uses in the core area of transit districts tend to achieve parking ratios that are lower by about one-half space per 1,000 square feet of leasable area than parking ratios for conventional suburban office developments. The design of the core area,

On-street parking and parking garages that are well integrated into the streetscape can accommodate automobiles without disturbing the pedestrian friendliness and urban atmosphere of planned transit districts.

its accessibility from transit stops, and the transit habits of employees influence the potential for lowering these parking ratios.

ULI's shared-parking methodology[4]—augmented with local data on transit use and propensities to walk and make linked trips—can be used to determine parking demand in a mixed-use transit district. Use of the shared-parking approach enables planners to set up a framework for the centralized management of parking within transit districts.

Some cities have waived requirements that development projects provide all needed parking spaces on site, opting instead to charge in-lieu fees that they use to provide shared parking in a central location. To manage centralized parking, some cities have turned to quasi-public parking districts or business improvement districts (BIDs) to handle the administrative tasks.

REGIONAL CONTEXT

Transit provides a rationale for increasing the intensity of land use at a particular location. But what is the right mix of land uses at the right scale of intensity depends on market realities and the capacity of the location to absorb growth. Transit stations and associated transit districts function within the metropolitan region of which they are a part. The planning of individual transit districts must take into account regional market forces and commuting patterns, as well as regional growth strategies.

Not all station areas will be suited for housing. Not all station areas will be able to support retail development. Careful consideration of the dynamics of the surrounding area is needed to provide a framework for integrating station area development into the wider context. The development program for a transit district should take advantage of the surrounding area and build off its strengths.

In built-up areas, the planning of transit districts can follow many of the same principles that have been discussed—mixing uses, developing at higher densities, and focusing on the pedestrian environment—

without aiming to end up with a transit village comprising a dense mixed-use core and surrounding housing. Planning for infill development at station areas along existing transit corridors may focus on such context-related concerns as the adaptive use of buildings, reductions in the use of park-and-ride facilities, and the expansion of employment uses. Planning for development around bus-transit stops/ stations in low-density suburban areas may identify a community need for a node of mixed-use development that could help create a sense of place where none exists.

REGIONAL POLICY SUPPORT

Regional land use and transportation-planning policies control the location of major transit corridors and draw the blueprints for metropolitan growth. A few regions—including Portland (Oregon), Seattle, and Ottawa—have adopted regionwide strategies to concentrate development in corridors served by transit. In North Carolina, a joint planning effort by the city of Charlotte and Mecklenburg County is seeking to channel future growth in a corridors-and-wedges pattern with higher-intensity development located around regional transit corridors. On the other hand, programs in the San Francisco and Chicago regions—both with highly developed transit systems and models of station area development—encourage development at transit stops but have not adopted regional policies that focus high-intensity growth on transit corridors.

In other words, the idea of concentrating development around transit stations is supported by public policies in some, but not all regions with regional transit systems. The main benefit of a regional policy that targets transit corridors for growth is that it provides a degree of certainty that the development of station areas will occur and establishes a predictable timetable for such development.

RESOURCES FOR PLANNING AND DEVELOPMENT

Even with regional policy support, developing around transit is a complex undertaking. However, a variety of resources are available to provide guidance. Guidance on planning for developing around transit is available from the federal government[5] and from planning manuals prepared by metropolitan planning organizations (MPOs, agencies that meet federal requirements for the regional coordination of transportation planning), transit agencies, and city planning departments. In many cases, financial assistance is available for the planning and implementation of development around transit. Such assistance includes planning grants from regional agencies, city redevelopment programs, and capital grants from federal and local governments.

Planning Information

Public agencies and communities publish planning guidelines for development around transit in order to communicate development standards and promote appropriate development. Such published guidelines offer a wealth of information on the planning and design of transit-oriented development. They also can offer insights into local and regional expectations. This helps developers design projects that are in tune with local expectations, which makes it easier to navigate the development approval process.

In a 1993 survey of 165 transit agencies in the United States and Canada, Robert Cervero investigated the use of guidelines to promote transit-supportive development.[6] At that time, guidelines had been prepared by 25 agencies and were under preparation by another 12 agencies. Cervero evaluated 19 of the guideline documents in terms of their organization and integration of concepts, the quality of the illustrations, the clarity of the technical information, and their overall effectiveness for reaching target audiences. Eight guidelines stood out in these categories. The Snohomish County (Washington) Transportation Authority's two-volume guidebook,[7] which is described in the following section, was one of these standout efforts to communicate information.

In the last decade, transit or planning agency guidelines for transit-oriented development have continued to evolve. A 2002 survey of transit agencies by Cervero found that almost half of rail-transit agencies—and 9 percent of bus-transit agencies—had formal pro-

grams to encourage transit-oriented development.[8] A number of newer documents have become more sophisticated in their message, content, and graphics. Two documents that are described in the following sections—*Creating Livable Communities*[9] from Denver's Regional Transportation District and *Planning and Design for Transit Handbook*[10] from Portland, Oregon's Tri-County Metropolitan Transportation District— exemplify this evolution. Both sets of guidelines are based on the respective regional agency's clearly articulated strategy for expanding and enhancing public transit, and are therefore focused and specific. A guidebook issued by the Minneapolis-St. Paul Metropolitan Council in 2000 represents a more recent example of improvement in the quality of guidelines for transit-oriented development.[11] These and similar guidelines provide a rich resource for the growing number of transit agencies with staff support for development programs as well as for developers and consultants involved in developing around transit.

The contents of three of the guidelines mentioned above are briefly described in the following sections.

Snohomish County Transportation Authority

Developed with funding from the U.S. Department of Transportation, the guidelines published by the Snohomish County Transportation Authority in Washington are highly respected and frequently used by other agencies as a model. Volume 1, which was first published in 1989 and updated in 1991, provides a rationale for developing around transit and includes ideas and examples. Volume 2, which was published in 1993, takes the reader from concept to specifics. It includes specific implementation strategies, drawings of preferred site designs, and model goals and policies. Written for a broad audience, both volumes tailor sections to particular interests. For example, a section for developers and planners includes criteria for transit-compatible land use activities and a summary chart, and a section for local officials steps them through a 15-year phasing strategy for the public improvements that would be needed to support transit-oriented redevelopment of an auto-oriented commercial strip.

TOD Markets and Initiatives Box Score

Support for development around transit can come from strong markets or from good planning. The following box score highlights trends in selected regional transit markets, including significant initiatives that have been undertaken to promote development near transit.

Primary Transit Markets

New York. Real estate especially hot in Manhattan and on the New Jersey waterfront—prime transit areas. Ambitious plans for subway extensions in Manhattan and to LaGuardia Airport under discussion. Strong urban turnaround in many New Jersey cities, and in Stamford, Connecticut.

Boston. Attractive opportunities in Boston and Cambridge—in the central areas, along the South Boston waterfront, and along the Central Artery (the Big Dig). Neighborhood opposition stymies development near suburban rail stations. State program adopted in 2004 seeks to expand the amount of affordable housing around transit.

Chicago. Housing market booming in downtown, in other parts of the city, and in suburban cities near train stations. Growing state and regional awareness of urban growth and development issues. In the works under the auspices of the Northeastern Illinois Planning Commission: an initiative to develop a comprehensive general plan for the region—which could orient development to the region's strong transit network.

Washington. Transit investment seeks to shape land use. Transit-served central-city and adjacent suburban markets appeal to residential and commercial markets. Signature transit-oriented projects—developed privately or under WMATA's joint development program—abound. Smart growth policies in effect in Arlington County, Virginia, and Montgomery County, Maryland. Growing public interest in capturing the benefits of transit in evidence in the District of Columbia, Prince George's County, Maryland, and Prince William County, Virginia.

San Francisco. A leader in promoting good planning and transportation concepts. A range of transit resources serve the central city, suburbs, and regional travelers. Extension of BART to high-growth areas in San Jose underway. Hot intown markets in San Francisco and Oakland support transit. In suburbs, support for development around transit in practice frequently falls way short of support in theory. New programs in Contra Costa and San Mateo Counties link local smart growth policies with local-option sales taxes that can be used to fund transportation.

Philadelphia. Downtown housing market healthy. State legislation authorizing transit revitalization districts pending. Transit-oriented development occurring along the new light-rail Delaware River Line connecting Trenton and Camden and the restored rail line between Philadelphia and Reading. State fiscal problems threaten the operation of several regional transit services.

Other Transit Markets

Portland. Most ambitious pushing of the market for density. Extensive agreements, regulations, and economic incentives encourage density levels that exceed those that would be accomplished through the normal development market. Growth boundary and regional government reinforce TOD strategies. Strong housing market in the city of Portland being met with industrial conversions. Suburban markets for higher-density living near transit remain untested.

Seattle. The regional policy of directing most growth to designated urban growth areas helps support bus-based transit. Innovative downtown bus tunnel, complemented by short Seattle monorail. Plans for a light-rail system moving ahead despite some controversy. Development near stations will be sought. Downtown housing market thriving.

Los Angeles. Undertaking an ambitious transit construction program combining light rail, heavy rail, and commuter rail. Blue Line to Long Beach goes through an industrial corridor with limited development potential. Alignment of newer Gold Line to Pasadena better relates to adjacent development. Worsening traffic congestion and air quality may force planners to more effectively use transit as a tool for shaping growth.

San Diego. In 1992, adopted the nation's first transit-oriented development ordinance to support the popular trolley system. Regional collaboration on growth issues occurs under aegis of SANDAG, which has been designated as the key agency for distributing transportation revenues from a regional sales tax. Once seedy downtown has been turned around. The light-rail line to Mission Valley has become a magnet for residential and commercial development.

Atlanta. MARTA achieves respectable rail ridership rates despite a pattern of dispersed low-density growth that is terrible for transit. (Compared with San Francisco's BART, MARTA system is half the length but carries two-thirds the ridership.) Strong market for transit-supportive intown housing. A growing movement for transit-oriented smart growth, exemplified by the regional council's Livable Centers Initiative.

Dallas. Development around transit occurring in suburbs, but not generally in the central city, which is the prime transit market. Developers closely watching the widely praised Mockingbird Station development in the city of Dallas, which is somewhat of an anomaly in the market. Regional council of governments preaches/teaches transit-oriented development. Suburban governments increasingly welcome prospective transit service for its development potential.

Denver. Transit station areas in the central city rezoned in accordance with a growth plan emphasizing support for transit. Downtown LoDo district adjacent to 16th Street transit mall is hot market for residential development. Much evidence of suburban support for developing around transit: a mixed-use development at the Englewood light-rail station; political support for development near stations planned in Arvada; expectations of major development along a multimodal corridor along I-70; and a ballot initiative scheduled for fall 2004 on local funding—including a new tax—for six transit lines.

Miami. High development densities and strong growth prospects—as well as a new heavy-rail system—should make Miami an ideal transit community. However, the new rail system, which follows transportation corridors, misses key destinations. And transit ridership failed to grow from 1980 and 2000. Little transit-supportive development has occurred, but a number of promising projects are in the works.

Englewood City-Center, located six miles south of Denver along the RTD light-rail corridor, combines a big-box store, other retail operations, offices, and housing into a successful transit district.

Regional Transportation District, Denver

Directed to an audience of local communities, the RTD's *Creating Livable Communities* is particularly strong in laying out the processes and tools needed to implement transit-oriented development. The roles of local government, the regional authority, and the development industry are described along with strategies for facilitating interaction. The publication provides an orientation to the region's transit network—including density and parking expectations at different locations within the network—and design guidelines that are meant to help communities review development proposals. A well-written local case study ties all the pieces together and highlights best practices. The narrative style of this publication makes it less useful for quick access to information, but builds an excellent case for the benefits and feasibility of developing around transit if both the public and private sectors plan early.

Tri-County Metropolitan Transportation District, Portland, Oregon

Assuming that the argument for transit has been made, Tri-Met's *Planning and Design for Transit Handbook* provides technical information for the next step—developing around transit—in two sections, each aimed at a distinct audience. The first section on land use and transportation lays out the regional vision for transit and development patterns. For each level in the transit hierarchy, it discusses the location and design of

transit centers and compatible land use activities and provides density tables. Unlike many TOD guidelines, the handbook specifies minimum densities for development at varying distances from transit centers. The handbook's second section, aimed at development professionals, focuses on site and building design guidelines. An effort has been made to focus on "tested" measures and "tested" examples in the standards that are proposed. The site design guidelines illustrate desired responses to different planning criteria, such as density or land use mix. Basic geometric, engineering, and service parameters and standards are detailed. Tri-Met intends to continue to update and revise the guidelines as the region develops.

Implementation Assistance

The following sections describe four of the most innovative programs in place for assisting with the implementation of transit-oriented development. While differing in emphasis, all four provide planning or capital grants to help cities support or encourage development related to transit. The programs in the Seattle and San Francisco regions are focused specifically on transit. Those in the Atlanta and Minneapolis-St. Paul regions are targeted more generally on livable communities and smart growth, but with an emphasis on transit.

Transit Station Communities Project, Seattle

The Puget Sound Regional Council's transit communities program has a regional component and a local component. Regionally, it seeks to raise the awareness of development opportunities around transit. The council has partnered with the 1000 Friends of Washington to provide an outreach program for local governments, developers, and the public that centers on opportunities to implement TOD. It also has developed a guidance document—*Creating Transit Station Communities: A Transit-Oriented Development Workbook* (1999)—that addresses station area planning and TOD feasibility and implementation. Locally, the transit communities program provides support for testing TOD strategies on demonstration sites. It provides technical assistance to local governments to help them identify opportunity sites near transit stops, conduct market research on transit-oriented development, and plan and design TODs.

Transportation for Livable Communities, San Francisco

The concept behind the Metropolitan Transportation Commission's Transportation for Livable Communities (TLC) program is that investments in small-scale transportation improvements can lead to larger-scale community revitalization. To that end, the TLC program funds community-oriented transportation projects that encourage pedestrian, transit, or bicycle travel or that support compact development patterns. The projects have to be community based, consistent with the community's plan, and developed through an inclusive planning process. Grants are provided for three categories of projects:

• planning efforts (funded at up to $75,000 per project);

• construction activities (funded at between $150,000 and $2 million per project); and

• financial incentives keyed to housing density and affordability.

TLC program funding comes from federal and state transportation funds allocated to the Bay Area. In its first five years (beginning in 1998), TLC provided approximately $2 million for 49 planning projects, just under $49 million for 59 capital projects, and $9 million for 31 housing incentive projects. It has built up an impressive record in terms of the number and variety of planning and implementation projects funded and in terms of the distribution of projects over the nine-county region. The Metropolitan Transportation Commission has noted that one of the crucial lessons it has learned is that partnerships among transit providers, regional and local government, and the public are needed in order to achieve these types of projects.[12]

Livable Centers Initiative, Atlanta

Directed at existing town centers and activity centers—areas that are less than half developed are excluded from the program—the Atlanta Regional Commission's Livable Centers Initiative (LCI) provides funding for study projects in the field of transit-oriented development. The program, which began in May 1999, has a budget of $5 million to be expended over a five-year period. Its goals are to encourage the development of residential uses, the mixing of uses, and improvements in connectivity within the region's

A streetcar line goes through the Pearl District—located in a formerly industrial neighborhood north of downtown Portland—which contains some of the highest-valued real estate in the city and qualifies as the densest transit-oriented development in the region.

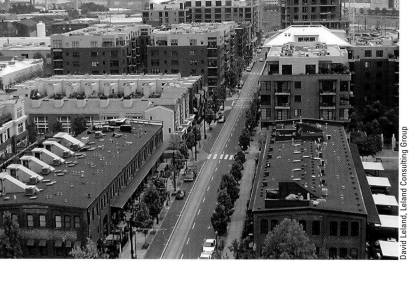

David Leland, Leland Consulting Group

activity centers and town centers. In its first three years of operation, LCI funded 32 planning studies, with planning grants averaging $85,000 per study.

A separate $350 million fund is available for the implementation of transportation projects identified in the planning studies. Projects that may be funded for implementation include the provision of pedestrian amenities, streetscape improvements, intersection improvements, the improvement of bicycle facilities, the provision of trails, parking improvements at stations, and bridge improvements.

In 2003, LCI launched a pilot project to explore opportunities for sustained mixed-use development on greenfield sites, that is, on sites of at least 250 acres that are less than half developed.

Livable Communities Demonstration Account, Minneapolis-St. Paul

The Metropolitan Council awards $6 million to $7 million per year in LCDA (Livable Communities Demonstration Account) grants to support residential or mixed-use development projects throughout the seven-county region. The competitively awarded grants go to projects that the council deems to be models for smart growth. The council awards planning grants as well to communities working to implement smart growth initiatives; these are given on a 50/50 match basis to a maximum of $150,000 per grant.

To receive a grant, projects must demonstrate connections to transit, a development density that can support future transit, walkable mixed-use areas, a range of housing choices in terms of type and affordability, and connections to adjacent neighborhoods and the larger community. Since its inception in 1996, the demonstration account has awarded 94 grants in 31 communities for a total of $44 million. The council calculates that this investment has leveraged more than $994 million in private development and $396 million in public investment. Projects funded by LCDA grants have provided 6,860 new housing units and 400 rehabilitated housing units. LCDA projects in core cities and inner-ring suburbs serve as models for walkable, mixed-use redevelopment and infill development

in built-up areas; those in newer suburbs serve as models for compact development in developing areas.

DEVELOPING WITHIN A TRANSIT DISTRICT PLANNING FRAMEWORK: EXAMPLES

Increasingly over the last ten years, governments and transit agencies have undertaken transit district planning to encourage private development around transit. And regional planning for transit corridors has provided the platform for successful transit-oriented development in a number of places. The planning framework is only one ingredient in a complicated recipe, although arguably a very important one that provides the basis for the process of developing around transit.

According to Timothy Rood, principal of Calthorpe Associates, a firm with a long history of work in transit-oriented development and regional planning for transit districts, the two projects that best exemplify TOD design within a regional planning process are Orenco Station in Hillsboro, Oregon, and the Crossings in Mountain View, California. The former is an outer-suburb greenfield development on a light-rail transit line. The latter is a suburban infill development on a commuter-rail corridor. (Calthorpe Associates was involved in the planning for the Crossings and not involved in the development of Orenco Station.) Rood suggests the following reasons for selecting these two projects as illustrative examples:

• In both cases, officially adopted plans had identified the project sites as potential locations for rail-oriented development—the Orenco Station site was identified in a regional growth plan and the Crossings site was identified in a city comprehensive plan.

• The local planning processes used to refine the developments were comprehensive, yet substantially different for the two sites.

• At each site, external influences greatly affected the ultimate design of the projects.

• Although their land use mixes differ, both projects are successful.

Both projects have been widely evaluated, making available wide-ranging information and documentation on each project's respective performance. Both projects exemplify a model of mixed-use development organized into a core area and secondary area. However, in each case that model has been modified to respond to the site and the regional context.

On the other side of the country, Arlington County in Virginia represents a premier example of planning a new transit system—the Washington region's Metrorail subway—to encourage supportive development. At the time that Metro was being planned, Arlington was in transformation from bedroom suburb to mixed housing and commerce suburb. The county took advantage of Metro access in its development policies and thus brought into existence a vibrant, mixed-use community along a formerly fading commercial corridor—in the process, enhancing its tax base, expanding transit ridership, and protecting many stable residential communities from unwanted change.

Orenco Station

Located in Hillsborough, Oregon, about 11 miles from downtown Portland, Orenco Station is a 190-acre development that contains a mixed-use town center and a diverse mix of residential properties designed in accordance with transit-supportive planning principles. In the 1990s, the project area—which had been planned in the 1980s for commercial/industrial uses in hopes of attracting high-tech development—was selected for a stop on Portland's Westside MAX light-rail line. In the *Portland Metro Area 2040 Plan,* the project area was designated a town center, after which it was rezoned as a "station community residential village" to support compact mixed-use development consistent with the requirements of the regional plan.

The 2040 plan established mandatory requirements for all Westside station areas for

- minimum densities;

- mixed-use development;

- pedestrian-oriented buildings;

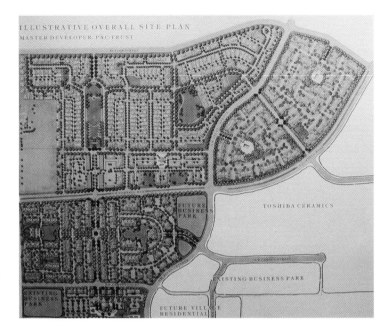

- prohibitions on auto-oriented land uses; and

- reductions in parking allowed.

Additionally, it set targets for minimum residential densities at varying distances from light-rail stops.

The transit stop at Orenco Station is located on the south edge of the site, one-quarter mile from the town center and one-half mile from the concentration of residential development north of the town center. It is connected to the town center by a landscaped north/south street that ends at a formal village green north of the town center. The mixed-use town center is located at the intersection of this street and Cornell Road, the east/west arterial through the development. The town center contains three-story mixed-use buildings and live/work and loft apartments. On-street as well as underground and behind-the-buildings parking is provided. A network of pedestrian pathways connects the open spaces in the project, and interconnects the development's residential and mixed-use areas and the transit stop.

The arrangement of land uses in Orenco Station grew out of the need to site the town center at a location that would provide both access to transit and, more importantly, access from nearby residential areas, thus making it a workable location for commercial land uses. Early in the project, PacTrust, which was one of the developers, elected to develop the northern portion of the site first. Because most transit-oriented communities that have relied primarily on transit traffic for their retail component have not fared well, PacTrust decided that it had to tap into traffic travel-

Supporting land uses outside the Orenco Station planned transit district help connect the entire suburban community of Hillsboro, Oregon, to the region's light-rail system.

ing Cornell Road, which does not run close to the station. This decision has proven to be a good one.

PacTrust and Orenco Station's other developer, Costa Pacific Homes, worked with the city of Hillsboro, Washington County, Metro (the regional planning agency), and Tri-Met (the regional transit agency) to establish the planning framework for the project. For example, an important agreement was reached with Washington County to retain Cornell Road as a five-lane road rather than widen it to seven lanes, thus allowing manageable pedestrian crossings in the town center, which are needed to provide pedestrian access to the transit station.

Completed in fall 2003, Orenco Station won the National Association of Home Builders' America's Community of the Year award in 1998 for its planning and design. Residential sales and commercial and apartment leasing have been strong. In late 2001, commercial rents in Orenco Station were about 10 percent higher than commercial rents in nearby areas and occupancies were high. Residential sale prices in 2001 were 20 to 30 percent above the area average.

The planning of Orenco Station made use of consumer focus groups involving 1,500 employees of nearby businesses to design the details of the project's residential and commercial offerings. The results of a 2002 study by Bruce Podobnik, a researcher at Lewis and Clark College, surveying the travel behavior of residents in Portland neighborhoods and their overall perceptions of the community in which they live reflect the success of this consumer focus.[13]

Podobnik found that residents of Orenco Station make more local trips by walking than do residents of comparison neighborhoods. He attributed the difference to Orenco Station's pedestrian-oriented design and compact arrangement of land uses. While Orenco Station residents do not make more commuting trips by transit than do the residents of comparison neighborhoods, almost 70 percent of the Orenco Station respondents reported that they use transit more than they did before moving to Orenco Station, a trend that was not present in other neighborhoods in the

survey. (Approximately 75 percent of commuting trips by Orenco Station residents are made by car.)

Podobnik's survey asked questions related to perceptions of social, health, and environmental conditions in Orenco Station in order to ascertain attitudes about the higher-density living experience. More than 90 percent of Orenco Station respondents say that the living experience in Orenco Station is better than in other suburbs, even though land prices are higher and lots are smaller. The reasons given most often for this preference relate to the attention to detail in the design of the living units, the sense of community in the neighborhood, and the community's overall organization—its open space, public amenities, pedestrian-friendly design, and town center.

The Crossings

In the early 1990s, the addition of a stop on the Caltrain commuter-rail line—which connects San Francisco and San Jose—adjacent to San Antonio Road in Mountain View provided the incentive for the city to seek redevelopment of the failing Old Mill Mall located on an 18-acre site in the southeast quadrant of the San Antonio Road/Central Expressway interchange, a site bordering the Caltrain tracks along its northern edge. In 1991, the city established a plan for the station area—*San Antonio Station Precise Plan*—covering four planning areas: the mall site, two adjacent fully developed areas, and an area to the west across San Antonio Road. Mountain View's plan predates the regional smart growth planning efforts that were undertaken in 2001–2002 by the Association of Bay Area Governments and the Metropolitan Transportation Commission, but is consistent with regional plans.

Mountain View's station area precise plan was used as a framework for a transit-oriented redevelopment of the area, including parking for the commuter-rail station. The plan provides for specific minimum and maximum densities and mixes of land uses in each of the four planning areas; and is most detailed concerning the site of the Old Mill Mall where it specifies access locations, minimum street rights-of-way and widths, and maximum (350 feet) and desired

Calthorpe Associates

Calthorpe Associates

(200 to 250 feet) block lengths. The precise plan for the Crossings includes performance criteria for walkability, integration with transit, landscaping, open space, building design, and building materials.

TPG Development engaged Calthorpe Associates to translate the precise plan requirements into a plan to recycle the mall (literally use its concrete and asphalt in foundations and fill for the new development) and redevelop the mall site as a pedestrian-friendly transit district with 358 housing units and a small amount of rider-oriented retail at the train station.

The Crossings contains a mixture of small-lot detached units with garages at the rear, rowhouses, and condominium units. Densities range from 11 to 70 units per acre. The retail uses are located at the corners opposite the station, in buildings that relate to adjacent rowhouses and provide a two-story streetscape for people walking to transit. Multiple small blocks

interspersed with parks and playgrounds are composed into a unified, walkable neighborhood. The street network provides connections to adjacent retail areas, allowing residents to access them without crossing arterial streets.

Because an adjacent roadway interchange and the rail corridor restricted access to the site and the transit station was located away from the available access points, the Crossings uses a small-block pattern to provide connectivity to the station. The site design defines the areas for different levels of residential density and provides walkable pedestrian routes from the residential areas to the station and to adjacent retail development.

Because the site is small and is surrounded by office and retail land uses, it did not make sense to develop large-scale employment and commercial uses at the Crossings. Instead, the synergy of different land uses that is the basis for the mixed-use model was achieved by a careful integration of the site's residential land uses with the office development and grocery store that are adjacent to the site. As Timothy Rood notes: "The Crossings filled in the missing pieces needed to make a great mixed-use neighborhood and connected them with walkable streets—a key strategy for creating transit-oriented neighborhoods in the existing suburban landscape."

Completed in 1998, the Crossings succeeded in selling out new units quickly and resale units continue to remain on the market for only a short time. While the Crossings has not been the subject of a cross-sectional study, how the development is perceived by its residents is a subject of ongoing interest that has been addressed by the press. The press occasionally expresses the view that the design may be too compact for suburban California, while acknowledging that the project's residents give high ratings to the walkability of the Crossings and the feeling of safety that this gives them.[14]

Arlington County

In the 1960s, the planning for a segment of the Washington area's Metrorail system through Arlington County, Virginia, helped focus the county's

The Crossings, an infill development on a commuter-rail corridor in Mountain View, California, combines residential and retail uses to create a relatively dense suburban neighborhood.

Some of the housing and retail in the 18-acre development is only a street width away from the Caltrain station.

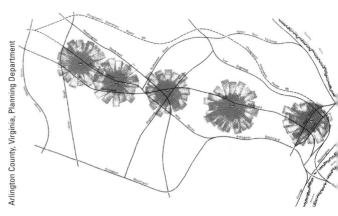

Arlington County, Virginia, Planning Department

Arlington County, Virginia, adopted a bull's-eye concept for development around stations along the Rosslyn-Ballston and U.S. 1 Metrorail corridors.

concerns over its growth. Located just across the Potomac River from downtown Washington, Arlington was a popular bedroom community for federal employees and other workers who had been flocking to the Washington area since the 1930s. It boasted stable neighborhoods, good schools, and many garden apartments. It also had a dramatically growing office sector spurred by a mushrooming federal presence—including the Pentagon, which was built during World War II.

However, Arlington's commercial districts by midcentury were generally seamy, marred by a hodgepodge of incompatible auto-related and industrial uses, distinctly downscale, and considered by many suitable for urban renewal. But the county shied away from federally supported renewal programs out of concern that they would involve public housing. Instead, it opted for a more flexible program oriented to encouraging private initiatives for redevelopment.

Unlike many of the other jurisdictions contemplated for Metrorail service, Arlington embraced the idea of the subway as a tool in its growth plans. Envisioning the rail route as an opportunity to cluster growth and revitalize its commercial core, the county lobbied strongly against the original proposal to align the tracks with I-66, a planned radial freeway bisecting the county. It proposed an alternative route beneath a failing commercial corridor, Wilson Boulevard.

First Try: Rosslyn

The redevelopment of the Rosslyn area within Arlington County provided planners with an object lesson in what not to do. In the early 1960s, Rosslyn was an unsightly mixture of pawnshops, lumberyards, oil tanks, and other marginal land uses with some key locational advantages including direct road and—on Washington's fading trolley system—light-rail access to the city, highway connections to suburban communities on the west and south, a planned interstate highway, affordable land, and the opportunity to build high-rise buildings with a view of downtown Washington. (Builders within the city could not provide such a view amenity because of a ten-story height limit.) Moreover, a Metrorail stop for Rosslyn was planned.

The market for commercial redevelopment in Rosslyn was supported by a shift in the space acquisition philosophy of the General Services Administration (GSA), the federal government's real estate arm, from ownership to leasing and by GSA's new value-conscious interest in suburban locations. The market was helped as well by the growing county's desire for commercial tax revenues to finance schools and other needed services. Arlington County adopted a sector plan to guide the location and character of development, and it imposed an exaction on developers to help pay for road and pedestrian circulation improvements.[15]

During the 1960s, 2.7 million square feet of office space, almost 600 residential units, and more than 600 hotel rooms were built. By 2003, according to the Arlington County Department of Community Planning and Development, the Rosslyn area contained almost 8 million square feet of office space, 4,600 residential units, 2,200 hotel rooms, and 665,000 square feet of retail space.

Rossyln's redevelopment proved to be a huge success in terms of commercial value and county revenues. But it was not a place-making success. Like many office nodes developed at the same time, Rosslyn's focus on the car produced a hostile environment for pedestrians. The elevated walkways never worked as planned. The area lacked a lively mix of shops and restaurants and died after 5:00 p.m. on weekdays. Al Eisenberg, a former member of the county board and now a state legislator, remembers thinking that the space-age Rosslyn site plan "looked like the Jetsons" and finds it ironic "that we tried to improve on what already worked—housing over the stores, common spaces, and an ability to walk. The model that served people well was abandoned in the last 50 years." The lessons of Rosslyn would help improve planning for the rest of the corridor.

A Corridor Vision

After Metrorail planners had reached a decision to build two lines radiating out from Rosslyn—one to the west generally along the then-proposed I-66 corridor, and one to the south along the U.S. 1 corridor—the county became actively engaged in locating the lines and stations to encourage transit-oriented development (even though the term was not yet in use) and protect neighborhoods. Wanting to take advantage of the rail line's potential to stimulate the kinds of development that could enrich the local economy and quality-of-life, the county lobbied hard for an underground route following the commercial corridor from Rosslyn to Ballston—rather than a less costly alignment in the median of the proposed freeway, the construction of which was under fire from community groups.

Outside of Rosslyn, which, as noted, stood in need of extensive redevelopment, the corridor traversed some of the wealthiest and most civic-minded neighborhoods in the county. In the 1970s, the county undertook an extensive citizen participation program. This examined a range of scenarios—from no growth (maintaining the county as an aging, residential enclave) to aggressive growth. The consensus result was a long-range plan that would concentrate high-density commercial and residential growth in the Rosslyn-Ballston and U.S. 1 corridors.

The plan sees stations as bull's-eyes located at the center of five rings of progressively less intense development extending a total distance of one-quarter mile from the station; and it provides for the protection of nearby residential areas. The general land use plan retains fairly low-density zoning but indicates the county's willingness to rezone in response to development proposals. Among the major policy goals of the long-range plan are

• a tax base consisting of a 50/50 mix of residential and commercial development;

• mixed-use development incorporating a significant amount of housing;

• the preservation of existing single-family neighborhoods and garden apartments; and

• an emphasis on redevelopment within one-quarter mile of Metrorail stations.

Beginning with Rosslyn in 1977 and continuing with Court House, Ballston, Virginia Square, and Clarendon in the 1980s, the county developed sector plans for each station district. (The Rosslyn plan updates the 1962 sector plan.) Each district is planned to serve a different function—Rosslyn as a major business center, Court House as the local government center, Clarendon as an urban village, Virginia Square as a cultural and educational center, and Ballston as Arlington's new downtown.

Development Success

Metrorail service to Arlington began in 1979 at an interim station in Ballston, the site of Arlington's first shopping center. At this time, the Ballston area was characterized by an amorphous mix of commercial uses accessed by car. The county's plans called for a mixed-use, pedestrian-oriented center with high-density commercial and residential development near the station featuring open space, shops, and walkways. Developers were offered density bonuses—up to FAR (floor/area ratio) 6 in FAR 3.5 zones—for certain amenities and additional bonuses for including housing, leading to a considerable amount of office, residential, and retail development. The county helped finance parking improvements, including Metrorail parking, at the shopping center, which was renamed

Arlington County considered a range of development densities for the Rosslyn-Ballston Metrorail corridor before adopting a mid-density general land use plan that has produced a compact mix of residential, office, and retail uses along the corridor.

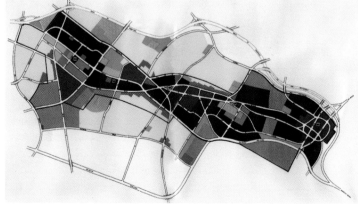

Arlington County, Virginia, Planning Department

The Rosslyn-Ballston corridor today boasts concentrated nodes of commercial and residential development, particularly around the Metrorail stations.

Ballston Mall. WMATA (the Washington Metropolitan Area Transit Authority) spearheaded the joint development of the nearby Ballston Metro Center.

Each station on Arlington's Rosslyn-Ballston and Jefferson Davis (U.S. 1) rail corridors offers a similar story. At the Pentagon City station, Pentagon Row is a successful new lifestyle main street center surrounded by a mix of housing and other retailing. The Fashion Center, a regional mall also located at the Pentagon City station, reports that about one-third of its business comes from Metro riders—which is to say that it captures customers not only from Arlington's neighborhoods, but also from retail-starved Capitol Hill in the city of Washington.

Even before Metrorail services were extended, the Rosslyn-Ballston corridor experienced much commercial development: 4.9 million square feet of office space, almost 500,000 square feet of retail space, and 2,000 hotel rooms between 1960 and 1980. The vast majority of this development occurred in Rosslyn, establishing it as a major uptown center. As Metrorail service was extended along the corridor and the county's planning matured, development gradually spread to Court House and then to Ballston. Clearly the market for commercial development, especially office, was strong.

But the county wanted a residential presence in the corridor in order to avoid creating another sterile office district that shut down at night and on weekends. The development community responded to the incentives that it offered for residential development. The county's land assembly program to combine small commercial parcels into more usable development sites was especially productive. In the 1980s, a rebounding economy, Metrorail access, and county incentives spurred the development of more than 8,500 housing units in Rosslyn-Ballston corridor station areas. Office and residential development were almost evenly matched (see figure 3-1).

Restaurants and bars have been attracted to the corridor by the many young singles moving in, which has created a thriving night life. Many of these uses have located in the corridor's large number of previously abandoned stores.

In the view of the county board, the corridor's initial failure to attract major retail development was a disappointment. In 2001, this disappointment was mitigated by the opening of the retail phase of the Market Common Clarendon, a mixed-use center. This project, which replaced a controversial Home Depot that had been proposed for the site, has been a financial success.

Almost 19 million square feet of office space and more than 2 million square feet of retail have been developed in the three-mile Rosslyn-Ballston corridor since 1960, as well as almost 20,000 residential units. The corridor is the equivalent of a city of 40,000 people with 80,000 jobs and a regional mall—all within a convenient walk of a Metrorail station. Perhaps more importantly, it offers attractive communities providing urban lifestyle choices for its residents and daytime population and has won the support of people who live in the more traditional residential neighborhoods around it.

Reflecting national market trends, residential development is currently so hot that county planners are trying to keep developers from going overboard in that direction, just as they kept the brakes on commercial development in the 1990s. The two Metrorail corridors in Arlington County represent 6 percent of the county's land and produce almost half its tax revenue.

Lee Quill, an area architect, says that "the clarity and intent of the county's plan on where commercial development can occur and its ability to work with developers on an approach that works with the market and the neighbors" have been largely responsible for development success. Over time, the county has gradually raised the bar for project approvals. For developers who remember the easier days, stricter requirements can be a challenge. County board member Chris Zimmerman reports that "in the early days, priming the pump was necessary to encourage development" and notes that "raising the bar can be difficult for developers whose expectations were set in the early stages of the corridor's development."

Transportation Success

Development in the Rosslyn-Ballston corridor has unquestionably spurred transit ridership. At the same time, it has not added significantly to traffic problems on local streets thanks to nearby highway construc-

Figure 3-1

DEVELOPMENT IN THE ROSSLYN-BALLSTON CORRIDOR, 1960–2003

Completed	Office GFA[1] (square feet)	Retail GFA[1] (square feet)	Housing Units	Hotel Rooms	Parking Spaces
1960–1969	3,845,242	333,235	1,263	1,134	10,900
1970–1979	1,070,263	135,655	378	872	3,782
1980–1989	8,542,520	1,150,782	8,524	572	29,762
1990–1999	3,461,971	334,201	6,179	458	13,876
2000–2003	1,671,849	191,312	3,180	189	9,418
1980–2003	13,676,340	1,676,295	17,883	1,219	53,056
1960–2003	18,591,845	2,145,185	19,524	3,225	67,738
Under Construction[2]	1,755,998	110,067	1,159	336	4,376
Approved[3]	3,392,810	741,846	4,700	660	17,700

1. Gross floor area.
2. As of December 31, 2003.
3. Approved, but not yet under construction.

Source: Arlington County Planning Division.

tion, local government policies encouraging transit use and carpooling, and the urban pattern of streets within the corridor.

Transit. Metrorail ridership is one measure of transit trends. Metrorail ridership in Arlington County increased by more than 40 percent (26,000 daily trips) between 1980 and 2003. In 1980, the top stations for ridership included the two end stations in the Rosslyn-Ballston corridor:

• Pentagon—a major government employment center (16,000 daily riders);

• Rosslyn—a major transfer station (almost 13,000 riders);

• Crystal City—a large-scale office development (8,200 riders);

• Ballston—in 1980, an interim terminal station (9,300 riders); and

• National Airport—an international airport (more than 5,600 riders).

As shown in figure 3-2, in 2003 the top four Arlington stations were Pentagon, Rosslyn, Crystal City, and Pentagon City, each with from 13,500 to 15,700 daily riders. Ballston was fifth with 11,300 riders. As a result of significant retail, office, and residential development, daily ridership at Pentagon City increased by 9,900 from 1980 to 2003. Development around the Crystal City and Court House stations translated to almost 5,400 and 4,200 additional daily riders, respectively. At Ballston, development attracted more riders while the extension of the Orange Line to Vienna in Fairfax County resulted in

Figure 3-2

AVERAGE WEEKDAY METRORAIL BOARDINGS AT ARLINGTON COUNTY STATIONS, 1977–2003

	1977	1980	1990	2000	2003	Ridership Growth 1980–2003	
						Number	Percent
Rosslyn	11,167	12,752	13,565	14,672	15,397	2,645	20.7%
Court House	–	2,825	5,310	7,079	7,066	4,241	150.1
Clarendon	–	1,899	3,078	2,752	2,927	1,028	54.1
Virginia Square-GMU	–	1,728	2,312	2,334	3,007	1,279	74.0
Ballston	–	9,352	9,531	10,450	11,262	1,910	20.4
Arlington Cemetery	140	362	1,102	1,759	1,441	1,079	298.1
Pentagon	10,558	16,123	20,687	15,548	15,726	–397	–2.5
Pentagon City	1,312	3,586	6,650	11,058	13,518	9,932	277.0
Crystal City	3,912	8,204	13,349	12,108	13,560	5,356	65.3
National Airport	2,479	5,605	5,657	5,039	4,659	–946	–16.9
All Stations	29,568	62,436	81,241	82,799	88,563	26,127	41.8

Source: Washington Metropolitan Area Transit Authority.

other riders staying on the train, for a net gain of only about 1,900 daily riders. Pentagon City and Court House—the stations experiencing the largest gains in ridership, with the exception of Arlington Cemetery, a sparsely used stop—both exemplify successful mixed-use development.

Robert Cervero (author of this book's Chapter Two) and Natasha Goguts, a graduate assistant at the University of California, studied the effects of commercial and residential development on the number of riders departing from or arriving at Arlington County stations. According to their model, every additional 1 million square feet of office and retail space within walking distance of a station adds about 500 daily boardings and alightings (250 round trips) and each additional housing unit adds about 0.5 daily boardings and alightings (0.25 round trips).[16]

The number of people entering the Rosslyn-Ballston corridor by either bus or rail is a second measure of transit trends. In 1979, prior to the extension of Metrorail to Ballston, about 7,000 daily bus riders entered the corridor during the morning peak-commuting period, half from Wilson Boulevard which traverses the center of the corridor and half from either U.S. 29/Lee Highway (north of the corridor) or Arlington Boulevard (south of the corridor). By 1981, after Metrorail service opened, total a.m. peak period transit ridership in the corridor reached 12,000, of which the bus share was under 2,000. These remaining bus riders arrived mostly from Lee Highway and Arlington Boulevard. By 1999, after Metrorail had been extended west to the end of the line, the number of transit riders entering the Rosslyn-Ballston corridor had doubled again to 24,000, but the bus component had dropped to a mere 200 (see figure 3-3).

This waning bus ridership reflects an agreement to cut back bus routes seen as competitive to Metrorail. Some bus trips that formerly went directly to downtown Washington now terminate at a rail station, which caused some grumbling and a temporary decline in total transit use by Virginia residents. However, continued development and growing traffic congestion have filled the missing seats and powered

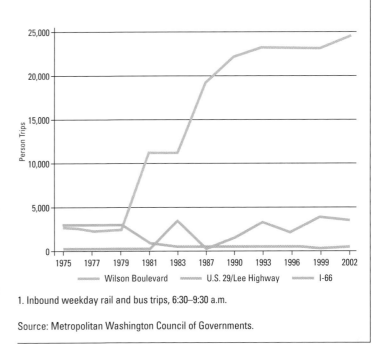

Figure 3-3
TRANSIT ARRIVALS IN ROSSLYN-BALLSTON CORRIDOR BY ROUTE, 1975–1999[1]

1. Inbound weekday rail and bus trips, 6:30–9:30 a.m.

Source: Metropolitan Washington Council of Governments.

strong gains in rail ridership. At the same time, the notion that rail transit could serve all transit needs in a close-in corridor is being rethought.

Service has been expanded for a Metrobus route that traverses the corridor, passes through Georgetown (which is not served by rail), and terminates in Washington's CBD. Recognizing that for some travelers there may be some appeal to seeing the sights, Metro markets its one bus route serving the corridor as "the Orange Line with a view." A new bus service, the Georgetown Shuttle, connecting the Rosslyn Metrorail station via Georgetown to the Dupont Circle Metrorail station in downtown D.C. offers frequent departures (every ten minutes) throughout the day. Underwritten in part by Arlington County to relieve congestion on the existing Metrorail route, the Georgetown Shuttle has been popular among tourists as well as workers and shoppers heading for Georgetown.

Recently the county has established Arlington Rapid Transit (ART), a bus service intended to support the county's emerging urban village concept, reduce car dependency in areas beyond Metrorail stations, and reduce the county's subsidy to WMATA, the regional transit operator. Three ART routes serve the Rosslyn-Ballston corridor, including one no-fare loop providing midday service between the Ballston and Virginia

Figure 3-4
PRIVATE CARS, TRUCKS, AND BUSES ENTERING ROSSLYN-BALLSTON CORRIDOR BY ROUTE, 1975–1999

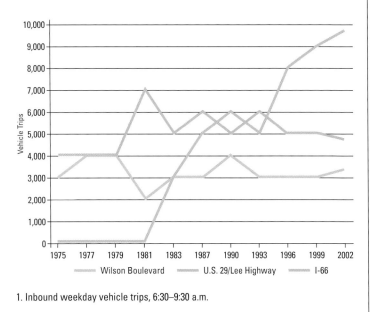

Vehicle Trips

— Wilson Boulevard   — U.S. 29/Lee Highway   — I-66

1. Inbound weekday vehicle trips, 6:30–9:30 a.m.

Source: Metropolitan Washington Council of Governments.

Square stations and another similar service between the Clarendon and Court House stations.

Traffic and Parking. The extensive redevelopment of the Rosslyn-Ballston corridor has, to the surprise of many observers, taken place without a corresponding increase in traffic. One reason is the construction of I-66 to the north, the use of which is restricted at peak hours to carpools and buses. This has helped siphon off some of the traffic generated by new development. By 1999, almost 9,000 vehicles carrying 17,000 people entered the corridor daily from I-66. (Commuter buses, most of them destined for the city of Washington, carry about 3,500 daily bus passengers on I-66.) Adjacent routes have experienced very little change in traffic. Another reason that the corridor's development has not created traffic problems is the county's requirement that employers and developers establish traffic management programs, including limits on parking and incentives for transit use or carpooling.

High transit use within the Metrorail corridors helps keep traffic under control. Commuters who live in these corridors use transit much more than do those who do not (see figure 3-5). Forty percent of corridor residents who commute do so by transit, 40 percent drive alone, and 10 percent walk. County residents

outside Metrorail corridors are more than three times as likely to drive alone as to use transit, but are somewhat more likely to carpool than are corridor residents.

The county's fine-grained street network also helps to limit the traffic impacts of development. The Rosslyn-Ballston corridor, for example, is served by at least four major radial streets and a number of cross streets offering a range of route choices. If traffic gets bad on one street, a back road is usually available.

Furthermore, strong outward growth over the last four decades has reduced the regional share of employment, entertainment, and retail land uses located in the District of Columbia—and thus has relieved the pressure of through traffic in Arlington and other first-tier suburbs within metropolitan Washington. Some of the additional traffic generated by development in the Rosslyn-Ballston corridor is counterbalanced by a reduction in the number of cars traveling from the outer suburbs for work, shopping, and entertainment purposes.

Appropriate parking also mitigates traffic. The county's parking requirements are on the low side. Its minimum one space per 1,000 square feet of office area resembles parking ratios in major downtowns. Such parking requirements are linked to public/private transportation demand management (TDM) programs that help keep driving levels below those outside the Metrorail corridors. In order to meet burgeoning nighttime entertainment parking needs, shared-parking deals with nearby office buildings have been worked out. The mixed-use Market Common Clarendon project was able to work such a deal up-front, reducing its parking needs from an estimated 1,600 spaces to 1,000 spaces.

Lessons

Development policy in the Rosslyn-Ballston corridor has had to both broaden its scope in order to deal with various related issues and narrow its focus in order to assure the evolution of a workable mixed-use district as opposed to simply a collection of nice developments. The pedestrian environment was an early issue. In Chris Zimmerman's view, the county's farsighted planning concepts committing the corridor to urban land uses were undermined by a street system that was designed on a suburban model with insufficient emphasis on pedestrian orientation. A solution was to offer development incentives under the site plan review process in exchange for specific developer-provided infrastructure and streetscape improvements.

Historic preservation, open space, and affordable housing have become issues in the corridor's redevelopment. Perhaps the most difficult of these is housing. Low-rise garden apartments and moderate-income houses have become attractive for high-rise redevelopment. Working with developers, the county has succeeded in designating parts of projects as historic, thus preserving a stock of affordable housing. A policy adopted in May 2004—to which the development community quickly responded with litigation —requires developers to allocate 10 percent of the floor area of new developments in Metrorail corridors for affordable housing.

Looking at the long-term, Arlington County's plan for developing around transit, which now is over three

decades old, not only represents an excellent success story, but also illustrates the evolution of the concept of transit districts from the 1960s to today. Many similar efforts in other jurisdictions have fallen short. Why did Arlington's efforts succeed? A number of factors seem to be key:

• *Development-Oriented Transit.* The decision to locate the rail line in the center of the corridor instead of in the median of the freeway, which would have limited opportunities for adjacent development, opened up vast potential for TOD.

• *A Receptive Population.* The many executive-level employees of the federal government and national and international nonprofit organizations who reside in Arlington County struggle with big-world problems at work. They are a large part of the county's progressive citizenry, which is inclined to support professional planning. It is no fluke that the fight against resistance to school integration in Virginia in the 1950s began in Arlington.

• *Location, Location, Location.* Lying directly in the path of growth, Arlington offered opportunities for developers to capitalize on views of the landmarks in the nation's capital city.

• *A Deteriorating Corridor.* Wilson Boulevard was ripe for redevelopment—or a candidate for becoming a suburban slum. The coming of Metrorail presented a golden opportunity for a revitalization effort.

• *Tax Base Potential.* Pressure was on the county to expand its commercial tax base in order to provide schools and other services demanded by residents. By turning the corridor's vacant, underused, and financially underachieving properties into prime real estate, the county filled its coffers and became the envy of jurisdictions in Northern Virginia. The county supports a well-financed economic development program to promote business attraction and retention.

• *Politics of Collaboration.* All the members of the country board are elected at large, and are less susceptible than neighborhood representatives might be to specific complaints about traffic and development. Furthermore, over long periods of time in recent years

Figure 3-5
COMMUTE MODES IN ARLINGTON COUNTY, 2000

	Countywide	Metrorail Corridor	Outside Metrorail Corridor
Drive Alone	54.9%	39.9%	60.5%
Carpool	11.5	7.8	12.9
Transit	23.3	39.1	17.4
Walk	5.6	10.0	3.9
Other Mode	1.4	1.0	1.5
Work at Home	3.4	2.2	3.8

Source: U.S. Bureau of the Census; data tabulated by Arlington County Planning Division.

they all have been from one party (Democratic). The chair rotates, which helps keep any one member from becoming too outspoken. The fact that the county manager is appointed by the board avoids the tension between elected legislative and executive officials that sometimes is seen at the local level. The generally nonconfrontational state of local politics makes possible consistent adherence to a big-picture plan over the years.

• *A Manageable Size.* The county covers only 26 square miles—making it possible for planners, local officials, and citizens to comprehend its totality and to focus on issues beyond their immediate neighborhoods. It has not been difficult to communicate the Rosslyn-Ballston transit-oriented corridor vision to most residents of the county, many of whom regularly patronize its new stores, restaurants, and other land uses.

CONCLUSIONS

Planning transit districts to encourage appropriate development around transit is an art that is still maturing. The planning techniques that have worked seek to balance the need to allow the creative responses to market forces that successful place making requires with the need to spell out development criteria that can achieve walkable, mixed-use centers that will generate transit ridership.

Transit is not the sole reason for developing around transit. To be successful, development around transit must entail a land use mix (including parking) that interacts with nearby development and fits strategically within the region. Certain planning elements— including connectivity, block size, building orientation, and density—can be specified to be more supportive of transit. But as concerns densities and mix of uses, there are no absolutes. There is more to developing around transit than physical form and adjacency. It takes a recognition on the part of public sector planners and private sector developers of the development opportunities that arise from transit—as well as an ability to be sufficiently flexible to capture those opportunities.

Notes

1. Peter Calthorpe, *The Next American Metropolis: Ecology, Community, and the American Dream* (New York: Princeton Architectural Press, 1993).

2. Calthorpe Associates, *Guidebook on Smart Growth: Planning More Livable Communities with Transit-Oriented Development* (St. Paul, Minnesota: Minneapolis-St. Paul Metropolitan Council, 2000).

3. Puget Sound Regional Council, Designation Criteria for Regional Growth and Manufacturing Centers (adopted June 26, 2003).

4. Mary S. Smith, *Shared Parking,* 2nd ed. (Washington, D.C.: ULI–the Urban Land Institute, forthcoming).

5. See, for example, Transit Cooperative Research Program, *Transit Focused Development, Synthesis 20* (Washington, D.C.: National Academy Press, 1997).

6. Robert Cervero, *Transit-Supportive Development in the United States: Experiences and Prospects,* DOT-T-94-08 (Washington, D.C.: U.S. Department of Transportation, December 1993).

7. Snohomish County Transportation Authority, *A Guide to Land Use and Public Transportation,* 2 vols. (Lynwood, Washington: Snohomish County Transportation Authority, 1991–1993).

8. Robert Cervero, *Transit-Oriented Development and Joint Development in the United States: A Stakeholder Analysis* (Berkeley, California: Institute of Urban and Regional Development, December 2002), p. 33.

9. Regional Transportation District, *Creating Livable Communities: A Transit-Friendly Approach* (Denver: Regional Transportation District, 1996).

10. Tri-County Metropolitan Transportation District, *Planning and Design for Transit Handbook: Guidelines for Implementing Transit-Supportive Development* (Portland, Oregon: Tri-County Metropolitan Transportation District, January 1996).

11. Calthorpe Associates, 2000 (see note 2).

12. Metropolitan Transportation Commission, *Transportation for Livable Communities: Program Overview* (Oakland, California: Metropolitan Transportation Commission, May 2002).

13. Bruce Podobnik, "The Social and Environmental Achievements of New Urbanism: Evidence from Orenco Station" (Portland, Oregon: Department of Sociology, Lewis and Clark College, November 7, 2002; http://www.lclark.edu/~podobnik/orenco02.pdf).

14. See, for example, John King, "Starting from Scratch, Mountain View Mall Transformed to Cozy?—Or Claustrophobic?—Mix of Houses, Condos, and Parks," *San Francisco Chronicle,* April 22, 1999.

15. See Douglas R. Porter, *Profiles in Growth Management* (Washington, D.C.: ULI–the Urban Land Insitute, 1996), pp. 202–204.

16. Robert Cervero et al., *Transit-Oriented Development in America: Experiences, Challenges, and Prospects* (Washington, D.C.: National Academy Press, forthcoming).

CHAPTER FOUR

MAUREEN McAVEY

URBAN OPPORTUNITIES

URBAN DEVELOPMENT ON INFILL SITES near transit lines in cities and higher-density suburbs is the best means of generating ridership for transit and offering people a choice of travel modes. The conundrum for transit-oriented development, however, is that development on such sites is often complex and problematic, requiring developers to overcome many hurdles they do not encounter on conventional suburban projects. Public agencies and private developers are gaining experience in generating success-ful projects around transit, however, and over time development around transit will no doubt become routine. In the meantime, promoting infill development in transit-served cities and first-ring suburbs often requires both positive incentives and the mitigation of negative factors. Land assembly and zoning and approval issues need special attention to encourage and speed the urban infill process. The market oppor-tunities for urban infill development are currently excellent in many older areas where young professionals and empty nesters are seeking a more urban lifestyle and employers are seeking neighborhoods offering more employee amenities.

The last decade has seen a resurgence in urban residential and retail/entertainment development. Mixed-use development has become commonplace and sophisticated. A large number of once suburban-only developers are now undertaking urban projects. Central cities and first-ring suburbs have been particularly strong markets for housing

The renovation of State Street in 1996 increased demand for retail and office space in downtown Chicago and provides ongoing support for the city's growing residential base.

tems around rail stations. However, only a handful of places offer a full array of transit choices. Transit in those places—the city and inner-ring suburbs of New York City, Chicago, Washington, D.C., San Francisco, Boston, and Philadelphia—exerts a dramatic influence on development and commuting patterns.

In older U.S. cities in the East and along the Great Lakes, long experience with transit has influenced development patterns and forms and given rise to a tradition of transit-supportive development. In New York City, land use and transit literally grew up together and it is here among U.S. urban areas that linkages between transit and development are the strongest. In most southern and western cities, on the other hand, development patterns and forms have been largely influenced by automobile travel and road networks. In these cities, the linkages between (relatively new) transit systems and land development are still very weak and land use, zoning, and density considerations have only recently been integrated into transit planning.

Transit-supportive urban infill development is considerably more difficult to implement than greenfield development. Assembling sufficient land for a major project can be a stumbling block. Often the neighbors object to density increases and higher buildings. Restrictive zoning may limit marketable mixed-use formats. Inflexible approval processes may delay projects. However, many central cities and close-in suburbs are currently updating their plans and ordinances to encourage mixed-use development, higher-density development, and development around transit. As developers, land planners, planning agencies, and transit officials gain a more sophisticated understanding of transit district opportunities and issues, urban infill development will become more successful at maximizing transit linkages. A small number of successful efforts by communities and developers working together to combine convenient access to transit with attractive urban amenities point the way for developing higher-density transit districts in many urban areas.

Transit-oriented infill development usually requires public sector commitment in the form of policy assis-

of all types—from multifamily units in converted warehouses and new apartment buildings to new upscale townhouses. Downtown housing from New York to San Jose commands some of the highest rents and sales prices in the country. Office markets too, while they are generally overbuilt, have remained stronger in downtown cores and close-in suburbs than in outer-edge communities.

Changing demographics, changing lifestyle preferences, and public and private investment in downtown and inner-suburb redevelopment over the last 30 years have all played a role in the revitalization of urban development markets. The availability of transit is clearly a piece of this picture.

In most large cities and first-ring suburbs there exists an array of transit options—including commuter rail serving outer suburbs; rapid rail serving the primary urban area; light rail serving key corridors into downtown; and buses, including shuttle or circulator sys-

tance or financial partnership—or both. Driven by an extremely strong market, mixed-use development around the DART Mockingbird Station in Dallas north of the CBD has proved an exception (see page 105 for details). Developers seeing market opportunities for transit-supportive infill development weigh the following factors before investing in a project:

• the community's history of and openness to development around transit;

• the transit agency's and planning agency's commitment to assisting development around transit;

• the flexibility of local codes and regulations as they pertain to mixed-use development, parking requirements, and other key issues involved in developing in transit districts;

• the potential availability of creative financing assistance from the city or transit agency; and

• the degree to which district design standards, planning guidelines, and planned public investments are likely to achieve an attractive, friendly, and walkable context for development.

This chapter discusses urban housing and office markets in general and then provides a number of specific examples of successful urban infill development projects in Bethesda, Maryland, a close-in suburb of Washington, D.C.; Atlanta; Chicago; Pasadena, California, in the Los Angeles region; Dallas; Minneapolis; and Milwaukee. The examples are followed by a discussion of public policies and programs that have proved useful in promoting urban infill development around transit, focusing on the Metropolitan Council's support for light-rail station area redevelopment in Minneapolis-St. Paul and transportation policy in Boston.

URBAN HOUSING AND OFFICE MARKETS

Many factors influence the location of residential and office development. The availability of transit is a key factor in the urban renaissance that has been gathering steam across the nation over the past decade. Development offering transit access makes market sense in transit-served central cities and close-in suburbs. Equally important, such development is expanding transit use.

Housing

The twin forces of congestion and changing demographics are spurring dramatic increases in urban residential development. Many cities are developing aggressive programs to add residents. Washington, D.C., for example, is planning to add 100,000 new residents over the next decade. St. Paul is seeking to add 5,000 new housing units in the next few years. In cities around the country, residential construction over the past few years far exceeds the average experienced in the last 30 years, when it could often be measured in the hundreds of units, not thousands. The dramatic growth that downtowns as diverse as Houston, Seattle, Chicago, Denver, and Portland experienced in the 1990s is shown in figure 1-1 in Chapter One. Because of shrinking household size and other factors, the population of many urban areas is static or declining at the same time that the number of housing units is on the rise.

One key factor is congestion, which has outpaced population growth in virtually all metropolitan areas

Bryant Park, New York City. High-quality transit and an attractive pedestrian environment help make this New York neighborhood an attractive area for living and working.

Bryant Park Restoration Corporation

The Special Design Challenges of Residential Projects near Transit

Transit-oriented housing has become a hot commodity in and around the nation's capital. Its development, however, often poses specific design challenges. Dorksy Hodgson & Partners, an architecture and planning firm, lists some of the challenges that it has encountered in its work at Metrorail stations in the Washington region.

Urban/Transit Context. Transit-oriented developments cannot be cookie-cutter projects. Each is unique. Planners must give careful consideration to a number of factors that differ from one transit district to another, including the station's location in relation to the project, vehicular and pedestrian flows, topographic conditions, and neighborhood character.

Constrained Sites. Site constraints are often a condition of locations near transit. The challenge is to

Bethesda Metro Center, a WMATA (Washington Metropolitan Area Transit Authority) joint development project, comprises three office towers and related retail space above a Red Line Metrorail station.

transform constraints into assets. Dorsky Hodgson did so for the 11-story Jefferson apartment tower, which is nearing completion one block from the Clarendon Metrorail station in Arlington County, Virginia. The triangular site is defined by three roadways, making placement of the front door, garage, service entries, and street-level retail spaces—totaling 14,000 square feet—a design challenge, which was solved by incorporating place-making architectural features at the three corners. These included roof structure design elements, accent lighting, and a public plaza with a clock tower. Some visual and functional separation of the housing component from the transit amenity was considered necessary to ensure residents' privacy. Among the solutions were a residential entrance and lobby separate from the retail entrances and the provision of resident-only amenities, including an outdoor pool and health club.

Community Concerns. NIMBY reactions can crop up everywhere, even in metropolitan Washington's prime transit districts. Dorsky Hodgson has found that a proactive approach—identifying key leaders early in the process,

over the last decade. People are increasingly desirous of spending less time in cars, particularly on their commutes. Surveys show that approximately 50 percent of households are willing to trade a smaller home for a shorter commute. The developers of urban housing consider proximity to transit as a marketing strength, and they feature it prominently in their Sunday display ads.

A number of demographic trends also are contributing factors. Propelled by high divorce rates, delayed childbearing, the aging of the baby boomers, and increased longevity, the number of childless households has nearly doubled over the last 30 years, and this category of household is expected to continue to increase as a percentage of all households for the next 20 years. Single- and two-person households are often attracted to relatively small housing units and walkable, mixed-use communities—that is, to an urban lifestyle.

Among primary transit markets, Chicago's central area growth has been extraordinary. According to the 2000 Census, housing in the area in or adjoining the Loop increased by almost 50,000 units between 1980 and 2000. The 12,549 housing units added between 1990

arranging community meetings, and reassuring neighbors that the proposed development will visually enhance the neighborhood—works best. The highly articulated, stepped design of the firm's 18-story Twin Oak residential tower near the Rosslyn, Virginia, station minimized the project's visual impact on an adjacent high-rise condominium and helped win the community's approval for the project, as did the project's inclusion of open space (made possible by providing underground parking for 350 cars), generous landscaping, an open plaza, and ground-floor retail serving the entire neighborhood. A local TOD developer from the area says: "For a residential, transit-oriented project to succeed, it must be attractive, look substantial, and be appropriately scaled, with plenty of curb appeal—while keeping everything within budget."

Nonresidential Uses. Attempts to mix uses to encourage 24/7 activity and to incorporate street-oriented retail in order to attract pedestrian activity and tap into foot traffic to and from Metrorail stations often encounter significant design challenges. Retail uses generally require a 15- to 18-foot floor-to-floor height, compared with eight to ten feet for residential uses, and providing a higher ceiling on the ground floor increases project costs. The placement of exhaust shafts for restaurant kitchens often must be decided before leases are signed. Not knowing the exact size and location of restaurant space requires designers to allow exhaust shafts to be put in several potential locations, which can reduce net leasable space. Mixed-use designs can be further complicated by the need to accommodate car- and bus-access lanes, transit tracks, and pedestrian walkways while addressing each site's geographic challenges and setback requirements.

Parking. Designing a garage to accommodate the parking needs of shoppers, office workers, and residents can eclipse all other design challenges in complexity. Many workers and shoppers arrive by Metrorail, but daytime parking spaces with easy pedestrian and elevator access to the development are needed for those who drive. Because parking security is a huge concern for residents, separate garage entrances for residents and shoppers might be required. The site configuration for the Residences at Rosedale Park—comprising a six-story building and an eight-story building on opposite sides of the street near the Bethesda, Maryland, station—allowed only one entry ramp for a garage and service area for both buildings. The solution was a three-level, 300-car garage that spans the underground space between the two buildings.

Source: Adapted from Sandy Silverman, "Designing the Urban Future," *Multifamily Trends* (Urban Land Institute), spring 2003.

---

and 2000 brought more than 20,000 additional residents into the Loop area, representing all age groups, but particularly the 25–35 and the 49–56 age cohorts.

Compared with many other downtowns, the Loop's retention of its employment base has been similarly remarkable. A downtown well served by transit, it seems, can capture a correspondingly large share of the metropolitan office employment market. For many residents of Chicago's Loop area, "a place in which to live, work, shop, and play" is not just a marketing slogan; it is a reality.

Some secondary transit markets, that is, cities with relatively high transit use, experienced even more dramatic residential gains in their central areas between 1990 and 2000. These include Seattle, Denver, Portland (Oregon), and Atlanta. Central area population growth has also occurred in some new transit markets. For example, Houston—a city not noted for either its urbanity or transit use—registered a spectacular two-thirds gain in its downtown population from 1990 to 2000. This growing downtown population represents a strong reinforcement for the region's light-rail system, which opened its first segment in 2004.

Figure 4-1

TRANSIT'S COMMUTE SHARE IN LARGE DOWNTOWN OFFICE MARKETS, 2000

	Office Inventory		Average Gross Rent (per square foot)	Transit's Share of Work Trips to the CBD	Monthly Parking Cost in the CBD
	Square Feet (thousands)	Share of Total Metro Inventory			
Midtown New York	252,009	44.4%	$61.57	75%	$450
Chicago	108,553	56.8	37.66	62	238
Washington	81,344	35.9	43.85	37[1]	230
Boston	56,789	41.0	53.50	55	408
San Francisco	53,245	33.6	61.13	49	375
Philadelphia	37,136	39.8	27.54	70	263
Houston	33,332	25.8	25.50	32	120
Los Angeles	32,176	19.2	27.85	20[2]	149
Seattle	31,366	45.8	37.54	35	210
Dallas	30,662	22.6	23.30	36	100
Atlanta	26,018	23.5	26.08	14[3]	100

1. Calculated by Surface Transportation Policy Project.
2. Calculated by Charles Purvis, Metropolitan Transportation Commission.
3. Calculated by Michael Meyer, Georgia Tech University.

Sources: Torto Wheaton Research (inventory); National Real Estate Index (rents); U.S. Bureau of the Census data compiled by local metropolitan planning organizations, except where indicated (transit share); and "Downtown Parking Costs Show Surprising Stability," *PR Newswire,* June 2002 (parking costs).

Office

Despite the explosive development of suburban office space in the last three decades, in most U.S. metropolitan areas the highest concentration of jobs continues to be located in traditional downtowns. In all the primary transit markets—New York, Chicago, Washington, Boston, San Francisco, and Philadelphia—one-third to more than one-half of the metropolitan office inventory is located downtown (see figure 4-1). Seattle also has a highly centralized office market, with downtown's share at 46 percent. Strong downtowns make good use of hub-and-spoke regional transit systems, which allow centrally located employers to draw employees from the entire metropolitan area.

Among large downtown office markets in the United States, those in the six primary transit markets (and Seattle) rank highest in terms of share of the metropolitan office market captured (see figure 4-1), indicating that downtowns in regions with strong transit systems tend to be strong office markets. Downtowns in cities in which transit captures a significant share of work trips can develop at high densities and capture a high share of the regional office market, which, in turn, reinforces the metropolitan centralization that is so good for hub-and-spoke transit systems.

For employers, the transportation benefits of a downtown location—accessibility to the regional labor force, including transit-dependent lower-wage workers;

less need to provide parking; and, often, subsidies available for assisting employees who use transit—can offset the generally higher property costs.

Transit-served downtown office markets offer advantages to developers and investors as well. Compared with suburban office submarkets, downtown space has generally achieved higher rents and higher occupancy rates throughout the recent recession (see figure 4-2). While many factors influence office vacancy rates, urban amenities, close-in housing, and transit all appear to help downtown office submarkets hold their own in difficult times.

Part of the story behind the superior performance of downtown office space and its durability in recession—features that appeal to developers, lenders, and investors—relates to the comparative difficulties of building in urban centers versus suburbs. To the degree that the barriers to entry in urban infill are high, new buildings that make it through the process (along with older ones) become more valuable. Downtown locations offer enduring attractions and appealing new amenities for major tenants, not the least of which is proximity to regional transit services.

Office for Metropolitan Architecture/Philippe Ruault

An "L" station at the McCormick Tribune Campus Center (designed by Rem Koolhaus) at the Illinois Institute of Technology enhances the revitalization potential of the campus neighborhood.

SUCCESSFUL TRANSIT-RELATED URBAN INFILL: EXAMPLES

A growing number of urban projects in a range of transit settings demonstrate the major ingredients—a good location, strong transit connections, visionary developers, and enlightened public agencies—of successfully developing around transit. Most of the urban infill examples of developing around transit have occurred in older cities around heavy-rail stations. Examples from the San Francisco (BART) and Washington (Metrorail) regions are often cited as success stories. Whether newer light-rail systems will exert a similar degree of influence on urban infill development remains to be seen.

The urban infill examples discussed in this section are associated with a range of transit facilities, from heavy rail to light rail to bus and trolley routes. The heavy-rail examples include Bethesda Row, a mixed-use development supporting and supported by Metro-rail transit in the Washington region; Lindbergh City Center, a 10 million-square-foot joint transit agency/private development at a MARTA station in midtown Atlanta; and the public/private development of a transit-rich site in downtown Chicago. The light-rail examples include transit-oriented development around Gold Line stations in Pasadena, California; and Mockingbird Station, a mixed-use activity center developed at a DART station in Dallas four miles north of the CBD. The final two examples discuss development in downtown Minneapolis associated with Nicollet Mall and planned urban village development at the Lake Street station of the recently opened Hiawatha Avenue light-rail line; and a housing development in the city of Milwaukee just outside the CBD.

Figure 4-2
DOWNTOWN AND SUBURBAN OFFICE VACANCY RATES, FOURTH QUARTER 2003

	Downtown Vacancy Rate	Suburban Vacancy Rate
Boston	12.1%	24.1%
Charlotte	10.2	18.7
Chicago	13.5	19.2
Philadelphia	12.3	19.5
Portland	10.0	20.0
San Francisco	18.5	25.1
Washington	7.8	10.5
U.S. Average	14.5	18.0

Source: CB Richard Ellis.

Work Trips around the World: Putting Transit First

More than 70 percent of commuters to Hong Kong arrive by transit.

The Louvre train station in Paris is heavily used by tourists and city residents alike.

In London, the majority of residents make use of public transportation.

Transit's commute share in many of the world's largest cities is considerably more significant than in any U.S. city with the exception of New York. In Toronto and in Montreal, for example, transit's commute share among central city residents is 38 percent and among central city residents in Ottawa it is 21 percent. In many European cities, the numbers are equally high. For example, transit's commute share in Paris is 36 percent. And cities in Asia achieve an even higher rate of transit use for commuting—74 percent in Hong Kong and 49 percent in Tokyo, for example. Furthermore, in many of these cities, bicycling and walking are important commute modes—making up, for example, 22 percent of work trips in Tokyo, 15 percent in Paris, and 17 percent in Hong Kong.

The community of Markham just north of Toronto provides an example of putting transit first. First settled in the late 18th century, Markham's growth in the last 30 years has been explosive and a master plan has been adopted to accommodate more than 1 million residents at full build-out. This plan calls for neighborhoods with a mix of apartments and single-family homes providing housing for households in a range of income levels. Transit services into Toronto and within Markham are being planned as an integral part of the community, and the planning and development of land uses and transit are being closely coordinated. In an effort to shorten the distances that residents have to travel for everyday errands, the master plan includes neighborhood retail and community services. An important lesson of Markham is that with careful master planning high-density land uses can work in a close-in suburban context. Another lesson is that integrated land planning and transit planning can promote development that creates livable places—new urbanist in design and transit-oriented in lifestyle.

In England, new light-rail systems using creative public/private financing have been built in Sheffield, Manchester, and Birmingham. They are providing reliable, high-quality service; and infill development is occurring around the stations. For example, the Midland Metro Line 1, a 12.6-mile route from Birmingham to Wolverhampton, carries more than 5.5 million passengers per year and two extensions to the line are being planned.

In London, where transit use is part of daily life, the construction of the London Tram, a £200 million (US$360 million), 28-kilometer (17-mile) light-rail system connecting downtown London with the borough of Croyden to the south, is seen as a new solution to traffic congestion. Part of this system—a £236 million ($425 million) line between Camden Town and King's Cross in north London to Peckham and Brixton south of the Thames—is expected to generate almost £5.6 billion ($10 billion) in redevelopment and new investment along its route. According to a study by DTZ Pieda Consulting, 6,700 units of affordable housing, 5,000 units of private housing, and 11.8 million square feet of office space will be developed over time on the 360 acres of land that will be released by the government for development as the route is completed. Strong population growth in London and the private sector development associated with this transit project combined with sustained public sector investment in infrastructure, transit linkages, and pedestrian amenities are expected to extend London's business district south of the river and bring sorely needed housing and employment to depressed areas.

Work Trips around the World *continued*

COMMUTE MODE IN SELECTED CITIES, EARLY 1990S

	Population (millions)	Commute Mode		
		Public Transit	Private Vehicle	Other[1]
Bogota	6.1	74.8%	8.8%	16.4%
Hong Kong	5.8	74.0	9.1	16.9
Curitiba	2.2	71.8	13.6	14.6
Nairobi	1.8	67.5	16.0	16.5
Cairo	9.7	58.2	10.5	31.3
Singapore	3.3	56.0	21.8	22.2
Santiago	4.9	54.3	15.8	29.9
Manila	9.3	54.2	28.0	17.8
Brasilia	1.8	53.0	45.0	2.0
Abidjan	2.8	49.1	15.8	35.1
Tokyo	27.0	48.9	29.4	21.7
London	7.1	47.0	39.0	14.0
Zurich	0.9	39.8	36.0	24.2
Jakarta	8.6	36.3	41.4	22.3
Paris	9.5	36.2	48.9	14.9
Toronto	4.3	30.1	64.6	5.3
Bangkok	6.5	30.0	60.0	10.0
Kuala Lumpur	1.2	25.5	57.6	16.9
Sydney	3.6	25.2	69.3	5.5
Amsterdam	1.1	25.0	40.0	35.0
Copenhagen	1.3	25.0	43.0	32.0
Vancouver	1.8	12.4	81.9	5.7

1. Includes commutes by foot, bicycle, and other modes.

Source: World Resources Institute.

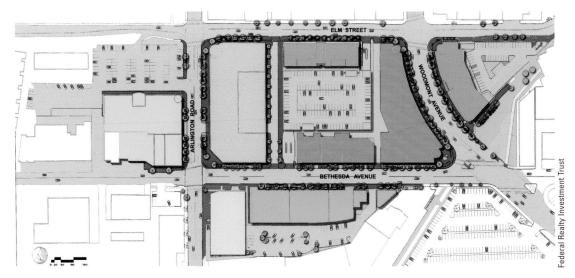

The development of Bethesda Row near the Bethesda station on the Washington-area Metrorail's Red Line was phased to allow maximum absorption and to assure the integration of the project into the community. Parking is publicly owned and operated.

Downtown Bethesda, Maryland

A comprehensive plan adopted in 1992 by Montgomery County, Maryland, sought to capitalize on the transit-oriented redevelopment of downtown Bethesda—an unincorporated first-ring suburb on the Washington Metrorail's Red Line. The county's general adherence to this plan over the subsequent decade provided developers with an understanding of the overall strategic vision for downtown Bethesda and a degree of comfort relative to public policy, thereby encouraging them to plan and build appropriate projects. As a result of this plan, Bethesda has become the downtown of southern Montgomery County.

Recognizing Bethesda as both a regional office center and a residential community, the plan called for office and a mix of residential development, a library and other public facilities, parks, strategically located public parking, and first-floor retail along major streets. The Bethesda Metrorail station is located on Wisconsin Avenue, below which runs the rail line. Development density (and height) would be greatest along Wisconsin Avenue, and would stairstep down to single-family neighborhoods three and four blocks off Wisconsin Avenue.

Today Bethesda has an employment base and residential base of a size that makes the downtown a busy place on weekdays and weekends alike. Downtown jobs number more than 40,000 and more than 125,000 people live within three miles of the Bethesda Metrorail station. Jobholders and local residents support thriving retail, restaurant, and personal services businesses. This combination of a strong residential base and a large workforce is essential for the success of a sizable retail and restaurant component in downtown.

In addition to the Metrorail station on Wisconsin Avenue, conveniently located public parking decks, good regional bus service to the transit district, and a local circulator bus route serve downtown Bethesda. A popular bike path—the Capital Crescent Trail—that goes throughout Bethesda is used for commuting as well as recreational purposes.

A coordinated parking strategy has been a key element in the implementation of the downtown Bethesda plan. The county established a parking taxing district to pay for public parking decks in the downtown area. The parking decks are generally located midblock, well signed, and lined by buildings on several sides. On-street parking is available on most streets at most times of the day. Because of the availability of sufficient parking as well as transit access, the county lowered its parking requirements for new projects, thus reducing development costs.

Sprinkling parking throughout Bethesda's downtown has enhanced street life. Many visitors arriving by car are willing to walk two or three blocks from where they park. This "park once" program has encouraged walking within the downtown district, reduced the amount of land allocated to parking, brought foot traffic to retailers, and reduced overall development costs for individual projects. A more lively street life has, in turn, made downtown Bethesda a place that people perceive to be fun and safe.

The quality of the comprehensive plan is one key element in the success of retail and housing development in the downtown Bethesda transit district. Another is the strength of the local market. The surrounding area has strong demographics. Approximately 400,000 people live within a five-mile radius, and their average income is high. Within a three-mile radius, average household income exceeds $125,000 (2002 data).

Downtown Bethesda's mostly white-collar employment base also adds market support.

Bethesda Row, a ten-building, mixed-use complex being developed in phases by Federal Realty Investment Trust, has been widely applauded as a successful transit-related, urban infill project. Located two blocks from the Bethesda Metrorail station and a block west of Wisconsin Avenue, Bethesda Row contains more than 250,000 square feet of retail space including a 30,500-square-foot art-film cinema, 13 restaurants totaling nearly 74,000 square feet, and nearly 181,000 square feet of office space; 210,000 square feet of apartment housing is planned (see figure 4-3).

In 1994, Federal Realty purchased the land—already assembled—and began the lengthy approval process. Phase 1—174,000 square feet of retail/restaurant and office space—opened in June 1997 and construction of the last component—housing—still awaits final public approval.

Except for providing public parking in the form of a nearly 1,000-space parking deck in the middle of the project, the county gave little direct subsidy to the developer. However, through its contributions to streetscape improvements and its flexibility and willingness to work with the developer in amending codes and regulations, the county made this project truly a public/private partnership.

For example, regulations were changed to allow sidewalk cafés that are physically detached from their main restaurant to serve liquor. The determination of parking ratios took into consideration the parking capacity provided by the county-managed parking

Figure 4-3

BETHESDA ROW DEVELOPMENT PHASES[1]

(Square feet)

	Office Uses	Retail Uses	Restaurant Uses	Residential Uses	Total
Phase 1	74,800	78,000	21,000	–	173,800
Phase 2	–	22,100	14,000	–	36,100
Phase 3	28,400	7,800	6,800	–	43,000
Phase 4	77,500	40,500[2]	12,000	–	130,000
Phase 5	–	61,000	–	–	61,000
Phase 6	–	41,000	20,000	210,000	271,000
Total Project					
Square Feet	180,700	250,400	73,800	210,000	714,900
Share	25%	35%	10%	29%	100%

1. As of early 2004, Phases 1 through 5 are completed and Phase 6 is awaiting final approvals.

2. Includes a 30,500-square-foot cinema.

Source: Federal Realty Investment Trust.

The Bethesda Row development includes offices, an art-film cinema, restaurants with outdoor dining, wide sidewalks, and abundant trees—all of which add to the pedestrian-orientation of downtown Bethesda.

Planning for Lindbergh Street near the MARTA Lindbergh Station in Buckhead emphasizes urban design and pedestrian amenities, rather than parking.

deck and on-street parking. The developer and the public sector coordinated on the widening of sidewalks, installation of street trees and furniture, provision of short-term on-street parking spaces enhanced by curbside landscaping, installation of lighting designed to enhance both the sidewalks and the street, and burying of utilities.

Among the planning and market elements that make Bethesda Row a model of urban infill development in a transit district:

• Parking is shared, and generally publicly built and managed and the central location of the public parking decks and on-street parking meters encourage park-and-walk visits to Bethesda Row and nearby destinations. As has been noted, well-planned parking helps make walking within central areas a popular way of getting from place to place.

• Street-level retail (including sidewalk cafés and summer kiosks) and close attention to detail and functionality at the pedestrian level (including wider sidewalks, benches, bike racks, and plantings) create a pedestrian orientation within the development's five blocks.

• The mix of uses serves existing markets—predominantly nearby residents, office employees, and the businesses housed in downtown Bethesda. The project's restaurants, office support services, and shops ranging from casual to elegant filled a retail void for the community within a three- to five-mile radius.

• Attention is paid to the establishment of attractive walking routes between Bethesda Row and nearby retail, office, and residential land uses. Walkability

has helped transform downtown Bethesda into a true urban center.

• Bicycle access is encouraged. As required under the county's downtown plan, the developer incorporated an extension of the Capital Crescent Trail into the project. The developer reinforces this travel option by providing bike racks and seeking retailers with offerings that serve bike riders. A plaza and fountain at the corner of Woodmont and Bethesda Avenues has become an informal gathering spot for bike riders (and others).

Lindbergh Station, Atlanta

Whereas Montgomery County, Maryland, relies on planning tools and incentives to encourage appropriate development in Bethesda's transit district, the Metropolitan Atlanta Rapid Transit Authority (MARTA) has acted more like an entrepreneur in promoting development around rail stations. For example, in 1998 MARTA put out a request for proposals (RFP) for a 47-acre site around the Lindbergh Station in Buckhead, the rail system's second busiest station and a major bus transfer point accommodating more than 600 buses daily. The site is bisected by the rail line and bordered by a single-family neighborhood, some multifamily developments, and a mix of other land uses.

MARTA's RFP called for intense residential and office mixed-use development. The agency chose a proposal from Carter Associates, an Atlanta-based, full-service commercial real estate firm. To maximize density on this transit-rich site, the Lindbergh City Center plan envisages more than 4.8 million square feet at full

Joint Development of the Atlantic Terminal, Brooklyn

The public/private redevelopment of the Atlantic Terminal site in downtown Brooklyn, a below-grade depot providing access to nine New York City subway lines and the Long Island Rail Road (LIRR), exemplifies the use of joint transit-station development to improve transit service and create profit-making development opportunities. New York City, the Metropolitan Transit Authority (MTA), and the LIRR are the public sector partners and Forest City Ratner Companies (FCRC) is the private sector partner.

The terminal is located in a commercial corridor that had been suffering from a lack of investment. FCRC decided in 2000 that the growing demand for retail and office space in the New York region and the fact that 40 million riders traversed the terminal annually warranted the site's redevelopment.

The initial plan envisaged a four-story, almost 400,000-square-foot retail complex and the potential addition

Retail uses line Atlantic Terminal's street-level facade, which eventually will also incorporate an entrance pavilion to the subway and LIRR station.

Forest City Ratner Companies

of an office building. While planning was proceeding, the Bank of New York (BNY) was seeking to disperse its employees and capital investments from Lower Manhattan—where they had been concentrated when the September 11, 2001, attacks took place—to locations throughout the city. It agreed to take office space at Atlantic Terminal. Thus, a ten-story office building was included in FCRC's final plan.

The project opened in July 2004. BNY will occupy 80 percent of the office space (to house almost 20 percent of its staff). Ninety percent of the retail space had been preleased by national tenants, including Target, which is opening its first store in the United States without parking facilities. With direct oversight over the project's design, the MTA and LIRR were able to coordinate shared parking with the adjacent shopping center, which FCRC had also developed. Public sector involvement in the design of the project also helped ensure that it would meet the needs, including visual enhancement, of the neighborhood.

The valuation of the site took into account the location's amenities—access to transit and high residential and employment densities—and the terminal redevelopment costs borne by the developer. The MTA reduced the lease payment to reflect the risk that the developer was taking and the MTA's lower costs for the redevelopment of the terminal because of private investment. (Without this investment, the cost of redeveloping the deteriorated terminal would have been prohibitive.) For its part, FCRC agreed to a revenue-sharing structure wherein any profits exceeding a certain threshold will be allocated to the MTA and the city.

It is likely that the benefits from the project will be significant for all the partners. While the MTA is not certain that the Atlantic Terminal development will lead to an increase in ridership, the terminal's repair will provide a better travel experience for current riders and the construction of a three-story entrance pavilion in the facade of the office tower will give the station increased visibility from the street. The city's benefits include the redevelopment of the site and its contribution to the revitalization of Brooklyn's downtown. The project's implementation has bolstered confidence in the redevelopment potential of Brooklyn and has provided support for the downtown Brooklyn plan, which aims to precipitate a significant increase in retail space, housing, and public open space. FCRC will reap benefits from its ownership of almost 800,000 square feet of leasable space in a dense, transit-accessible, and revitalized commercial corridor.

buildout, incorporating retail, office, hotel, and a mix of residential uses. The current program comprises 2.4 million square feet of office space, 225,000 square feet of retail space, more than 700 residential units, a 190-room hotel, and related parking. MARTA estimates that the development will generate 8,000 new daily transit trips.

The focus of the project is a new pedestrian-oriented main street that bridges the MARTA platform. Its 1,200 linear feet of street frontage will house a mix of large and small tenants, including a grocery store. Above the retail will be two stories of office and residential space and behind it, with a 45-foot setback, will be office towers. Twin 17-story residential buildings and a hotel and multiplex cinema will terminate the main street.

Carter is developing the office and retail components and Harold Dawson Company is developing the residential elements. Originally, Carter partnered with three other developers to deliver the project. Although the team approach makes sense from the perspective of risk management and skills, it presented some master planning and deal-making challenges and required extensive negotiations and legal agreements. This project has involved the creation of multilayered public/private partnerships involving the city, MARTA, Carter, and Bell South, the office development's lead tenant.

The economic engine of the Lindbergh City Center development is the office component. As the lead tenant, Bell South has committed to occupying more than 1 million square feet in twin 14-story towers, and has an option on an additional 1.2 million square feet. The first office building was delivered in August 2002, about four years from the date of the initial RFP. The completion of the first phase of Lindbergh City Center has signaled that such a complicated project can succeed. Weakened market conditions have delayed the start of a second-phase, nine-story multitenant building. The long-term prospects for the development, however, remain strong.

The original zoning allowed high-density commercial, mixed residential, and—in the area adjoining the CSX rail line—industrial uses. Rezoning of the industrial

Advantages of a Transit District Location for Bell South

Bell South is an active supporter of the Metropolitan Atlanta Rapid Transit Authority's Partnership Program through which MARTA offers discounted TransCard passes to employers that distribute them to employees who commute on MARTA. The company is locating major offices at three MARTA stations so that its employees can travel between offices as well as commute to work on transit.

Bell South has concluded that a location adjacent to transit is a measurable employee benefit that gives it a significant recruiting edge. This is because congestion in Atlanta is growing apace. The share of all freeway lanes considered to be congested, for example, rose from 30 percent in 1991 to almost 70 percent in 1999.

Having reached this conclusion, Bell South initially programmed a total of 6 million square feet in three MARTA locations. However, the fallout in the telecom industry has caused the company to scale back its new space requirements for the foreseeable future.

area to residential created a residential buffer for adjacent single-family neighborhoods that was critical to the success of the project.

Bell South's aggressive move-in schedule forced Carter to move expeditiously in resolving planning, zoning, and entitlement issues. The developer's willingness to participate in countless meetings in living rooms, libraries, city hall, and MARTA offices helped it to resolve neighborhood disputes, lawsuits, and site logistics and to move the project along reasonably well. Carter thus exemplifies a developer prerequisite for meeting budget and schedule in projects like Lindbergh City Center—a combination of flexibility with hard-headed practicality.

The need to accommodate parking and a bus transfer interface added complexity to the Lindbergh City Center project. The determination of the size and location of parking decks was based partly on the following estimates of how rail passengers would access the station: The majority of those who worked or lived within 300 feet of the station would walk; 40 percent of those within 2,000 feet would walk; and most of those more than 3,000 feet away would take a shuttle or bus. Because of its transit connections, Lindbergh City Center was permitted to reduce the normally required number of parking spaces by almost 30 percent.

Bus operations on the site present transit district design challenges and market opportunities. Potential retail tenants may find the opportunity to tap into the bus-to-rail transferee market attractive, but their ability to do so will require a change in MARTA's standard transfer policy.

Lindbergh City Center exemplifies many of the special challenges of developing around transit in urban areas. Market conditions varied by project component—office, housing, and retail—and each use had its own financing requirements and developer. The complexity of the project required timely decisions by all parties. Even the simple maintenance of effective communication and coordination within the development team has been a major undertaking. The city government and the transit agency were involved as "codevelopers" of the project in the sense that they have financial interests in its success and its success depends in part on their zoning and permitting decisions and infrastructure investments. Community involvement

as well has been sought throughout the development process, and the need to resolve neighborhood opposition and other political considerations have affected the development timetable.

Lindbergh City Center also represents the significant benefits of developing intensive land uses around transit in urban areas. In MARTA's view, the primary benefits are increased transit ridership and reduced traffic congestion. In the city of Atlanta's view, the major benefits include the renewal of the neighborhood; the retention of major employers, such as Bell South, within the city; an increase in the tax base; the development of underutilized land; and bragging rights to a nationally recognized mixed-use development.

Block 37, Chicago

Bordered by State, Dearborn, Washington and Monroe Streets, Block 37 in downtown Chicago is transit rich by anyone's definition. It is served by 20 bus lines and is located within three blocks of 11 "L" stations, including the Blue Line to O'Hare Airport. Pedestrian counts and vehicular counts on all four block faces

---

Public Sector Value Capture in Transit

Infill transit-related developments like Lindbergh City Center generally require some public subsidy, and this is an issue that frequently is raised in public meetings. The Metropolitan Atlanta Rapid Transit Authority (MARTA) has been creative in trying to capture some of the financial value created by its transit investments and transit-related development. For example, the agency generally leases rather than sells its land, and thus receives annual lease payments.

The still developing Lindbergh City Center project has not yet produced the revenues to MARTA that are projected. Other MARTA projects, however, give some indication of its financial potential. Resurgens Plaza, for example, a 400,000-square-foot mixed-use office/retail building adjoining the Lenox Station on land leased from MARTA, generated approximately $177,000 in land lease payments to the agency in 2001. (In addition, development around the Lenox Station generates an estimated 5,775 transit passengers, representing farebox revenue.)

Similarly, the Washington Metropolitan Area Transit Authority (WMATA) has entered into a number of joint development projects in which it assembled land, leased land to developers, and provided assistance for transit-related developments. Significant returns have been realized. As of 2003, WMATA had participated in 56 joint development projects with a market value of $4 billion. These projects were providing the transit agency with annual revenues of $4 million and an aggregate total of $150 million over the terms of the agreements—as well as generating an estimated 50,000 new transit riders and more than 25,000 new jobs.

are among the highest in the city. Block 37 is a prime linkage block in downtown, abutting the government center (home to city, county, and state offices); financial office towers to the south; the burgeoning theater district to the northwest; and the historic State Street retail district and Marshall Field's original flagship store to the east.

Despite its important location, Block 37 has been vacant since 1990, when the city finished demolishing the existing structures in order to clear the way for a planned 2 million- to 3 million-square-foot mixed-use office/retail redevelopment. The city had issued a request for proposals for the site in 1983, chosen a developer, and begun planning with high hopes. It purchased the land in 1986.

However, the formulation of a development plan that would meet both the city's and the developer's requirements proved impossible. The city hoped to have the entire site built in one phase, but the weak office market precluded this approach. Despite extensive negotiations and the offer of several alternative plans, the site languished. The long vacancy of Block 37 is

strong evidence that while transit can be a magnet for development, successful transit-oriented development requires favorable market conditions, a strong development team, and rational public policies.

In 2002, the city of Chicago embarked on a new process to encourage the development of Block 37. Its recognition that the site might be developed in phases with a multiplicity of uses has gotten the project back on track. The city has selected the Mills Corporation as principal developer, and project planning, design, and financing are currently underway. The current plan calls for the construction of transit and pedestrian connections along with a retail podium as the initial phase, and for the construction of three towers—containing office and hotel uses—above the podium in later phases.

The master plan requires the developer to fully integrate transit access into the development. Pedestrian amenities, midblock and diagonal pedestrian connections, and multilevel pedestrian access are all part of the fundamental infrastructure planning for the site. The city is limiting parking to a minimum for each designated land use.

The city's new direction for Block 37 allows for more flexible and realistic development. Total square footage will likely be reduced from earlier plans. The project will be developed in phases. Major mixed-use developments often cannot be developed without phasing. At any point in time, each of the major land uses can be at a different level of market demand and absorption. For example, there may be a glut of hotels, making them impossible to finance, at a time when the market for apartment development is strong—and, if this is the case, a proposed mixed hotel/apartment tower will be delayed or will require creative financing to keep both components on the desired schedule and financially viable.

The Block 37 experience demonstrates an important lesson: In urban infill development, even the most attractive transit access cannot make up for soft market conditions or unrealistic development expectations.

Block 37 in Chicago. Vacant for more than ten years, this site serves as a reminder that excellent transit access is not enough to secure development financing, which requires strong market demand as well as accessibility.

OWP/P Architects

The development of Holly Street Village, a mixed-use project in Pasadena, California, was a response to the city's general plan calling for transit-oriented development located next to light-rail stations.

Art Cueto

Transit-Oriented Development in Pasadena

Del Mar Station in downtown Pasadena, California, is a mixed-use residential project at a station by the same name on the newly completed 13.7-mile Los Angeles to Pasadena light-rail line—the Gold Line. Located on the historic Atchison-Topeka and Santa Fe railroad line, Pasadena has had a history of building around rail. During the decade when the Gold Line was being approved, financed, and constructed, the city planned for station area development. Its planning has been well met by proposals from creative and sophisticated developers who understand the market potential of locations near light rail.

The city of Pasadena, the Los Angeles County Metropolitan Transportation Authority (MTA), and the Los Angeles-Pasadena Metro Blue Line Construction Authority (the special authority created to build the light-rail line) cooperated in the planning and development of station amenities and infrastructure.

The city's plan for the Del Mar Station area promotes the development of an urban village through a mix of uses, a mix of housing types, and a pedestrian-oriented environment. A number of transit-related developments—predominantly housing and park-and-ride facilities—have occurred or are planned within

the urban village. Planners and transit advocates expect that these will increase ridership and lead to further mixed-use development in downtown Pasadena. The success of transit-oriented development in downtown Pasadena reflects a number of factors—including early planning, effective local policy initiatives, the availability of development subsidies, land assembly opportunities, favorable market conditions, and the presence of sophisticated developers.

A number of developers constructed transit-oriented projects in advance of the opening of the Gold Line. Del Mar Station, which was developed by Los Angeles–based Urban Partners on a 4.4-acre site is one such project. It comprises 374 apartment units in four separate buildings, 11,000 square feet of retail shops and restaurants—most located in the fully restored Santa Fe Depot—and a 1,210-car underground parking facility, with 600 spaces designated for transit users. It opened for occupancy in spring 2004, with its four levels of subterranean parking having been opened earlier. With the Gold Line operating 200 daily trips (carrying 14,000 passengers) over a 22-hour period from 4:00 a.m. to 2:00 a.m., the residents of Del Mar Station enjoy convenient access (taking approximately 15 minutes) to downtown Los Angeles.

Hollywood and Highland: Underperforming Entertainment Complex

Hollywood loves a blockbuster and so does transit. But the challenges of developing around urban transit can make investors nervous. This was the case for Hollywood and Highland, a 1.3 million-square-foot entertainment center anchored by the 3,500-seat Kodak Theater, the new home of the Academy Awards ceremony. The project, which opened in November 2001, contains 375,000 square feet of retail space, a 640-room Renaissance hotel, a six-plex movie theater, a 40,000-square-foot event space, a 7,000-square-foot broadcast studio, and a 3,000-space parking garage (which is publicly financed and owned). It is oriented around a large public courtyard with a direct connection to the Hollywood/Highland Station on the Los Angeles Red Line MTA subway.

Good development around transit requires good transit as well as successful development. Hollywood and Highland failed to deliver on the successful development side. Underperforming real estate leads to underperforming transit. The Hollywood/Highland Station would clearly be attracting more than the 4,600 daily riders it currently serves had development occurred as planned.

Hollywood and Highland suffered from the temporary disappearance of the tourist market after the 9/11 terrorist attacks.

Hollywood and Highland was designed to appeal to the tourist market in Los Angeles, with expectations of capturing the estimated 8 million to 10 million visitors a year to the famous Chinese Theater adjoining the complex as well as a share of the regional entertainment market. It was jointly developed by TrizecHahn on land owned by the Los Angeles County Metropolitan Transit Authority (MTA) and additional property obtained by the city's Community Redevelopment Agency.

The temporary disappearance of the tourist market after the 9/11 terrorist attacks on the United States, which occurred only a few weeks before the project opened, was crippling to the property. TrizecHahn, which had already made a decision to sell all its retail properties, adopted a strategy of leasing the property as quickly as possible to an undifferentiated collection of retailers. This resulted in a loss of much of the project's unique character. The new project now had to compete with numerous malls in the Los Angeles marketplace.

Although MTA picked up more than $100 million of the costs for its facilities on the site, cost overruns drove the project development costs to $650 million, of which TrizecHahn paid $540 million. The project has now been sold—for $201 million—to the CIM Group, which specializes in commercial leasing and mixed-use development in urban areas, and Calpers, the state employee retirement fund, which includes urban investment among its missions. They will be repositioning the project by implementing an entertainment-related tenant mix that reflects the unique character and location of the complex.

The prospects for the Hollywood and Highland entertainment complex have improved in the past year.

Market changes posed one great challenge to the development of Hollywood and Highland. TrizecHahn's conversion to a real estate investment trust (REIT) and its subsequent disposition of its shopping center properties posed another challenge. REITs generally seek to be long-term owners of plain-vanilla real estate investments with stable cash flows, not developers of risky, high-profile projects. These challenges resulted in an underperforming property in a superior transit location. The project's difficulties were unrelated to the transit.

Meanwhile, the prospects for the Hollywood and Highland entertainment complex are looking better. The year 2003 closed with a 10 percent hike in retail sales over 2002 and seven straight months of monthly sales increases. In the long run, it may prove to be a financial success. It has certainly helped turn around a once seedy area of Hollywood and added visibility and ridership to the MTA's subway line. Meanwhile, TrizecHahn reports that its disposition of Hollywood and Highland marked the completion of its transformation to a REIT specializing in office properties.

Designed by Nadel Architects (Los Angeles) and Moule & Polyzoides (Pasadena), Del Mar Station offers more urban and pedestrian amenities than most developments in the Los Angeles/Pasadena area. The light-rail transitway bisects the site and forms the center street of the development. Walkability is a central element of the design. Public courtyards link to private areas and apartment entrances. A large public plaza facing the retail shops is intended to draw in the commuter market as well as project residents. The project's architecture reflects the richness of Pasadena's Spanish colonial, art deco, Craftsman, and industrial modern architectural heritage. The four- to seven-story buildings contain several types of apartment units, including stacked flats, courtyard units, and walk-up lofts.

Mission Meridian Village is another transit-oriented development along the Gold Line. Located next to the Mission Street Station in South Pasadena, this 212,000-square-foot housing/retail development, which will be completed in early 2005, includes a mix of housing—14 artist lofts, 50 Mission style townhouses, and three single-family houses—retail space, a small grocery store, and 324 underground parking stalls, half of which are set aside for Gold Line commuters. Bicycle storage areas and a bike repair shop are included in the plans.

The $22 million project is publicly supported through $5 million in public grants—a $2.5 million grant from the MTA under its program to support developments that relieve traffic; $1.5 million from the state of California to pay for commuter parking; and $500,000 each from the city of South Pasadena and the state for burying utilities.

Strong sales—the project's 67 units sold out in little more than a week—indicate market interest in transit villages. The units are affordable by Los Angeles standards: The 800-square-foot artist lofts sold for $355,000 and the three-bedroom patio homes sold for $839,500. To minimize potential noise problems, the developer retained acoustical engineers and will install commercial-grade acoustical window systems in the lofts that face Meridian Avenue and the light-rail station and dual-paned windows in the remainder of the project.

UC Urban

Mockingbird Station, Dallas

Mockingbird Station, a mixed-use, urban infill development driven more by strong market forces than by public planning and incentives, is a pioneering project next to the Dallas Area Rapid Transit (DART) Mockingbird light-rail station, which is four miles north of the Dallas CBD. Completed in 2002, the project includes 211 loft apartments; 140,000 square feet of office space; and 180,000 square feet of restaurants, entertainment uses, and destination and convenience retail stores. It was developed by Dallas-based UC Urban. Ken Hughes, president of UC Urban, says he sought to create a place reminiscent of the bustling, kinetic train stations he remembers from his youth.

The initial segment of the DART light-rail system opened in 1996. Light-rail ridership currently stands at around 60,000 passengers per day and officials project 185,000 passengers per day by 2010. Since opening day, local authorities estimate that more than $800 million of commercial and residential development has occurred within walking distance of DART stations. In the city of Dallas, development around light rail is driven by strong market forces and does not require public subsidies; the good offices of real estate staff at the transit agency; or explicitly supportive policies by the regional planning agency, the city of Dallas, or DART. (Compare the experiences of

Mockingbird Station, a mixed-use development adjoining the DART Mockingbird Lane Station in Dallas.

development around DART stations in the suburban communities of Plano and Richardson, as described in Chapter Five, where public planning and density incentives played an important role.)

Located at the intersection of Mockingbird Lane, which is an east/west arterial, and the North Central Expressway, the Mockingbird Lane Station is eight minutes by rail from downtown Dallas. The station is also a major bus transfer center. Dedicated shuttles serve the nearby 165-acre Southern Methodist University campus, including such activity-generating attractions as the Meadows Museum and the 32,000-seat Gerald J. Ford Stadium. The presence of these activity generators encouraged the developer to make retail development a significant component of the Mockingbird Station project. The project's market assessment considered the site's transit connections to be a key factor.

As is usually the case for urban infill development, land assembly posed significant challenges. Negotiations with land owners were lengthy and costly, and the assistance of the public sector was needed to keep land assembly costs within the financial parameters of the project. In 1997, a year after service to the Mockingbird Lane Station had commenced, UC Urban purchased seven acres that included an abandoned Western Electric three-story, brick-and-concrete assembly plant located next to the DART platform. In 1998, the developer purchased three neighboring acres that offered direct access to and visibility from the North Central Expressway.

Mockingbird Station is directly linked to the DART station by means of a UC Urban–designed and –built pedestrian bridge, elevators, and escalators to the boarding platform. The below-grade passenger platform becomes, in effect, the project's front door. Several gardens and a public courtyard with a waterfall—as well as the landscaped bridge to the transit platform—are among Mockingbird Station's impressive pedestrian amenities.

A key element of the development—and one made possible by the expansion of the site from seven to ten acres—is its 1,150-space underground parking

garage serving residents, office workers, shoppers, and visitors. A portion of the parking deck that had provided station area parking could then be converted to ground-floor retail space, which is now the home of a Virgin Records megastore.

Four stories were added to the 1947 Western Electric building, which was converted to 200,000 square feet of loft apartments with exposed brick walls—an unusual amenity in the Dallas apartment market. An arched roof recalling 19th century railroad terminals was added to this building. The roof deck accommodates a garden and a 25-meter Olympic swimming pool. At ground level are 45,000 square feet of retail space. The development of a boutique hotel is planned.

The loft apartments are upscale, appealing mostly to 30- to 45-year-old professionals who earn incomes sufficient to purchase housing, but who prefer to rent. The transit linkage is important to this market, as are Mockingbird Station's restaurants, cafés, movie theaters (an eight-screen art-house Angelika Film Center), and retail offerings (including, in addition to Virgin Records, the Gap, Urban Outfitters, and Ann Taylor Loft).

Atypically for transit-oriented developments, Mockingbird Station is almost totally privately financed. The developer footed the bill for pedestrian amenities and transit linkages, with the exception of federal contributions toward local infrastructure; for constructing links to the Katy hiking and biking trail; for public sidewalks and landscaping; and even for upgrade improvements to the DART station.

The developer was required not only to build the project's infrastructure, but also was required to build arguably too much parking. For most transit-oriented, mixed-use developments, the appropriate amount of parking is a difficult negotiation point for local planning agencies and developers. The city of Dallas did recognize the shared nature of parking for Mockingbird Station, and required 1,600 spaces rather than the 2,200 that would have been required were each use considered separately. In the developer's estimation, only 1,300 spaces would have been required if transit usage had been fully credited.

To date, it appears that Mockingbird Station's residential component has established the strongest relationship with transit. The retail component is predominantly auto-oriented, while the office component generates car travel and DART ridership in relatively equal proportions. Mockingbird Station demonstrates the private commitment necessary to create a new product and the sheer persistence required to coordinate all the complex linkages and communication with public local agencies and transit authorities.

Downtown Minneapolis

The 11.6-mile Hiawatha light-rail line opened in July 2004, the first installment in a planned Twin Cities regional transit system that calls for the development of two light-rail lines, two commuter-rail lines, and four or five busways for bus rapid transit. Four downtown Minneapolis stations on this initial segment connect downtown with major activity centers and offer opportunities for new development.

Nicollet Mall runs along the historic office and retail spine of downtown Minneapolis. In the 1960s, under the leadership of the local business community, Nicollet Avenue through the downtown was redesigned as a pedestrian-oriented office and retail activity center. Traffic was restricted to buses and taxis, sidewalks were widened and public art added, and a network of second-story skybridges was constructed. In addition to the physical amenities, programmed activities such as parades and open air markets along the Mall became part of the downtown culture. Nicollet Mall is now served by a Hiawatha line station, at 5th Street.

Downtown Minneapolis—particularly Nicollet Mall—has continued to be a competitive business and retail location despite the growth of suburban submarkets. Office tenants like the central location and access to transit for their employees. In the opinion of local planners, without the commitment to transit in downtown many major employers would have been lost to the suburbs. Over the last five years, Nicollet Mall has seen an unprecedented amount of headquarters redevelopment, inspired in large part by the location's access to transit, including the Hiawatha light-rail

Metropolitan Council

line, which will extend from downtown to the region's two international airports by December 2004.

Recent redevelopment in downtown includes a $400 million, three-phase development by Minneapolis-based Ryan Companies in conjunction with Ellerbe Beckett Architects: 1) Target Plaza, a 1.8 million-square-foot, two-tower headquarters for Target (formerly Dayton Hudson) in the 1000 block of Nicollet Mall; 2) an 822,000-square-foot complex comprising a two-story Target store, an 841-space underground parking ramp, and an 11-story office building in the 900 block; and 3) a 929,000-square-foot office tower for U.S. Bancorp Center in the 800 block, which was completed in June 2001. In conjunction with this development, local businesses funded a $4 million Minneapolis Beautiful project to upgrade public art and streetscape elements on the 800 to 1000 blocks of Nicollet Mall. In addition to being the address for six major corporate headquarters—Target, U.S. Bancorp, Pipper Jaffray, Retek, Xcel Energy, and Ryan Companies—Nicollet Mall is also the home of the landmark office tower, IDS Center. This corporate presence is frequently attributed to the region's commitment to transit, which is indicated by the fact that approximately 40 percent of work trips into downtown Minneapolis are made by transit.

Unlike many other downtowns, Minneapolis has retained its retail core, which boasts some home-grown major stores—including Marshall Field's (a former Dayton's store renamed when Dayton Hudson acquired the Marshall Field's stores) and Target. Downtown's office and retail node acts as an activity link between the arts district—including the Walker Art Center, the Minneapolis Sculpture Garden, and the Guthrie Theater—to the west; and residential neighborhoods,

A light-rail station at Nicollet Mall in downtown Minneapolis. Investment in a light-rail system for the Minneapolis-St. Paul region helped spur the construction of more than 2 million square feet of office space in downtown Minneapolis over the past decade.

Greater Milwaukee Convention and Visitors Bureau

Milwaukee's "old world" Third Street district in downtown is a transit-accessible cultural, retail, and restaurant destination for the entire region.

the main branch of the public library, and governmental offices to the east.

The addition of light-rail service is expected to expand opportunities for residential development near downtown as well as give downtown employees and visitors transit access to cultural activities. According to Metropolitan Council estimates, jobs in downtown will grow from 140,000 today to 185,600 by 2020; and the number of people living downtown will grow more than 20 percent, from 25,000 today to more than 31,000 by 2020.

Hiawatha Avenue, the primary light-rail line route, goes north/south from downtown to the airports. Land use along this corridor within Minneapolis city limits is a mix of fairly low-density apartments and commercial uses, with few examples of dense development and many examples of inadequate investment in maintenance and infrastructure. For development around the Hiawatha light-rail line to achieve its full potential here, the public sector, the development community, area residents, and the transit agencies will need to craft a common vision and strategy for implementation.

The city of Minneapolis is planning a model urban village at the intersection of Lake and Hiawatha Streets, a major intersection that has had its share of urban development ups and downs. Lake Street connects Minneapolis to Saint Paul on the east and to residential suburbs on the west. The city's plan calls for as many as 1,000 units of housing and 30,000 square feet of retail oriented to a light-rail and bus transit hub. As experience with urban infill transit-oriented development elsewhere shows, the realization of this vision depends on some important public sector actions, including land assembly, development and approval of a master plan, and the selection of competent developers.

Lake Street and other close-in stops on the Hiawatha line offer opportunities for the development of strong, neighborhood-oriented transit villages. To move beyond the planning stage, transit-oriented development requires leadership to bring together human and financial resources and craft a common vision. In downtown Minneapolis, such leadership has historically

come from the private sector. For transit-oriented development outside of downtown, the needed leadership may come from neighborhoods, enlightened developers, or public planning and transit agencies.

Infill in Downtown Milwaukee

The city of Milwaukee has been promoting urban infill housing in downtown for more than a decade. A master plan for downtown calls for the construction of 13,000 housing units over 20 years to accommodate almost 20,000 people—mostly empty nesters. Housing is indeed a growing market in downtown Milwaukee. Downtown typically absorbs about 20 percent of the metropolitan area's annual multifamily construction (or 300 out of an annual total of 1,500 to 2,000 units), but in 2003, 800 units were under construction in downtown. The continued redevelopment of downtown and nearby neighborhoods—with retail, restaurants, other urban amenities, and a mix of housing—is whetting demand for close-in housing.

Multimodal mobility is a key element of redevelopment planning in Milwaukee. Improved linkages between downtown and nearby neighborhoods have played a role in the recent upsurge in the downtown housing market. The accessibility of downtown and close-in neighborhoods is being enhanced through improvements to the RiverWalk (a pedestrian path along the Milwaukee River), upgraded bike trails, and trolley service that operates in the summer months. The rubber-tired trolley travels in a loop through downtown and nearby points. Making 22 stops, it runs Wednesday through Sunday—every 20 minutes from 11:00 a.m. to 10:00 p.m. (to midnight on weekends).

The downtown plan calls for the removal of the Park East Freeway, which has made available 26 acres (about 11 blocks) of developable land. The Park East Freeway site, which overlooks the Milwaukee River and lies just outside the CBD, is being planned for mixed-use development.

The Mandel Group is a Milwaukee area regional developer that thinks that close-in sites abutting transit offer attractive residential and mixed-use opportunities. In 2001, the developer purchased a 7.5-acre brownfield site—formerly the home of a U.S. Leather shoe manufacturing facility—out of bankruptcy court. It is located across the street from the Park East Freeway site. U.S. Leather had received a $900,000 grant to cover a portion of the environmental remediation costs.

This riverside location offers easy access to downtown by car, bus, trolley, foot, bike, or boat. Upon completion, the U.S. Leather development will include 560 housing units—rental apartments and condominiums —20,000 square feet of retail space, and 875 structured parking spaces.

The Mandel Group intends to construct a 1,400-linear-foot section of the RiverWalk in order to close a gap in the walkway. Residents of the development will be able to bike, walk, canoe, or kayak to downtown, and to catch buses and trolleys from stops located on its southeastern edge. The project's planning emphasizes these travel options by including storage space for kayaks, canoes, and bicycles and providing good pedestrian linkages to the bus and trolley stops. The availability of multiple travel options reduces the amount of parking that will be required. The developer plans 1.5 structured-parking spaces per housing unit and no dedicated parking for the retail uses. Issues regarding on-street parking still need to be resolved with the city.

While urban infill development takes time and adds complexity to the development process, Mandel continues to seek urban sites because there is pride in their successful development, as well as an enhanced reputation and financial rewards. The relatively small Milwaukee market can easily become overbuilt, which, in Mandel's view, makes urban locations more attractive because they appeal to a larger demographic base than do suburban locations and thus offer greater long-term market potential. Furthermore, the difficulty of developing in the city of Milwaukee limits

the competition. For the Mandel Group, a development firm with a long-term, portfolio perspective, developing in transit-served urban locations makes sense.

PUBLIC POLICY AND PROGRAMS

A number of communities have adopted policies and programs that encourage suitable development—that is, more intense, pedestrian-friendly development— around transit stations. For example, many communities have applied flexible zoning regulations, shared-parking standards, and transfer of development rights within transit-station areas in order to improve the economics of development around transit.

In Seattle, for example, the city's Strategic Planning Office in partnership with Sound Transit, Seattle's regional transit agency, launched a three-year station area planning (SAP) program in 1998. The program's goal was to formulate a vision and development guidelines for the areas within a quarter mile of eight pro-

Public library building in Seattle, designed by Rem Koolhaas. Residents and visitors are drawn to Seattle by its vibrant neighborhoods, attractive downtown, and convenient transit.

Ross Tilghman/courtesy of TDA

posed light-rail stations in the city. The planning effort involved a number of city departments, community and neighborhood representatives, and partner agencies. Station area advisory committees were established to involve local residents in station area planning and the design of the stations. From 1999 to March 2001, 95 advisory committee meetings took place. In addition, 200 community meetings, 150 interviews, and a number of focus group sessions further informed the process. More than 800 participants attended station area planning open houses. In July 2001, the city council adopted a station area overlay district ordinance and rezoned the land around the future light-rail stations to accommodate higher-density development and walkable neighborhoods. Reaching a consensus on the shape of station area development-to-be was the result of an arduous process that demanded extensive time commitments on the part of city and transit agency staffs. The payoff was the resultant rezoning, which assures developers that conforming, transit-supportive proposals will receive approval and thus should expedite suitable development around the city's light-rail stations.

Another example of public programs to encourage transit-supportive development is provided by the city of Denver's reduced parking requirements at transit-served development projects. In practice, Denver tries to limit parking in downtown office projects to one space per 1,000 square feet of office space. (Suburban office developers in Denver generally provide five to six parking spaces per 1,000 square feet of office space.) A new district that is well served by transit is taking shape in the area behind Union Station, where a considerable amount of office, residential, and retail development is extending the 16th Street Mall. The city has capped parking within this district at 2.4 spaces per 1,000 square feet of development.

A number of cities including Chicago and San Francisco support transit-oriented housing through location-efficient mortgage programs and subsidies for transportation-related community improvements and for the development of higher-density housing near transit. In San Francisco, the Metropolitan Transportation Commission offers a housing incentive program (HIP) providing grants for new projects within one-

third mile of transit. HIP subsidizes the costs of streetscape improvements, bicycle facilities, pedestrian plazas, and other improvements that support transit use. For projects built at high densities, HIP provides direct funding: $1,000 per bedroom in projects with 25 units/acre, $1,500 per bedroom for those with 40 units/acre, and $2,000 per bedroom for those with 60 units/acre—plus an additional $500 per bedroom for all affordable units.

The following sections discuss the specifics of transit-supportive public policies and programs in the Twin Cities (Minneapolis and St. Paul) and Boston.

Twin Cities

Regional planning and implementation in the Minneapolis-St. Paul region is far in advance of regional mechanisms in place in most other metropolitan areas, and a regional planning context has contributed to the overall economic health of the two central cities and prevented some degree of urban disinvestment. More than 20 years ago, the state of Minnesota created the Metropolitan Council, joining the fate of the surrounding urbanized counties with that of the Twin Cities. Subsequently, the state enacted fiscal disparities legislation that provided urbanized areas with a share of tax revenues deriving from new development in suburban areas. But even with a strong regional perspective in place, the Twin Cities are still battling to restrain edge development, contain sprawl, and focus development in built-up areas and around transit.

As part of its regional planning mission, the Metropolitan Council is encouraging the development of transit "hubs" or villages centered around light-rail stations in the suburbs. Former park-and-ride lots are now being redeveloped with residential and community uses, such as daycare and retail. To encourage specific station areas to develop as true mixed-use hubs, the Metropolitan Council has awarded more than $10 million in grants to local jurisdictions, money that can be used for planning, infrastructure, and incentives for the development of higher-density, mixed-use projects and projects with a wide mix of housing. Burnsville has received $1.1 million; Eden Prairie $1.3 million; Eagan $1 million; and Minneapolis, Richfield, and Burlington together have received $7.7 million for urban village planning along the route of the Hiawatha light-rail line.

Boston

Boston, where the close integration of land use and transit has been a fact of life for so long that it is now part of the local DNA, teaches a number of important lessons on the subject of successful urban transit policy. A small city of 48.4 square miles—that is constrained in area by natural growth barriers like Boston Harbor and the Charles River and has acquired the "density habit" through its history of rapid, immi-

gration-led growth—Boston practiced smart growth long before the term was coined.

Among central cities, Boston ranks third in transit's share (33 percent) of work trips and is one of a small number of older cities that gained population (2.6 percent) between 1990 and 2000. The city of Boston's tradition of development linked to transit extends to the near suburbs and transit use is high in Brookline, Somerville, Cambridge, Chelsea, and Malden.

Boston offers the full complement of transit choices—heavy rail, extensive bus routes, streetcars, and commuter rail. It is one of the few cities to retain

Boston public transit map.

Metropolitan Boston Transit Authority

Goody Clancy Architects

Tent City in Boston is a successful mixed-income housing development that is within walking distance of several transit lines and steps away from major Back Bay employers.

its traditional trolleys. Recently, ferry services and a bus rapid-transit service (the Silver Line) have been introduced. The market for transit receives a boost from a large tourist population and the students and staff affiliated with the more than 45 colleges and universities in the metropolitan area.

As has happened in many other communities, transit in Boston has gained support from the resurgence of downtown development. In many ways, however, the really interesting transit story in Boston involves its neighborhoods. Boston has always had strong ethnic neighborhoods fiercely protective of local institutions and development patterns. In the 1950s and 1960s, many of these neighborhoods were destroyed in the name of urban renewal and progress. The Massachusetts Turnpike made a machete cut through the heart of downtown, driving households and businesses to the wealthy western suburbs. By the early 1970s, a powerful coalition of aggrieved voters—environmentalists, the lunch-bucket crowd, and historic preservationists —formed to protect and restore the neighborhoods

they remembered and loved. The agenda of neighborhood improvement pushed by this coalition of conservative, preservationist, and green voices became and still is a powerful political force in Boston.

In the view of public officials, modernization of the public transit system was the first step in the improvement of the city's neighborhoods. This would require rethinking the state's transportation plan, which focused available funding on the expansion of freeways into the suburbs. The governor of Massachusetts at the time, Frank Sargent, who had been a highway advocate, was persuaded to establish a moratorium on the construction of new highways inside Route 128 and to then spearhead the enactment of federal legislation allowing the use of interstate highway funds for transit improvements. With funding available for transit, Boston soon extended the Red Line subway to Braintree (1980) and Alewife (1985) and completed construction of the Orange Line (1987). These transit extensions stimulated the development of station-related office parks in the suburbs and infill mixed-use developments around downtown and close-in suburban stations.

The modernization of the public transit system received another boost from Michael Dukakis, who, as governor, worked to substantially revitalize the Metropolitan Boston Transit Authority (MBTA). As a result, commuter-rail lines were reopened, subway lines within the city were extended, rail rolling stock and buses were renovated, and new vehicles were added to the fleets. It helped that Governor Dukakis frequently was spotted on the train, commuting from Brookline to the statehouse.

Another public policy element that has greatly impacted transit use and development patterns in Boston was the 1973 imposition of a freeze in the number of allocated parking spaces—that is, spaces built for the exclusive use of building tenants—in downtown. The freeze was negotiated by Alan Altshuler, the state transportation secretary, and Fred Salvucci, transportation adviser to then-mayor Thomas White, with the federal Environmental Protection Agency (EPA) in order to bring Boston into compliance with air quality standards.

The number of allocated spaces was frozen at 35,000 (the 1973 level). The city of Boston maintains a list of all downtown parking spaces and is parsimonious in permitting the construction of new parking. Permits for private, off-street parking for residential, hotel, employee, or visitor use must meet a strict needs test; and parking for residential use is allowed only if the developer can demonstrate that the public will be excluded from using the new facility. Because of parking restrictions, the number of frozen and exempt spaces in downtown grew slowly between 1977 (51,000 spaces) and 1997 (59,100 spaces).

The parking rule has had profound effects on development patterns, transit use, and quality of life in Boston. Some communities around Boston, notably Cambridge, also have enacted limits on the construction of parking. While the parking freeze receives a lot of criticism from developers and city residents, developers and planners tend to give it much of the credit for the significant improvement in the quality of community life in Boston that has occurred since the 1970s. The intensification of development patterns around transit stations in Boston can be traced back to the parking freeze and other transit-supportive actions starting in the 1970s.

(It should be noted that two West Coast cities—Portland and Los Angeles—also negotiated parking freeze agreements with EPA, after which Congress, under intense lobbying pressure, chose to join the fray by forbidding any other such EPA-city agreements. Parking restrictions must now be locally enacted, a step that generally requires more political courage or powers of persuasion than most city governments can muster.)

In addition to securing federal funding for transit, revitalizing MBTA, and freezing parking, the city undertook to construct new MBTA stations with little or no parking. At these stations, the importance of pedestrian connections was elevated. The new pedestrian-oriented MBTA stations have been credited with improving streetscapes, encouraging the retention of neighborhood retail operations, and enhancing the quality of community life.

In more recent years, MBTA and the city of Boston have sought out joint development opportunities in order to bring suitable development to transit districts. A private real estate consultant hired by MBTA identified 23 potential joint development opportunities, of which five or six were considered priority near-term prospects. Some of the joint development opportunities on the list are modest, neighborhood-scale projects.

Much transit-related development has occurred in Boston since the 1970s modernization of its transit system. At Ashmont Square Station, for example, MBTA leased land to a developer for the construction of 150 housing units. MBTA has worked with a number of developers to enhance connections to their projects from the "T"—as the subway is known locally. In Cambridge, for example, CambridgeSide Galleria, a retail mall, runs shuttle-buses from two nearby "T" stops at half-hour intervals—and nearly 50 percent of CambridgeSide shoppers arrive by foot or transit.

In 2001, the Ritz-Carlton Hotel and Towers, the largest development downtown Boston had seen in some time, opened at a transit-rich location across from the Boston Common. Developed by Millennium Partners, the $500 million, 1.8 million-square-foot project includes a 191-room luxury hotel, 309 high-end condominiums, 63 extended-stay apartments, a 19-screen cinema, a fitness center, and a restaurant and luxury retail shops.

Because of the site's access to three transit lines as well as plentiful bus and cab service as well as pedestrian connections to Newberry Street and other Back Bay and downtown attractions that make walking a pleasant experience, only about 20 percent of trips generated by the Ritz-Carlton Hotel and Towers are expected to be by private car, according to early traffic studies. The city allowed Millennium to construct only 1,100 parking spaces, and the developer estimates that the cost savings of not having had to provide a conventional amount of parking for such a large, luxury project exceeded $60 million.

Pioneer Court-
house Square—
known as Port-
land's "living
room"—is sur-
rounded by transit.
Almost 8 million
people visit the
area annually.

The Boston experience provides some important lessons for cities trying to orient their transit policies to achieve revitalization and redevelopment goals:

• Leadership counts. Boston's revitalization was led by a coalition of passionate neighborhood activists and public officials on the city and state levels who recognized the key role that transit could play in overall revitalization. And it has been supported by the participation of the private sector in the form of location-appropriate development.

• Investment in transit is a powerful tool for urban redevelopment, but one that requires time to take its full effect. Market forces ebb and flow, investment climates change, transit improvements are made over time. The Boston story is impressive because the city and close-in suburbs recognized early on that the march to the suburbs was destroying community life; and they decided—four decades ago—to redirect their efforts to existing neighborhoods; and they stayed the course.

Boston's investments in transit and urban redevelopment have paid off in terms of a strong downtown office market (downtown's share of the metropolitan area office inventory stands at 41 percent), widespread transit use (among central cities, Boston ranks third in the country in transit's share of work trips, behind New York and not far behind second-place Washington, D.C.), and healthy and vital neighborhoods.

CONCLUSIONS

As the examples throughout this book show, it takes time for development around transit to achieve its full potential. Urban areas offer the most potential for transit-oriented development, while the often intimidating context for development in urban areas makes achieving that potential difficult. Probably the two most important lessons that successful urban infill projects offer for transit advocates are that the public sector needs to facilitate private development and that transit benefits most from development that promotes the evolution of 24/7 urban neighborhoods.

Public sector participation is a necessary element of infill development around transit in urban areas. Infill

development takes longer and is generally more expensive than greenfield development, and must therefore often be subsidized in order to make project economics work. The public sector role may include the provision of parking, streetscape improvements, utilities, or other infrastructure components; programs that offer financial incentives for development; tax-abatement or tax-credit programs; and assistance in expediting the approval process.

Many developers complain about the "brain damage" and long development periods associated with urban infill and say that the uncertain profits are not worth the aggravation. It is important for local officials to get behind proposed projects that support their transit and transit district goals, and to push to gain timely approvals from neighbors and review agencies and boards at all levels. If it takes three or more years to get approval, proposed projects can fall by the wayside as costs escalate by 20 percent or more and local market conditions change. Public officials often need to be more aggressive in assisting good projects through the neighborhood review process—not by limiting local input or negotiation on design details, but by providing a public voice that explains the importance of the project to the future of the larger community. By sharing the political risk of a development, city governments can make development in central cities more attractive.

To be successful, urban transit districts need to be safe, attractive, and lively—which means that they must incorporate restaurant and retail uses, which means, in turn, that they require residential and office development in significant quantities. Housing alone may generate transit ridership, but it cannot support a critical mass of retail and entertainment uses. Office-dominated districts generally fail to attract more than a minimum of retailers and restaurants, because they cannot survive on lunchtime employee traffic alone. They become deserted in the evenings and on weekends and do not generate the ridership they could were they rounded out by the addition of a resident population.

Land assembly and critical mass count. Large projects, such as Lindbergh City Center, have an opportunity to be more successful by all measures simply because of their ability to plan for an integrated whole. Bethesda Row benefited not only from its five-block land assembly but also from the careful planning and implementation of the surrounding blocks. By adding new uses and substantial square footage to a transit district, development projects start to change the district. If proper attention has been paid to the pedestrian environment, the development or redevelopment of adjoining areas occurs and a transit village starts to emerge. Success in urban infill development around transit takes leadership, land assembly, critical mass, an appropriate mix of uses, good transit service, and time.

CHAPTER FIVE

DOUGLAS R. PORTER

SUBURBAN CHALLENGES

DEVELOPING AROUND TRANSIT SEEMS TO GO AGAINST THE GRAIN of suburban patterns of growth. Most suburban towns and cities have grown up without access to transit. Suburban areas are designed for people who travel by car, and mobility in them depends on street and highway capacities. The only transit services that are available in most suburbs consist of a few bus routes. Little wonder then that developers and public officials, asked to consider the concept of development around suburban transit, might well respond with two questions: "What transit?" and "Why worry about transit when everyone here drives?"

The advocates of smart growth, new urbanism, and other theories of better ways of community development are putting forth answers to these questions with increasing vigor. They are proposing that communities be designed to be transit friendly and pedestrian friendly. And they are succeeding in turning public attention toward the creation or extension of transit services to supplement the highway construction that has long been the mainstay of new suburban development.

For smart growth advocates, the answer to "What transit?" is to promote access to existing bus and rail facilities and to build new transit systems where none are now

Menlo Park, a residential suburb in Silicon Valley, has effectively integrated a transit station into the community.

available. Their response to "Why worry about transit?" is to point out that traffic congestion is on the increase in most metropolitan areas, that automobile emissions threaten air quality, and that a wider choice of travel options could be of great benefit to people in their everyday lives. Since most metropolitan growth is taking place in suburban areas, transit advocates believe that it is important to develop them in ways that allow the use of transit—rather than continue to build only for the car.

This chapter shows by means of examples that developing around suburban transit represents an economically viable opportunity for developers and communities. Development around transit is occurring in many suburban jurisdictions. This chapter identifies the particular conditions that are necessary for such development to succeed and describes measures by which these conditions may be created and enhanced. Examples of development around transit in the suburban jurisdictions listed in the sidebar on the opposite page illustrate the why, where, what, and when of development next to transit.

TRANSIT IN SUBURBAN SETTINGS

Dictionaries define "suburb" as an outlying part of a city or town or a district, especially a residential one, adjacent to a city. The areas around central cities that are commonly referred to as "a city's suburbs" exhibit a great deal of variety. While U.S. suburbs contain many areas corresponding to what most Americans traditionally think of as "suburban"—pleasant residential neighborhoods that are characterized by low densities of development, plenty of trees and green grass, and a relaxed style of living—they also contain

cities as well as rural communities. And the governing units found in suburbs are equally varied, from municipalities large and small, to urban or rural counties, to community associations.

In the 19th and early 20th centuries, many U.S. cities, especially in the East and Midwest, developed a belt of suburbs, which now are sometimes called first-ring suburbs. Today, some older, first-ring suburbs are affluent communities equipped with reputable school systems, high-end shopping centers, and numerous parks and golf courses. Such communities are considered highly desirable in the marketplace. Other first-ring suburbs that were developed to be affordable for blue-collar households offer fewer amenities, and many of them suffer from inadequate tax bases and competition from outlying suburbs. Over the years, some of these suburban jurisdictions have become little more than slums.

In post–World War II America, a wave of suburbanization began, sweeping past the first-ring suburbs that surrounded older, mostly northeastern and midwestern cities. Suburbanization continues to advance the metropolitan envelope of development, with many communities springing up seemingly overnight. Many outer-ring suburban jurisdictions in U.S. metropolitan areas are still in an early stage of development, while others have become almost completely built out.

The ways in which suburban development patterns relate (or do not relate) to transit vary in the same ways that suburbs vary. Many inner-ring suburban jurisdictions grew up when rail transit was a common mode of travel. Shaker Heights (Cleveland area), Arlington Heights (Chicago area), Chevy Chase (Washington area), and New Rochelle (New York area), for example, were established on a trolley or rail line. With residential areas clustered close to stations and streets and walks providing direct access to stations, these suburbs attracted residents who wanted to live in a semirural community and commute to jobs downtown. The rail service that spurred the development of these communities is still in operation in many of them—like Shaker Heights, Arlington Heights, and New Rochelle—and their residents (and the residents of adjoining communities) still ride the trains to downtown jobs. In many trolley suburbs, on the other hand, bus service long ago replaced light-rail service. In some of these, however, like Chevy Chase, new rail services have been added in recent years.

Post–World War II suburbs, in contrast, grew up when travel by car became widespread, and few suburbs built in the last 60 years offer any significant transportation facilities other than roads and highways. These suburbs are designed to serve and be served by cars. Their spread-out development and segregation of land uses create long distances between daily destinations that make the car-travel option convenient and the walking-to-transit option unattractive. Their lack of continuous sidewalks discourages walking. These suburbs may contain sizable concentrations of shopping and employment that might make a transit option practical, but typically these nodes are designed in ways that make car access more convenient and pedestrian navigation within them akin to running an obstacle course. Shopping and employment complexes frequently are inaccessible from adjoining residential areas—because of fences or a lack of pathways and sidewalks. The design of suburban street systems with few connections among neighborhoods further complicates access to bus stops and (potential) transit stations.

One consequence of a low-density, disconnected pattern of suburban development is that the provision of transit service is expensive. Transit must cover too many miles for too few riders. Another consequence is that transit service is inconvenient and uncomfortable because bus routes and rail lines often fail to connect the dots, that is, to serve most people's daily destinations—work, shopping, school—without time-

Redevelopment of the area around the Metra commuter-rail station in Arlington Heights has helped revitalize the Chicago suburb's downtown.

Metra

Palatine's hand-
some new Metra
commuter-rail
station in the
Chicago suburbs
sets the design
standard for rede-
velopment around
the station, which
is now underway.

consuming connections. Suburban transit services—if there are any —tend to be limited to bus routes that meander through neighbor-hoods and connect to employment and shopping centers. Because they compete with cars on con-gested streets and highways, the buses often are slow and infrequent. Bus patrons stand exposed to sun, rain, and the fumes and noise of passing cars as they wait at bus stops, which usu-ally consist of a patch of scruffy grass or bare dirt next to a busy highway. No wonder that people living in the suburbs tend to think of transit chiefly as an inexpedient mode of travel that mostly serves people who do not drive because they are too poor or too infirm.

Patterns of development around many older suburban transit stations and lines generally reflect this view of transit—as well as the lure of highway-accessible locations elsewhere in the community. In some older suburbs that developed around rail stations or bus terminals, the commercial areas near these facilities have become derelict places, their once thriving businesses having moved to highway-oriented cen-ters or disappeared altogether and their commercial buildings having been torn down to provide parking for commuters. Often, private disinvestment in these areas is rivaled by the public sector's neglect of the maintenance of streets, sidewalks, and parks.

Such was the situation around the commuter-rail station in Palatine, Illinois, which is located about 25 miles from downtown Chicago. Founded in 1856, Palatine was one of many farm-market towns that dotted the Union Pacific rail line. The rail-station area attracted commercial development that served the surrounding agricultural areas. Beginning in the 1950s, the town attracted residential development and the station served residents who commuted by rail to work in downtown Chicago.

But although suburbanization attracted affluent households, it failed to prop up the economy of Palatine's diminutive town center, which was scaled and oriented to serve a small-town market. A high-

way bypass constructed north of the town center ensured its continued stagnation. By the 1980s, the rail station sat in the center of a deteriorated and unlovely area. Many commercial buildings had been torn down to create parking lots for commuters and the few remaining businesses struggled to survive. (As discussed on page 148, station area development in Palatine has very recently taken another turn, this time for the better.)

The unfriendliness of most suburbs to transit is not entirely the fault of local land use policies. Sometimes transit agencies choose to provide rail service on ex-isting rail lines that are flanked by industrial proper-ties, many of them abandoned, or by other land uses that provide little incentive for new transit-oriented development. San Diego's light-rail Blue Line, for ex-ample, winds through rundown residential neighbor-hoods. In the Washington region, sections of the Metrorail system run along freight-rail tracks that are lined with warehouses, car dealerships, trash transfer stations, and abandoned industrial properties.

DEVELOPMENT AROUND SUBURBAN TRANSIT: MOTIVATIONS

Development that occurs around transit access points may or may not be transit-supportive. It may be sim-ply a response to market demand in the area that pays little attention to the presence of transit; or it may be programmed, sited, oriented, and designed to achieve a mutually beneficial relationship with transit. That is, the development can include land uses that would gain in value because of a location near transit (see Chap-ter Two); and it can be specifically planned to gener-ate significant ridership for transit (see Chapter Three).

According to a number of studies, transit ridership increases markedly when the density of residential development reaches at least 15 dwelling units per acre and the density of commercial and office development reaches at least 75 employees per acre. Such density levels are uncommon in American suburbs. What would motivate developers, public officials, and transit agencies to alter the usual patterns of suburban development in order to meet the distance, diversity, density, and design criteria of successful transit districts as described in Chapter Three? The following sections explore the interests of developers, public officials, and transit agencies in making the suburban development/transit connection.

For Developers

Developers look for market support for any development they undertake, including development around transit. Location, location, location is the critical factor. For residential development in suburban areas, the market values locations near or within highly desirable neighborhoods with good schools, pleasant parks and recreation areas, and convenient access to attractive shopping and employment areas. For commercial, office, and other nonresidential development, the most sought-after locations are near high-income neighborhoods or on highway corridors that provide convenient access to and from such neighborhoods.

Market Forces

Despite patterns of development that are generally unfriendly to transit, in some ways suburbs offer ideal conditions for development around transit. A climate of growth and change characterizes many suburban jurisdictions. New development—especially revenue-generating development—is sought and supported as a matter of public policy in many growing suburbs. Growing suburbs promise expanding markets for development and support a cadre of investors and developers on the lookout for development opportunities.

Within sprawling suburbs, possibilities for infill and redevelopment generally exceed those found in built-up urban areas. Suburban communities in Portland, Denver, and Dallas, for example, offer plenty of vacant or underused land near transit stations located in growing areas.

A number of successfully developed suburban transit districts provide evidence of the importance of general market forces in development around transit. Transit-station area development in Arlington County, Virginia, across the Potomac River from the District of Columbia is a case in point. During planning for the Washington region's Metrorail system, county officials insisted on a route that linked the Rosslyn-Ballston corridor to downtown Washington, D.C., rather than a route along an existing rail line that would not have served planned and existing commercial centers. Banking on a strong local economy and supportive public policies, developers subsequently created a series of dense, mixed-use complexes at each of the five station sites along the line. Market forces propelled the development and public policy promoted its clustering around stations. (See Chapter Three for details on development along the Rosslyn-Ballston line.)

Cited by transit village advocates Michael Bernick and Robert Cervero as "one of the best examples of suburban transit-oriented development in the United States,"[1] the Pleasant Hill station area on the BART rapid-rail line in Contra Costa County, California, east of San Francisco provides another example of the key role of market forces in development around transit. Between 1988 and 2002, more than 2,400 housing units, offices for more than 4,000 employees, and two hotels were built within walking distance of the Pleasant Hill station.

Transit-oriented development in Arlington Heights—which is one station closer than Palatine to downtown Chicago on the Metra commuter-rail line—has been stimulated by a surge of construction that is transforming the city's downtown.

Strong market interest in station area locations in Arlington County, Contra Costa County, and Arlington Heights was absolutely essential to the success of development around the stations. Station area revitalization in these and other suburban jurisdictions has been supported by robust local and regional economies, by the location of stations within high-income communities, and by the availability of sites with good access to major roads and highways in the region.

The 11.6-mile Hiawatha light-rail line that opened in 2004 in Minnesota's Twin Cities region is applying this lesson in the location of its 17 stations. Most of the suburban station areas already boast significant development and hold promise for more. Among the suburban stations planned are ones at the Lindberg and Humphrey airports, the Bloomington Corporate Center, the Mall of America, a number of educational and medical complexes, and three regional parks. A market study predicts that by 2020 nearly 7,000 new housing units, more than 19 million square feet of new commercial space, and up to 68,000 new jobs will be located within a half mile of the stations.

It deserves notice that not all successful locations for high-intensity development make convenient, feasible, or politically acceptable locations for transit stations. Tysons Corner, Virginia, a major shopping and employment center in the Washington region, is oriented to a network of major highways, is not near the primary routes for Metrorail subway service and—because it consists of megaprojects spread over a large area—cannot be easily retrofitted for transit service. Current planning for the extension of rail transit along the Dulles Airport corridor through Tysons

Corner has found it difficult to identify centroids of activity that would both provide good station sites in terms of potential ridership and also retain quick service to the airport, which is 15 miles from Tysons Corner.

The south corridor of a planned light-rail system radiating from downtown Charlotte, North Carolina, is expected to use an existing rail line—a route that will not offer direct service to South Park, the region's premier shopping and employment district, which is located about one mile east of the line. Although shuttle-bus service might furnish a connection, it is unlikely to generate the ridership that a station located within South Park would attract.

The unfeasibility of siting transit at some locations where it could benefit from a strong development market is illustrated, finally, by the case of Nassau County on Long Island, New York. With more than 14 million square feet of retail, office, and industrial space plus two universities, the so-called Nassau Hub constitutes the county's largest shopping and employment center. It has developed along decidedly suburban lines for half a century and today is afflicted with a typical suburban problem—rampant traffic congestion attributable to the half a million trips a day (to, from, and within) that it generates.

To address the problem, the Regional Plan Association of New York and the Long Island Regional Planning Board proposed a plan for retrofitting the existing center as a more transit-friendly, 21st century suburban center to be served by a new light-rail circulator line connected to an existing commuter-rail line. But support for the plan failed to materialize. It had originated from the county and involved the Long Island Rail Road—two entities that were not perceived as credible sources of thoughtful solutions to local issues. Some residents objected to the potential traffic impacts of a planned park-and-ride facility. The business community in general was apathetic. And many Long Islanders doubted that a problem requiring a solution existed.

Light-rail stop in downtown Minneapolis. The new Hiawatha line will eventually connect suburban locations around the Minneapolis-St. Paul region to downtown Minneapolis and two other major regional nodes—the airport and the Mall of America.

Metropolitan Council

Transit Access

Transit access is an obvious motivation for development around transit. But do transit facilities provide a strong magnet for development in suburban areas? Research as well as experience show that access to transit service is considerably less significant as a market force than other locational characteristics, such as access to major highways or the quality of nearby residential and commercial neighborhoods. Among homebuyers, for example, unit size and cost are decision factors that trump transportation factors, much less transit access factors. Even the generally positive Cervero studies on the effects of a transit accessible location on property values (see Chapter Two) showed mixed results—commercial properties near light-rail stations in San Diego's Mission Valley, for example, enjoyed significant sale price premiums while in Los Angeles commercial properties located near transit but in redevelopment districts sold at price discounts, all other factors being equal.

The specific value of a location near transit for different kinds of development is a case of "it depends." In most instances, transit-conferred values are unlikely to outweigh the values conferred by other locational factors. Furthermore, it is clear that transit access is more important for development in built-up areas than in suburban areas where the car is king and patterns of development favor travel by car.

Because transit access is not generally a strong locational asset for development in suburban locations— though it may still be an amenity—it behooves suburban jurisdictions and transit agencies that are interested in promoting development around transit facilities to

• identify market conditions in station areas that would favor development with or without transit access; or

• create favorable market conditions in station areas through public programs that reduce the costs and risks of projects and thus boost development.

Utah Transit Authority

Downtown Mountain View, California, offers evidence that transit access—provided here by VTA light rail—is becoming a marketable amenity in suburban areas.

Urban Amenities Market

Among young adults and baby boomers reaching empty-nest or retirement years, interest in living in mixed-use, often older, higher-density neighborhoods that offer urban amenities and shorter commutes is surging. This return-to-the-city phenomenon is playing a significant role in attracting development to areas served by transit in both cities and suburbs. Households in the urban amenities market crave a lifestyle that puts them close to restaurants and shops, cultural activities, and sports facilities. They are less interested in large yards and good schools, and more interested in fashionable lofts and historic or architecturally distinctive buildings and spaces. They represent a sizable share of the market for development around suburban transit stations, perhaps especially in the many older suburbs that have a significant stock of historic buildings dating from the late 1800s. Many of the recent developments around suburban transit that have been successful clearly are intended to play to the urban amenities market.

For Public Officials

For public officials, there may be two kinds of motivations for promoting development around suburban transit stations. One is its potential for relieving traffic pressures and the other is its potential for contributing to the betterment of the community.

Varieties of Station Area Development in Two Texas Cities: Plano and Richardson

The variety of development opportunities presented by the new rail-transit services in suburban areas is well illustrated by the development planned and taking place in Plano and Richardson around stations along the DART (Dallas Area Rapid Transit) light-rail Red Line.

In 1989, DART proposed a northward extension to the suburban communities of Richardson and Plano, and service on the Red Line to Richardson began in early 2002 and to Plano in late 2002. Recognizing opportunities for achieving community development goals around the new stations, these two jurisdictions paved the way for transit-focused development by tailoring plans and zoning for current and projected development to the individual qualities of each station area. (For this purpose, Plano sought the advice of a ULI advisory panel at a session of the 1998 ULI annual meeting held in Dallas; and Richardson sponsored a full-scale ULI advisory services panel that took place in June 2000.)

Both cities lie within the North Dallas high-technology corridor along the Central Expressway (Highway 75), where high-technology industries experienced vigorous rates of growth over the past two or three decades, at least up to the time of the technology bust. Employers in Richardson, population 95,650, provide almost 95,000 jobs; those in Plano, population 238,000, account for 115,000 jobs. Both cities expect continued growth, in part due to the new President George Bush Turnpike (Highway 190) located along the boundary between the two cities. This road, which has become an important high-tech corridor for the Dallas region, provides east/west access and links to the north/south Central Expressway.

Between 1992 and 1997, traffic congestion in Dallas increased by 41 percent, according to the Texas Transportation Institute. Richardson and Plano are among the 14 local governments that supported establishment of the DART system in 1983, and both are members of the DART board and contribute sales tax revenue ($.01 per $1 of sales) to the agency.

Four Red Line DART light-rail stations—from south to north, Spring Valley, Arapaho Center, Galatyn Park, and Bush Turnpike—are located in Richardson and a fifth—Main Street—is proposed one mile north of Spring Valley.

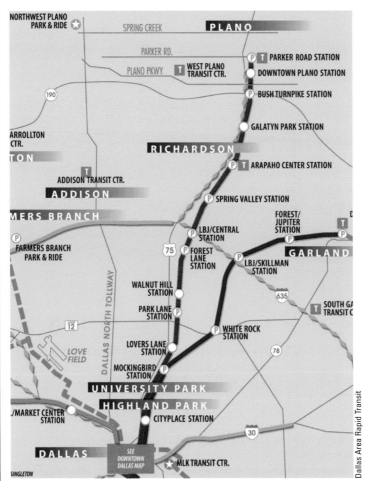

DART's northern lines. The extension of light-rail service to the suburbs has widened commuting choices, created development opportunities, and enhanced the value of nearby real estate.

Dallas Area Rapid Transit

continued

Two Red Line stations—Downtown Plano and Parker Road—are located in Plano. (The Bush Turnpike station area extends beyond the border of Richardson into Plano.) Existing and planned development differs greatly from one station to another, reflecting station area market opportunities, existing development conditions, property ownership, and public development goals and policies.

Spring Valley

The station is surrounded by a wide mix of uses and very little vacant land. To the north and northwest, manufacturing and distribution activities predominate. Apartments and the city's oldest single-family houses occupy the east and northeast sectors. Mixed commercial, employment, and warehouse uses fill out the southern sector.

Preliminary plans for the station area focus on the redevelopment of some distribution and commercial properties north and west of the station. Probable new uses include medium- to high-density housing, which would add to the residential qualities of the area without encroaching on nearby low-density neighborhoods. Development of the Spring Valley station area will likely require proactive city assistance in land assemblage, street improvements, and other actions to stimulate redevelopment.

Main Street

The proposed Main Street station is near Richardson's Old Town district. The station area is mostly built out, primarily with auto-related commercial uses but also with some office and low-density residential uses. Assuming DART finds construction of the station to be feasible, plans call for development that can augment the commercial, small-store character of Main Street, provide links to the Asian-themed retail center east of the station, and add to the residential character of the surrounding neighborhood. Station area redevelopment is likely to require development incentives from the city.

Arapaho Center

Although this station area also features a broad mix of uses, it has, according to the ULI advisory services panel, three special advantages that will stimulate and shape future development:[1]

• a location at the intersection of two major fiber-optic trunk lines, making it an ideal location for telecommunications companies;

• the availability of relatively large parcels of land; and

• a location with good access to the Central Expressway, a DART regional bus transit center, and a DART light-rail station—thus offering a choice of travel modes.

These advantages suggest that future growth should center on the development of office and retail uses.

Galatyn Park

The Galatyn Park station is a transit village in the making. It is being developed with a mix of uses at a scale that can make this station area a major regional center. Zoning allows more than 1 million square feet of development, and permits residential densities as high as 90 units per acre on four acres of the 12.4-acre site next to the station. Nortel Networks and MCI have built large office and research complexes just east and southeast of the station. A new high-end hotel and conference center and a new performing-arts center overlook a public plaza that leads east from the station toward the office/research complexes. A nearby woodland preserve and trail system add amenities. Plans call for more entertainment, office, and residential development close to the

continued

station and additional office and research facilities to the south. Galatyn Park is a brawny, Texas style development complex with a difference—it incorporates a light-rail station. (See "Public Financial Participation" sidebar on page 150 for details on the development of the Galatyn Park station area.)

Bush Turnpike

Located under and beside the President George Bush Turnpike overpass at its interchange with the Central Expressway and functioning as Plano's southernmost and Richardson's northernmost station, the Bush Turnpike station is planned as a major park-and-ride destination for the time being, with much of the parking tucked under the turnpike. Most of the land within a mile of the station is vacant and no firm plans for its development have been drawn up. However, since the land is controlled by only a few property owners, development will undoubtedly take place when the market for this area matures. City involvement in development probably will need to go little further than zoning guidance.

Downtown Plano

The city of Plano was heavily involved in planning the downtown station's location. It seized the opportunity presented by the advent of transit service to kick off a downtown redevelopment program, a central theme of which is to preserve the historic character of downtown by expansion through infill and selective redevelopment. The goal is to develop a mixed-use, pedestrian-oriented downtown. (See "Using Transit Service as a Catalyst" sidebar on pages 128–129 for details on development around the Downtown Plano station.)

Parker Road

Located at the end of the Red Line, the Parker Road station was planned as a major park-and-ride facility with almost 1,500 parking spaces for commuters and as a bus transfer hub. Commercial and industrial uses, including two new big-box stores, and a number of vacant properties occupy the station area. Given the dominance of highway-oriented land uses in the station area, planners do not foresee that extensive rail-oriented development will soon occur. Like the Bush Turnpike station area, the Parker Road station area is viewed as a land bank for the development that will eventually happen when the market matures and when the rail line is (perhaps) extended.

The vision for development at the Parker Road station has not fully formed, but the city of Plano and DART are preparing for future opportunities by buying land near the station. DART bought ten acres immediately north of the station in early 2002 when a building supply company closed, and Plano purchased four acres adjoining the southeast corner of the platform in late 2002 to keep it from being subdivided into pad sites. Both Plano and DART think that the land should be reserved for true transit-oriented development. The Red Line will likely be extended north and Parker Road will then no longer be the end of the line. This will reduce parking demand and open significant development opportunity around the station. Plano hopes that one more Red Line station will be built in Plano approximately two miles north of the Parker Road station at Spring Creek Parkway. The city and DART are already working with the property owner of the preferred location to plan development.

Note

1. *Transit System Opportunities for Richardson, Texas,* ULI Panel Advisory Services Report (Washington, D.C.: ULI–the Urban Land Institute, June 2000).

Traffic Impacts

The possibility that adding transit options or encouraging transit-supportive development might relieve traffic pressures on local highways—which is an enticing goal that can be counted upon to garner citizen support—is a potential motivation for promoting development near transit.

However, the possibility of attaining significant reductions in traffic volume is often very slight. One problem is that as fast as some drivers shift to transit, other drivers arrive to crowd the roads. Also, many of the riders attracted to new rail-transit systems are former bus riders, so that the increase in total transit ridership achieved by the addition of rail-transit services may be modest. Furthermore, given that transit seldom carries more than 5 to 10 percent of all trips in metropolitan areas, the dent that transit makes in overall traffic volume is rather small. It seems certain that as long as most people in suburban areas depend on cars for most of their daily travel, traffic and traffic congestion will continue to increase.

In some suburban situations, however, adding transit options can make a discernible difference to traffic. Transit offers an alternative means of travel for many erstwhile drivers who otherwise would add their cars to the daily flow of traffic—and even a 5 percent rise in car trips could wreak havoc in some travel corridors. In certain travel corridors—particularly those handling a heavy volume of commuting trips from suburbs to the downtown or other major employment centers—transit options can help avoid or relieve traffic congestion. The share of trips made by transit in such corridors is often significant, even in metropolitan areas with low overall transit shares.

The argument that is often raised in this regard is that the fastest-growing segments of metropolitan travel—suburb-to-suburb trips and nonwork trips—are much more difficult for transit to capture than are commuting trips to major employment centers. But transit could improve its capture rate if development were more clustered around transit, creating suburban concentrations that are easier to serve by transit and putting more potential transit riders near transit facilities. Such development would reduce the

Utah Transit Authority

suburban dependence on cars. Even designing suburban development to support the future availability of transit service could help to delay the onset of traffic congestion.

Community Impacts

Public officials may be motivated to support development near transit by the potentially positive effects of such development on the local economy, declining business centers and neighborhoods, and the community's quality of life. To the extent that developers consider transit access as an amenity, a community's ability to offer such access can help it attract the kind of high-quality development that will improve its tax base, add jobs, and serve to diversify housing choices. Transit can help bring private development to areas targeted by the community for revitalization. Public officials may be motivated by the potential to develop or redevelop station areas as important centers of community life.

In the minds of some suburban public officials, however, development around transit offers few benefits. They and their constituents often oppose proposals to develop the kinds of projects that might prosper by proximity to rail service and react with alarm to the notion that new transit service might stimulate development, especially development of a different (not "suburban") character. They envision increased traffic congestion, not improved travel options. They fear that transit-oriented development will intrude on settled and stable neighborhoods, and they fail to consider that it may be an enriching, welcome addition to the quality of life of the community.

Developers have found that older communities located along commuter-rail lines are often disinter-

The Utah Transit Authority's University Line, west of downtown Salt Lake City. By reducing the number of cars entering or exiting suburban residential and business districts —most of which have a limited number of entry and exit points— transit can play an important role in alleviating traffic congestion.

Using Transit Service as a Catalyst for Downtown Development: Plano, Texas

To take advantage of the opportunities that transit offers suburban communities, city officials in Plano, Texas, decided to promote development around a proposed rail station in its town center. Although the city had experienced strong growth since the 1950s through the development of decidedly upscale residential neighborhoods, major retail centers, and major corporate office centers, its downtown had grown hardly at all. Downtown investment over the past two or three decades had been mostly limited to municipal office expansions, the establishment of a small number of boutique and antique shops, and the construction of city-owned parking lots.

 Various efforts undertaken to stimulate private reinvestment in downtown—including streetscape improvements and park expansions financed by bonds approved by voters in 1984, improvements to two major downtown streets, municipal commitments to remain in downtown, and the preparation in 1991 of a downtown plan—failed to do the job.

However, the 1991 downtown plan set guidelines for new development aimed at creating a compact urban center. These guidelines emphasized

- preservation of the historic character of downtown;

- expansion through infill and redevelopment of areas adjacent to the historic center; and

- compact, mixed-use, pedestrian-oriented design.

Still, private interest in downtown redevelopment failed to materialize until 1997, when a decision had to be made on where to locate a transit platform. The new DART light-rail system had achieved unexpected success in Dallas, quickly drawing ridership and interest in station area development. Originally, DART had planned to extend service to Plano in 2010, but it advanced the schedule to 2003 and finally 2002.

The urgent need to agree on a downtown location for a station became the catalyst for an intensive planning effort that launched an ambitious city program for downtown redevelopment. The city's role included assembling city-owned property and land acquired by DART with privately acquired properties, adopting appropriate zoning regulations, providing funding assistance, and facilitating intensive public/private collaboration. The city set a goal of 1,000 new dwelling units and 50,000 square feet of new retail space within a quarter mile of the station platform.

continued

Using Transit *continued*

City officials sought a downtown location for Plano's new DART station and then took aggressive steps to ensure that it would attract development to downtown.

By December 2002, when DART Red Line rail service to Plano began,

• the station was flanked on the east by Eastside I, a three- and four-story urban density apartment and retail development wrapped around a parking structure;

• Eastside II, a second mixed-use project, had been developed a block away, taking the city halfway to its goal of 1,000 station-oriented dwelling units and adding 40,000 square feet of commercial space;

• new and old businesses had begun investing in the renovation of buildings along the main downtown streets; and

• west of the station, a city-supported arts and theater complex was taking shape.

Construction began in 2004 on 15th Street Village, the first owner-occupied housing in the downtown. The project site includes 1.1 acres that were sold to the developer by the city.

The coming of rail service, in the view of city officials, was a call to action for downtown redevelopment. The city's energetic response was founded on the recommendations of the 1991 downtown plan and wove together many ideas for redevelopment that centered on the station location. Transit has succeeded in helping to transform downtown Plano into a bustling residential and commercial center with an urban character not seen elsewhere in the city.

The Rutherford, New Jersey, rail station has historically operated as a hub for trains going to New York City from throughout New Jersey. Recently designated a "transit village" by the state of New Jersey, the station area will be redeveloped with housing, retail, daycare facilities, and parking.

ested in, if not antagonistic to, the redevelopment of station areas to accommodate more intensive land uses. Even if the businesses remaining in the station area are barely surviving and numerous storefronts have become vacant, residents fear that new development will add to traffic congestion and change the character of the town. They may approve station restorations and minor landscaping and streetscape improvements, but adamantly oppose additional development.

That form of developmental limbo hinders transit-oriented development in suburban station areas in metropolitan areas with extensive commuter-rail systems—including New York, Philadelphia, and Boston. If a development proposal wins approval, it is often at a much smaller scale than initially proposed. For example, community pressure forced public officials to halve the density of a proposed residential development at the VTA (Santa Clara County) light-rail Whisman station in Mountain View, California, and eliminate all rental units. The 500-unit project that was built is considered a success, but its potential transit benefits were severely reduced by the failure to build 500 additional units.[2]

For Transit Agencies

Transit agencies tend to actively encourage development around transit in suburban locations. They are motivated by their understanding that increased development can boost ridership and therefore help to underwrite the costs of providing transit service. They also have found that station properties represent salable (or leasable) assets that can generate revenues. A number of transit agencies serving suburban markets have promoted the joint public/private development of property in station areas.

The proclivity of transit agencies to build surface park-and-ride facilities at the outer stations of rail lines has opened up a number of joint development opportunities. Land purchased—at relatively low cost—for parking essentially creates a land bank that can be drawn upon for development when the supply of building sites shrinks and land prices go up. San Francisco's BART agency, for example, welcomes opportunities to free up land next to stations for development by replacing surface lots with parking structures. The agency operating the Metra commuter-rail system in the Chicago region cooperates with municipalities that propose to redevelop commuter parking lots that were acquired jointly with Metra.

Although bus terminals exert only a minor gravitational pull for development, transit agencies in a number of suburban areas are working with local governments to promote development around bus depots located in town centers and employment complexes. Their motivations are expanded ridership and, in some cases, income from salable (or leasable) property.

DEVELOPMENT AROUND SUBURBAN TRANSIT: ELEMENTS

Substantial preparation is required to create successful transit districts. The developers, public officials, and transit agencies that are involved must build a compelling case for the special kinds of development that can benefit from locations near transit and they must put in place innovative policies and incentives to promote these kinds of development.

Generally, advocates for transit-oriented development will be proposing development projects that in type, design, and density differ from what is usual in the suburban marketplace and may be in conflict with many of the public policies and regulations that guide development in suburban jurisdictions. Responses—

both private and public—to development opportunities near transit will tend to be timid as long as such forms of development remain unfamiliar. The hurdles facing development around suburban transit can be overcome only with intensive effort by all parties—over a long period of time. Suburban jurisdictions can help immensely by adopting initiatives that lay a solid policy framework for transit-oriented development and offer incentives to developers entering this special development arena.

The scale of effort required is illustrated by the transit-related developments profiled in this chapter, many of which have required up to ten years of preparation—in public planning and consensus building, the adoption of appropriate zoning regulations and funding mechanisms, collaborative partnering between public officials and developers, and, for developers, assembling the necessary professional expertise and funding.

Advance Planning

The two basic forms of public sector planning and regulation for community development are 1) to let the private development process proceed with only minimal regulatory nudges and course corrections, or 2) to guide development through a more disciplined and proactive planning and regulatory process. Juris-

dictions that want to ensure that development clusters around transit in ways that provide advantages for both transit and development must take the latter approach. A disciplined and proactive planning and regulatory process can ensure that developers who propose transit-oriented projects will find a welcoming regulatory climate and can also guide the location and design of development to make best use of available transit service.

The transit-related development projects described in this chapter have profited from the commitment of public officials to comprehensive public strategies for stimulating certain kinds of development in the right places. An effective public strategy for development around suburban transit usually includes proactive plans that provide direction and lay the policy groundwork for public and private actions. Specifically, an effective public strategy will

• offer a persuasive rationale for concentrating development next to transit by spelling out the economic, community, fiscal, and regional benefits of transit district development;

• identify the qualities of development that will draw on specific local and regional demands for development and support a close relationship to transit;

• make the public policy and regulatory adjustments, including zoning and permitting changes, that will be necessary to attract those qualities of development; and

• adopt public investment and regulatory incentives that can assist in realizing the plan.

Proactive planning takes time and thought. Many suburban jurisdictions have relatively little experience in proactive planning and regulation, and their residents and political leaders must be brought up on the learning curve to appreciate the benefits of such a strategy. Jurisdictions need to target and plan specific development areas and to work out innovative types of public actions. The substantial time and energy needed to make a plan come together pay off because a plan gives public officials and private developers a predictable road map that can guide their efforts to develop around transit.

Utah Transit Authority

Affordable housing and streetscape improvements have been added to the **MARTA** station area in the city of Decatur, a suburb of Atlanta, as a result of a study funded by a regional initiative to concentrate development into activity and town centers.

Strictly Suburban: Development around Metrorail in Miami-Dade County

Miami-Dade Transit (MDT)—the regional transit agency that operates various transit services, including Metrorail, a 22-mile, single-line rapid-rail service between downtown Miami and suburban Dade County locations, and Metromover, a light-rail people mover with closely spaced stops around downtown Miami—promotes the joint development of MDT-owned land and parking lots around Metrorail stations. Until recently, it has not worked closely with local jurisdictions to encourage transit-oriented development beyond the agency's own land holdings. Therefore, although MDT has succeeded in generating substantial development around the Dadeland North and Dadeland South stations—the two southernmost Metrorail stations—the amount of development has been limited by how much land MDT can make available as well as by the general disinterest of local jurisdictions in promoting the redevelopment of built-up districts near the stations.

Dadeland North

The Dadeland North station is located next to the tremendously successful Dadeland Mall. With 185 stores, it is one of the largest shopping centers in the nation. Characteristically for a suburban mall, the shopping center is oriented to highway access rather than Metrorail access. In 1994, MDT and the county commission approved the lease of a 9.2-acre parking site next to the station for the development of Dadeland Station, a multiuse project.

Phase 1 of Dadeland Station, which opened in 1996, consists of a three-level, 320,000-square-foot shopping mall housing five big-box retailers, a few small shops and restaurants, and a six-level garage to serve both mall and transit parking needs. The county expects to realize from $40 million to $100 million over the course of the lease from the guaranteed minimum annual rent ($500,000) and a percentage of gross income. In 2000, a 48-unit apartment project was completed on a Dadeland Station outparcel.

Future phases of the Dadeland Station project may include additional residential development and hotel and office buildings. A 218-unit, 25-story apartment tower was announced in 2001. Downtown Dadeland, a complex

continued

Dadeland Station, a three-level, big-box shopping mall, is sited next to the Dadeland North Metrorail stop. A market-rate apartment tower (the building on the left) is under construction.

containing 375 condominium units and 150,000 square feet of retail space, has been proposed. The design of each project component is auto-oriented, with road access given high priority, and each component has been designed as a distinct project rather than as part of a larger plan. As a result, the Dadeland North station attracts only 5,500 trips per weekday (July 2001), which constitute a minor fraction of car trips to and from the area.

However, the city of Kendall has adopted a plan that proposes to create a "proper" town center around the station. This plan promises that future projects in the station area will have a more pedestrian-friendly design.

Datran Center, a joint development project encompassing office, retail, and hotel uses, provides access to the Dadeland South station through an office building. The transit agency receives an annual return of approximately $800,000 from the project.

Bobbie C. Crichton/Miami-Dade Transit

Dadeland South

In 1984, development around the Dadeland South station was initiated by the first phase of Datran Center, a transit-oriented, joint development on a 6.5-acre county-owned site adjacent to the station. The tightly clustered development currently includes a 305-room luxury Marriott hotel, three Class A office buildings totaling 600,000 square feet, 35,000 square feet of retail space, and parking for 3,500 cars (with 1,000 spaces reserved for Metrorail riders). Access to the transit station is provided through one of the office buildings.

Under the ground lease agreement, which involves a share of the project's income, the extremely successful Datran Center has been providing the county with approximately $800,000 annually. The recent addition of a 21,500-square-foot conference space may increase this return. The final phase of development—an office building and a hotel—is currently under construction.

The Dadeland South station is the northern terminal for an 8.2-mile busway (bus-only roadway) that opened in 1997. Thirty stations are located at intersections along the busway, and several of them offer free parking nearby. Thanks in part to the busway connection, Dadeland South attracts 4,700 trips per weekday (July 2001).

Strictly Suburban

Development around the Dadeland stations represents a variant on the common model for transit-oriented development. Strictly suburban in character, the development—much of it retailing—focuses on land uses that thrive on highway access and depend little on transit service. That focus and the auto-oriented design of the development to date make transit an accessory use rather than a significant stimulus for development. Whether transit's function at these stations changes over time will depend on how the transit districts mature—on whether a mix of uses that can benefit more from transit access evolves and whether the areas can be made more pedestrian-friendly through site design.

Joint Development at a Bus Depot: Eden Prairie, Minnesota

Southwest Metro Transit, the bus transit agency serving the Minneapolis-St. Paul region, has attracted private development to land it sold around its Southwest Metro transit terminal in Eden Prairie, Minnesota. The original 22-acre site was excess right-of-way property acquired by the Minnesota Department of Transportation and transferred to Southwest Metro for development purposes in 1996. In 1999, Southwest Metro completed a $7 million depot and a $10 million, 900-stall parking deck to serve park-and-ride commuters.

The agency started selling land around the transit complex for retail and residential development in 2001. On the east side, a 40,000-square-foot complex of restaurants and convenience shops opened in late 2003. On the west side, a 250-unit, market-rate apartment and townhouse project is under construction, with the first of three buildings scheduled to be open and leasing by summer 2004.

Southwest Metro had three goals in undertaking the joint development of its land:

• generate income from the sale of land;

• generate transit ridership from the depot and parking improvements and from transit-supportive development around the depot; and

• increase the supply of affordable housing in the area.

The agency will recoup about $5 million from the sale of land and hopes to attract riders from up to half of the apartments being developed. Southwest Metro is seeking to identify similar joint development opportunities in other maturing suburbs near Minneapolis.

Southwest Station in Eden Prairie, Minnesota, combines an enclosed passenger terminal, a six-bay bus loading platform, and structured parking. Retail and condominium housing have been developed in the station area on land sold by the transit agency to private developers.

Renton, Washington, provides an example of a city-led planning and multiphased implementation program for a transit-oriented redevelopment of a downtown area. (See "Planning for a Transit-Friendly Downtown" sidebar on the next page.) The city formulated a plan, assembled funding from a variety of sources, worked closely with property owners to relocate existing uses, and worked with developers and the county transportation department on several major projects.

The development of Orenco Station project in Hillsboro, Oregon, represents a virtual primer for planning development around suburban transit. Tri-Met (Portland's regional transit agency) and Metro (Portland's regional planning agency) worked closely over several years with county and city officials to plan transit-supportive development around the station. Metro designated the station area as a town center for which mixed-use development and target residential densities were mandated, and the city zoned the site as a "station community residential village" and adopted design guidelines that ensured a mix of housing types and land uses. (See discussion of planning for Orenco Station on page 73 in Chapter Three.)

All the other examples of development around suburban transit that are discussed in this chapter benefited from hands-on planning and coordination by the local government involved.

Transit-Friendly Design

Development around suburban transit will not achieve the objective of getting people out of their cars and into transit unless it is designed to be transit friendly —on the level of the transit district as well as on the level of the individual project. This requires suburban jurisdictions to plan for and work to achieve an appropriate diversity of uses and appropriate development densities within transit districts and to provide a pedestrian-friendly network of streets, sidewalks and other pathways, and open spaces.

Density

Development density is relative. Just as Manhattan densities are not suitable for Topeka, urban densities are not necessarily appropriate from either a market or political perspective for suburban transit districts.

Nevertheless, transit-supportive development needs to be at a certain minimum density, and the minimum required is not out of reach for suburban development.

The gross density of Orenco Station in Hillsboro, Oregon, is 7.3 dwelling units per acre and the net density in the development's residential sections averages almost 11 units per acre. Residential development around the BART Pleasant Hill station in Contra Costa County, California, averages about 40 units per net residential acre. Suburban residential projects built at such densities have proved highly marketable, with many selling or renting faster than projections. Some suburban communities have approved projects around transit facilities that exceed 50 residential units per acre and more than 75 employees per acre. The Eastside I and II apartment projects in Plano, Texas, achieve about 100 units per acre, a density never before dreamed possible in suburban Dallas.

Achieving transit-supportive employment densities in suburban transit districts may be more problematic. Suburban office parks and shopping centers seldom reach densities of 75 or more employees per acre, and those that do may not be located within walking distance of transit. Near the Galatyn Park station in Richardson, Texas, for example, most of the 24-acre Nortel campus, which is planned for 10,000 employees, was built before the detailed planning for extending the DART line through Richardson had taken place. Most of Nortel's office space is located beyond a quarter mile of the station and much of the campus that falls within the quarter-mile radius is occupied by parking garages. However, although the distances involved are longer than ideal, the Galatyn Park station area has been designed to maximize access to Nortel from the station.

The new Galatyn Park Urban Center at the Galatyn Park DART light-rail station in Richardson, Texas, contains hotel, conference, and performing-arts uses. Large-scale projects like this can market their transit-accessible locations.

Planning for a Transit-Friendly Suburban Downtown: Renton, Washington

Renton is a city of 46,000 residents and 43,000 jobs wrapped around the southeast end of Lake Washington in the Seattle metropolitan area. Its largest employer, the Boeing Corporation, is its main reason for being. In the mid-1990s, the city began planning for the revitalization of downtown, which was chiefly noted for a plenitude of car dealerships and aging buildings. In 1995, it adopted a "downtown element" and "urban center policies" as part of its comprehensive plan, and in 1997 in its *Downtown Core Strategic Implementation Plan,* the city called for the multiphase development of transit-friendly land uses and a new civic open space arranged around a bus transit center to be built by King County Metro Transit.

To create a redevelopment site, the city of Renton acquired five acres of downtown property for $1 million in 1996; and sponsored zoning changes and waived street vacation fees to assist the occupants—car dealerships —in relocating to a new auto mall adjacent to I-405. The city sold part of the five acres in 1997 to Dally Homes for development of an $8 million project—Renaissance—that opened in December 1999. Renaissance comprises three stories (110 units) of luxury apartments above covered parking and 4,700 square feet of street-level retail space. It has been a market success.

The development of the $1.4 million regional transit center, for which the city provided some funding, involved the reconstruction of a Metro Transit bus terminal, new bus layover and loading areas, and pedestrian improvements and landscaping. The terminal, which is a hub for 17 bus routes, opened for service in September 2001.

In 2002, Dally Homes completed Metropolitan Place—90 apartments atop 4,000 square feet of ground-level retail space and a 240-car, two-story parking garage —built on a privately assembled site flanking the terminal. Almost two-thirds of the parking spaces are leased by Metro Transit for use by bus riders. Dally Homes supplies a free annual bus pass to each apartment.

To enhance the pedestrian environment of this emerging transit district, the city developed a central park called the Piazza, created a small gateway park that serves as a decorative entryway to development around the transit center, and provided streetscape improvements along the main street. Downtown Renton's rejuvenation in progress is a testament to the potential effectiveness of advance public planning for the public/private development of transit districts.

As part of its downtown plan, the city of Renton has promoted the development of transit-friendly land uses and provided civic open space around a bus transit center.

Renton's new transit center is a major hub for local buses and an attractive addition to downtown.

Projects built at transit-supportive densities need not overwhelm their suburban settings. Office campuses located near stations and designed tightly with some mix of uses can generate substantial ridership for transit. Housing well under high-rise proportions can easily reach the prescribed density threshold. A combination of three- and four-story multiplexes, some townhouses, and even some single-family houses on small lots can yield an average density of well over 12 units per acre.

Because suburban jurisdictions are inclined to set densities below transit thresholds, even in commercial areas, zoning changes frequently are necessary to achieve an appropriate intensity of development around transit. For example, Eastside I and II in Plano, Texas, each required a zoning amendment; and transit-related projects at the BART Pleasant Hill station in Contra Costa County and the VTA light-rail Ohlone/Chynoweth station in San Jose were approved only after station area specific plans, with related zoning, had been adopted.

Context and Connectivity

Development around most suburban transit stations will be accomplished project by project, an approach that makes the public connective tissue of streets, sidewalks and other pathways, and open spaces a highly significant element in guiding development. Many suburban transit districts—like the areas around Miami-Dade Transit's Dadeland North and Dadeland South stations—lack the kind of grid street systems that create small blocks and provide walkable connections between transit and nearby buildings in more urban patterns of development. It is, therefore, important to include a walkable network of public spaces, streets, and walkways in suburban transit district plans, in order to strengthen the relationship between transit and private (and public) development in the district.

Making walking convenient is key to transit-friendly design. The planning for Orenco Station in Hillsboro, Oregon, on Tri-Met's light-rail line exemplifies good pedestrian connectivity. Almost all of the 500-acre

Eastside I, a mixed-use housing/retail development across the street from the DART station in downtown Plano, Texas, includes retail frontage that generates activity along the street. It was the first project developed under the city's station area redevelopment program.

development is within a half-mile radius of the transit station, and streets have been planned to provide convenient pedestrian access to the station despite its location just beyond the southern edge of the development. A landscaped central boulevard that runs from the station to the northern border of the development also provides a clear-cut walking route directly from the station through the heart of the development.

Pedestrian connectivity was a key objective in planning for the area around the DART light-rail station in Plano, Texas. City officials planned the first downtown redevelopment project—Eastside I, an apartment and retail combination—to plug the gap between the station and downtown's main shopping street and they designed an attractive pedestrian streetscape to reinforce that connection. The city closed part of a street to provide open space and rebuilt sidewalks in order to link the transit platform to Main Street, while the developer designed the building with a welcoming facade and incorporated retail uses.

Developers or their architects tend to want to design projects as stand-alone entities that reflect their own vision more than they tend to want to focus on the project's compatibility with surrounding development or its relationship to nearby transit. To encourage developers to tailor the scale and design of their transit-district projects to the local context, suburban jurisdictions can adopt design guidelines and add design reviews to the project approval process.

Design guidelines and other initiatives to achieve compatible design often take their cue from the concept of place making—that is, the establishment of a distinctive, identifiable character for the community. Place making may focus on establishing a certain architectural character for important clusters of buildings, such as town centers, or on designing a

Development Difficulties around BART's Pleasant Hill Station

Efforts to spur transit-focused development around the suburban, sparsely developed Pleasant Hill station (on the San Francisco Bay Area's BART rapid-rail system) were launched in 1977, when the county adopted a general plan amendment for transit-oriented development. By 1981, however, little development had taken place around the station.

To get the ball rolling, a committee comprising representatives of Contra Costa County, the nearby cities of Walnut Creek and Pleasant Hill (the station lies on unincorporated county land), and BART commissioned Sedway Cooke and Associates to prepare a specific plan for the 140 acres within a quarter mile of the station. The plan for what is now called Contra Costa Centre focused on a concentration of high-intensity office uses within 700 feet of the station and multifamily housing beyond—together with retail uses and public open space that would be mingled with the office and residential uses.

Under the guidance of a new marketing/management entity, the Contra Costa Centre Association, and with the help of property assemblage and infrastructure improvements implemented by the county redevelopment agency, development gradually occurred around the station according to the plan. By the end of 1994, more than 1,600 residential units, 1.5 million square feet of office space, and a 249-room hotel were located within a quarter mile of the station. A transit village was beginning to take shape.

continued

Infill development that is planned for the Pleasant Hill station district will substantially improve its pedestrian friendliness.

Development Difficulties *continued*

Nevertheless, by 1996 more than half the land in the station area remained undeveloped, including three large parcels near the station, according to an analysis by Michael Bernick and Robert Cervero. Furthermore, the buildings that had been developed were unconnected to each other and to the station, and retail uses and public open space were "conspicuous by [their] absence."[1] Two large parking lots adjacent to the BART station and two major streets interrupted pedestrian flows.

Among the reasons for these shortcomings in the evolution of the station area as a transit village were the active opposition of nearby neighborhood organizations to dense development and the efforts of the cities of Walnut Creek and Pleasant Hill to lure development to their downtown areas rather than promote development around the station. Also, the 1989 Loma Prieta earthquake and the real estate recession of the late 1980s and early 1990s had caused the postponement of several planned projects, bringing development around the station to a halt.

In 1995 in an attempt to jump-start additional development, BART issued an RFP for the development of 11.4 acres of parking lots within its 18.8-acre station property. The agency selected a proposal from a development team headed by Millennium Partners for a massive entertainment complex that would establish the Pleasant Hill station area as a destination point. But the proposed complex ran into a buzzsaw of opposition and was put on indefinite hold.

In 1997, the county began a two-year process of amending the specific plan for the station area. The amendments that were made reduced allowable development densities and called for community participation in planning for the development of the site. As a result, a series of design charrettes took place over several months in 2001, attracting participation from more than 500 people. The station area plan that came out of this process was accepted by the county supervisors in 2002. The new plan calls for a compact transit district containing 467,000 square feet of office space, about 30,000 square feet of ground-floor retail shops and restaurants, 255 residential units, a town square and community green, and about 3,500 square feet of civic uses. With buildings lining the streets and rail lines, grouped around open spaces, and clustered close to the station, the site design is walkable and bikable.

Millennium Partners hopes to negotiate approval for developing a project on the BART site that is compatible with the new plan. In any event, station area development is now likely to occur because there is a politically acceptable plan in place that also fits the market. As the Pleasant Hill experience demonstrates, transit-friendly development in a suburban context is not likely to occur in the absence of detailed station area plans that reflect both development realities and community concerns about the intensity and design of development.

Note

1. Michael Bernick and Robert Cervero, *Transit Villages in the 21st Century* (New York: McGraw-Hill, 1996), p. 195.

sequence of streetscapes and civic open spaces that provides a setting for a lively community. Transit stations can be a key element in place making. The cities of Plano (Texas), Hillsboro (Oregon), and Renton (Washington), for example, have made their respective transit station or terminal an important identifier of the city's distinctive quality of life—by prominently displaying the city's name on the station and clustering important elements of the community around the station.

Diversity of Uses

The experience of suburban communities with mixing uses around transit demonstrates that it can be done, but that adequate market support—by whatever travel mode it arrives and from whatever distance it comes—must be available for each component of the mix. The theory of mixing uses around transit, as has been noted, is that people are more likely to use transit if they can satisfy multiple trip needs at their destination, whether it is shopping for everyday items on the way home, patronizing a dry cleaner during the lunch break, or dropping kids off at a daycare center on the way to work. Concentrations of jobs, restaurants, shops, and services around transit stations provide these opportunities. Special destinations such as entertainment centers and sports complexes also have proven attractive for transit users.

Even just a small convenience center at the residential end of a commuter trip can make transit use more attractive. That was the thinking of Southwest Metro Transit when it sold land next to its new bus terminal in Eden Prairie, Minnesota, for both residential and convenience retail/restaurant development. The transit agency hopes that easy access to the retail center will attract more people to travel by bus.

Many of the communities planning for development around suburban transit stations have emphasized new residential development as part of the mix. They are expecting not only to ride the wave of increased interest in urban style living, but also to generate substantial transit ridership. Southwest Metro Transit predicts that one-third to one-half of the residents of the apartment project under construction on the

land that it sold adjacent to the Eden Prairie bus terminal will use the bus system regularly. In the Chicago region, the cities of Palatine and Arlington Heights estimate that the Metra commuter-rail stations in their redeveloping town centers will draw regular riders from 25 to 40 percent of the residential units located nearby.

Adding residential development to a transit-oriented town center benefits the businesses located there and helps make it a 24-hour place. In Arlington Heights, for example, the residents of housing that has recently been developed in the town center are providing patronage for the new Town Square retail shops, offices, and movie theaters; as well as for older retail and service establishments.

Some communities are taking steps to develop performing-arts centers, museums, and other civic uses around suburban transit stations. A complex recently opened at the Galatyn Park station in Richardson, Texas, for example, includes the Charles W. Eisemann Center for Performing Arts and Corporate Presentations. Built by the city of Richardson on land contributed by the project developer, Galatyn Park Corporation, the performing-arts center features a 1,550-seat performance hall, an adaptable theater space that can seat up to 400 people, and a multiuse room. The project's other components include a conference center and a hotel. (See "Public Financial Participation" sidebar on page 150.) Three other full-service hotels are located within a half-mile of the Galatyn Park station. City officials expect that Galatyn Park will attract considerable attention as a conference and performing-arts center for the North Dallas region, with good connections to downtown Dallas.

In Arlington Heights, Illinois, a performing-arts theater as well as an extremely popular multiscreen movie theater are part of the land use mix in the redeveloping town center adjacent to a Metra commuter-rail station. These uses have enlivened the town center, especially on weekends. In Rockville, Maryland, a multiscreen theater that is part of the first phase of a multiuse redevelopment project has proved to be a successful addition to the city's transit-served town center.

Many of the residential projects that have been developed around suburban transit stations incorporate ground-floor retail space. The intention is to add to the liveliness of the transit district. This is a worthy goal, but often the number of housing units that are developed cannot support a great amount of new retail space, especially if existing businesses can capture part of the demand from the new housing. In many suburban transit districts, the leasing of new retail space has been slow.

A lesson learned the hard way in Rockville, Maryland, is that a suburban town center may not be able to support 350,000 square feet of retail space. (See "Developing a Town Center" sidebar on the next page.) An office complex is planned to replace a foreclosed retail mall near the WMATA Metrorail rapid-rail transit station in Rockville. Phase 1, a 104,000-square-foot retail development anchored by a multiscreen movie theater has been completed and is relatively successful. But more retail development must await the completion of office space, which has been delayed by the currently slow office market. Any developing transit district may find that leasing large amounts of ground-floor retail space is troublesome. The ability to support retail development may depend on the maturing of the transit district as a town center to the point at which it can draw substantial patronage from outside the area.

Public/Private Redevelopment

In suburban communities with transit stations located in existing town centers or older neighborhoods, redevelopment strategies for underused land and buildings have promoted appropriate development around transit. A focus on redevelopment puts local governments in a leadership role that requires close collaboration with private sector developers. These public/private relationships have proved successful in many communities.

Redevelopment efforts frequently focus on assembling sites for potential development. Site assembly in built-up areas is a task that private developers often do not want to tackle because of the many potential problems that they may encounter—not the least of

which is paying top dollar for property. Public redevelopment agencies can use the power of eminent domain if necessary and usually are willing to write down initial site costs to help private projects pencil out.

Publicly owned land or buildings—including park-and-ride lots owned by transit agencies—often are the major component of redevelopment sites that public agencies assemble around suburban transit stations. In fact, planners and transit agencies have come to view transit-station parking lots—which are a necessary and low-cost adjunct of many suburban transit stations in their initial years of service—as land bank deposits, which will be held for more intensive reuse as opportunities arise. Suburban jurisdictions have not been reluctant to supplement publicly owned land resources with the targeted acquisition, through eminent domain if necessary, of other properties needed to round out redevelopment sites or to create amenities to spur redevelopment.

One common redevelopment scenario is to sell or lease a portion of a park-and-ride lot for mixed-use development and to replace some of the lost parking by the construction of a parking structure. Among the transit stations where this type of public/private development has occurred are the Southwest Metro bus transit terminal in Eden Prairie, Minnesota; the King County Metro Transit bus terminals in Renton and Redmond, Washington; various BART rapid-rail stations in suburban San Francisco; and various Metra commuter-rail stations in the Chicago metropolitan area. At the Ohlone/Chynoweth VTA light-rail station in San Jose, a portion of a surface-parking lot was redeveloped as housing and a portion was retained in surface parking for transit riders.

The city of Arlington Heights, Illinois, has based much of its town center redevelopment strategy on recycling land resources originally acquired for commuter parking at the Metra commuter-rail station. Over the years, with some help from the Northeast Illinois Regional Commuter Railroad Corporation, the agency that operates Metra, the city had acquired five acres for commuter parking and built four parking garages for the use of commuters and visitors

Developing a Town Center near a Transit Station: Rockville, Maryland

The county seat of Montgomery County, Maryland, Rockville is a city of 47,388 that is situated in the center of the I-270 high-technology corridor. However, the core of the city has, in the words of the 2001 Town Center Master Plan, "struggled to capitalize on the vitality evident elsewhere in Rockville."

Not that Rockville has ignored the state of its downtown. In the early 1960s, it was the second community in Maryland to initiate a federally supported urban renewal project. The plan was to construct a new downtown in anticipation of the economic stimulus to be provided by a proposed Metrorail rapid-rail station that would connect Rockville to downtown Washington, D.C. The centerpiece of the urban renewal project was the development of Rockville Mall, a 350,000-square-foot retail center built over a 1,560-space pub-

Sited on a pedestrian-friendly street within the Rockville Metrorail station district, the retail component of Rockville Center has been quite successful. The stalled office and residential components are awaiting a strengthening of the market.

licly funded garage. The center opened in 1972 and when the Rockville Metrorail station was finished the center was connected to it by a pedestrian bridge over the main highway, Maryland Route 355.

However, Rockville Mall was not competitive in its market. The original anchor tenant, a department store, went bankrupt within a year of its opening and the mall never recovered. After years of only partial occupancy, the lenders foreclosed in the early 1990s.

At that point, the area designated as the town center in the city's plans consisted of an unimpressive cluster of government and civic buildings, a few office buildings, a few apartment buildings, some scattered retail shops, and a considerable amount of surface parking. After the Rockville Mall foreclosure, city officials stepped in to reinvent the town center. Marine Midland Bank acquired the foreclosed mall and proposed to rebuild it as Rockville Center. The city contributed the mall's parking structure and approved a development plan that called for replacement of the mall by new development organized around a traditional grid system of streets. Work on extending streets to create the grid began in 1995 and the mall was demolished in 1997.

A 104,000-square-foot retail building anchored by a 13-screen Regal cinema opened in 1998 and has been quite successful. The other components planned for Rockville Center include three office buildings totaling 1.2 million square feet and a 117-unit apartment building—with ground-floor retail to be provided in all components. These are to be constructed along a pedestrian-friendly street opposite the center's retail building. The softening of the regional office market beginning in 2000 put a damper on office construction. One office building has been approved, but construction is awaiting a renewal of market interest.

Rockville's 2001 town center plan accommodates the development of 1.6 million square feet of new office space, 350,000 square feet of new retail space, and 700 to 1,200 new residential units over the next ten to 15 years. The plan's guiding principles specify the importance of the Metrorail station as a significant presence in the town center. The city plans to implement streetscape and connectivity improvements to improve pedestrian access to the station.

Within the town center outside the stalled Rockville Center development, some recent residential and office development has taken place, guided by the 2001 plan. The first building of Rockville Metro Plaza, a planned complex totaling 597,000 square feet of office space and 23,000 square feet of retail space, is under construction. Negotiations are underway for a major mixed-use project nearby.

continued

Developing a Town Center *continued*

Rockville's experience demonstrates the overriding importance of the real estate market in achieving successful station area development. It also indicates the long-term political tenacity that sometimes is required to carry out major redevelopment around suburban transit stations. The city's first try, involving radical surgery to replace its original town center, was undercut by the vigorous commercial development taking place along the Maryland 355 corridor south of Rockville. The second attempt, which was initiated almost 25 years later, has produced a new but limited retail core and several new office buildings. Development has slackened in the face of an oversupply of office space in the region, but the city is still pursuing its ambitious plan and officials are hopeful that the market will be there to support its implementation when the national economy recovers from the last recession.

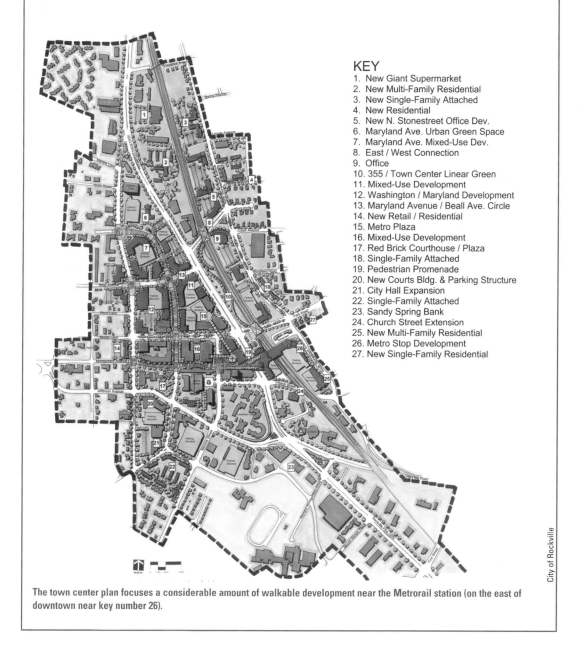

KEY
1. New Giant Supermarket
2. New Multi-Family Residential
3. New Single-Family Attached
4. New Residential
5. New N. Stonestreet Office Dev.
6. Maryland Ave. Urban Green Space
7. Maryland Ave. Mixed-Use Dev.
8. East / West Connection
9. Office
10. 355 / Town Center Linear Green
11. Mixed-Use Development
12. Washington / Maryland Development
13. Maryland Avenue / Beall Ave. Circle
14. New Retail / Residential
15. Metro Plaza
16. Mixed-Use Development
17. Red Brick Courthouse / Plaza
18. Single-Family Attached
19. Pedestrian Promenade
20. New Courts Bldg. & Parking Structure
21. City Hall Expansion
22. Single-Family Attached
23. Sandy Spring Bank
24. Church Street Extension
25. New Multi-Family Residential
26. Metro Stop Development
27. New Single-Family Residential

City of Rockville

The town center plan focuses a considerable amount of walkable development near the Metrorail station (on the east of downtown near key number 26).

The Overlake Station area of Redmond, a high-tech employment center and residential suburb of Seattle, has benefited from the addition of a bus transit center, affordable housing, and a daycare facility within its commercial corridor.

to downtown. The city's redevelopment program began with a 3.75-acre site, 40 percent of which was city-owned surface-parking lots and the remainder of which was acquired by the developer that was selected on the basis of an RFP to develop Arlington Town Square. The project includes a six-screen movie theater, 72,000 square feet of retail space, 26,000 square feet of office space above the retail shops, 94 condominium units in a 13-story tower, and an urban plaza. An underground parking structure provides 325 spaces for public use and 124 reserved spaces.

The city has joined in the development of other projects on former parking lots. These include Village Green with 235 condominium units and 42,000 square feet of retail space; and the Metropolis Performing Arts complex with a 350-seat theater, 32,000 square feet of retail space, an equal amount of office space, and 63 loft condominium units. An 816-space public parking garage serves the Metropolis project and park-and-ride commuters.

A moderate-income rental housing project built on air rights above a parking structure at the Overlake Metro Transit bus station in Redmond, Washington, was a pilot project for King County's office of transit-oriented development, which leased the air rights to the developer. It opened in 2002. Overlake, the site of Microsoft's main campus, is a major employment center with about 600 firms and 22,600 employees. King County, the King County Housing Authority, and a private developer collaborated on the development of the Village at Overlake Station. It includes two levels of covered parking with 536 parking stalls; a 308-unit, four-story apartment building designed to look like townhouses; and a 2,400-square-foot daycare facility. Retail and service establishments, including grocery stores, are located within a short walking distance. The apartments are affordable to households earning 60 percent of the area's median income. The developer encourages bus use by donating an annual bus pass to every apartment unit. The

parking serves bus riders as well as Village at Overlake Station residents, the latter at a parking ratio of one-half space per apartment.

Infrastructure and Other Cost-Sharing Incentives

Suburban communities have supported station area development and redevelopment through programs for upgrading infrastructure. The city of Renton, Washington, built a park and gateway feature to add pizzazz to the redevelopment area around the King County Metro Transit bus terminal and improved the downtown water system to accommodate future redevelopment. The city of Arlington Heights, Illinois, developed an urban park to support redevelopment in the town center and funded a portion of the costs of rebuilding the Metra commuter-rail station and improving pedestrian and bicycle amenities in the station area. The city of Rockville, Maryland, is building new streets to create a more urban setting for redevelopment and has sited a new regional library in a central location. Many communities have made extensive streetscape improvements around suburban transit.

Tax-increment financing (TIF) is a popular tool for funding redevelopment, and many of the examples of development around suburban transit discussed in this chapter have been supported by infrastructure improvements and land-cost subsidies funded by TIF. How this works is that the local government designates the transit district as a TIF district in which all or part of the increased property tax revenues stemming from new development is earmarked for improvements within the district. Often, the local government leverages the promise of future revenues to issue bonds that it pays off from the stream of earmarked revenues.

Arlington Heights, Illinois, established a TIF district for its town center redevelopment and issued bonds for $27 million to be repaid through TIF revenues. The $27 million has been used to provide funds for the construction of parking garages, grants and loans to about 35 building owners for facade and interior renovations, some business relocation grants, and gap financing for four development projects—including the rebuilding of the train station. The TIF has exceeded expectations: With $133 million invested by private developers in the TIF district so far and more private investment projected, the TIF bonds may be paid off by 2006, well ahead of the planned date.

The city of Plano, Texas, established a single TIF district to support development in all three of its DART light-rail station areas—including the Bush Turnpike station, which is located on the Plano/Richardson border. TIF revenues from the entire district are available to help fund improvements around the downtown station, which is the focus of the city's station area activities at this time. (See "Using Transit Service as a Catalyst" sidebar on pages 128–129.) In the future, TIF revenues—which will have increased substantially over the years—can be drawn upon for funding improvements and land-cost write-downs around Plano's other stations.

Regulatory Incentives

The special and "unsuburban" types of development that are most supportive of transit are typically difficult to undertake in many suburban jurisdictions because of regulatory factors—especially zoning, parking requirements, and permitting procedures. Jurisdictions can amend their regulations in ways that can spur developers to undertake the types of development that are suitable for transit districts.

Zoning

Specialized zoning districts with a limited number of uses allowed by right are characteristic of suburban zoning. The mixing of residential and commercial uses is generally viewed as undesirable. And strict limits are usually imposed on how much higher-density development of any kind may occur—and on where it may occur.

The development of compact, multiuse suburban transit districts thus usually requires that jurisdictions amend their zoning ordinances to allow compact, multiuse development in transit districts. In 1993, before a DART light-rail station was planned for downtown Plano, Texas, the city adopted a business/government zoning district for downtown that allowed residential development—with a residential density ceiling of 40 units per acre. When the Eastside I apartment/retail development was proposed at a density of 100 units per acre, it was seen as the kind of transit-supportive development that Plano wanted to encourage. Based on the project's design quality and support from surrounding neighborhoods, the city council amended the zoning to accommodate this density.

Zoning around transit facilities should provide incentives for the development of relatively higher density, mixed-use projects—preferably by right (that is, requiring only administrative review) or involving minimal special review procedures. Some communities have established overlay zones for transit station areas that allow, for example, smaller lot sizes, higher floor/area ratios, or other modifications to the base zoning. Some communities in which transit stations were or are under development have established overlay zones in order to prevent the development of projects considered unsuitable for transit districts. The city of Hillsboro, Oregon, for example, established a station community residential village zone that not only encourages a mix of land uses in the Orenco Station

The Orenco Station light-rail transit district, located in Hillsboro, Oregon, just outside Portland, includes a mix of housing, open space, and a pedestrian-friendly and community-oriented retail center.

transit district, but also keeps out development that is not transit oriented. A further use of overlay zones is to establish design guidelines and other special regulations to guide the quality of development.

"One size fits all" is not, experience shows, true in zoning for development around transit. Jurisdictions with more than one transit station have found it better to tailor-zone transit districts to the needs of individual station areas. California jurisdictions often craft transit districts through adoption of a specific plan—that is the official adoption and mapping of zoning provisions for a specific area based on a plan worked out by public officials and the developers selected for a project.

In Montgomery County, Maryland, floating zones— permitting density bonuses either for residential uses or for commercial uses, depending on the orientation of the zone—are applied to rail-station areas. The zoning districts allow a mix of uses with density options for station-related development. If developers mix uses and provide amenities—such as open space or public art—they are permitted to develop to greater densities and other requirements may be relaxed. This optional method entails an intensive and often lengthy review process during which special features or design changes may be negotiated. Developers have proved willing to subject themselves to this arduous process in order to receive the additional densities allowed.

In Atlanta, the zoning ordinance contains a Chinese restaurant menu of zoning subdistricts in which variations from permitted uses, densities, and other requirements within base zones are allowed. Sets of subdistricts are assembled to form overlay zones for specific station areas. This type of approach has proved useful in some transit districts.

Parking Requirements

Suburban jurisdictions often reduce parking requirements for development around transit, which reduces development costs. They reason that developments that are accessible to transit require less parking and that reductions in the supply of parking can discourage the use of automobiles. Montgomery County, Mary-

land, reduces parking requirements for office uses based on their proximity to rail-transit stations. For the most urbanized part of the county, parking can be reduced from 2.4 spaces per 1,000 gross square feet of office space beyond 1,600 feet of a station to 1.9 spaces per 1,000 gross square feet of office space within 800 feet of a station.

The city of Beaverton, Oregon, granted a parking variance for a 211-unit townhouse project near its MAX light-rail transit station that reduced the required number of parking spaces from two per unit to 1.8 per unit. The city of Plano, Texas, lowered its parking standards for land uses in the downtown transit-station area some years ago. Parking requirements for nonresidential space were set at 75 percent of previous levels and the requirements for residential projects were set at one space for one-bedroom units, 1.5 spaces for two-bedroom units, and two spaces for three-bedroom units. The city also adopted a phased parking management plan that progressively increases the area in downtown in which parking is limited to a four-hour maximum.

Many jurisdictions promote shared parking near suburban transit stations, with transit patrons using park-and-ride facilities heavily during weekday days and local residents and patrons of local commercial establishments using the same facilities heavily during the evenings and weekends. The parking facility

Bethesda Urban Partnership

at the Village at Overlake Station affordable housing development in Redmond, Washington, for example, is also a park-and-ride facility for Metro Transit bus riders, with the parking allocated to residents set at a low one-half space per housing unit based on the development's proximity to the bus terminal and the issuance of an annual bus pass to every apartment.

At Metropolitan Place, a 90-unit apartment/retail development near the regional bus transit terminal in Renton, Washington, 30 of the 150 park-and-ride spaces leased by King County Metro Transit are made available for residents' use during off-peak hours. Ninety additional spaces are allocated for resident parking, for a total of 1.3 spaces per unit.

Parking requirements for the Ohlone/Chynoweth Commons affordable housing project in San Jose (see "Targeting a Transit Station" sidebar on page 149) were reduced by 5 percent because of its proximity to a VTA light-rail station. In Bloomington, Minnesota, planning for an expansion of the Mall of America is taking into account the park-and-ride spaces at the Mall of America station on the Hiawatha light-rail line that recently opened in the Twin Cities region, spaces that can be shared during evenings and weekends to reduce total parking requirements for the shopping center.

Permitting Process

Appropriate development around suburban transit stations in many cases depends on the willingness of local officials to help guide project proposals through the approval process. All of the development projects profiled in this chapter have benefited from the close, cooperative involvement of local officials in their permitting.

Public sector help in project approvals has taken the form of case-by-case amendments of comprehensive plans and zoning regulations in order to accommodate transit-friendly types of development, the waiver of permit fees, and the expediting of project reviews and formal approvals. Nearly all the projects profiled in this chapter required various zoning amendments and variances. The Ohlone/Chynoweth Commons affordable housing project in San Jose, for example,

was exempted from most fees related to plan review, building permits, and infrastructure.

Making Development Happen

For local jurisdictions and regional transit agencies, the proactive promotion of development around suburban transit means learning how to engage in public/private development and calls for a willingness to lead instead of follow development. The station area development programs that served as examples for this chapter came about through determined leadership —usually an administrative official as point person backed by a supportive council or agency board. These examples demonstrate the immeasurable value of having a champion in pursuing a development program that will stretch over several years or even decades.

In Renton, Washington, for example, Sue Carlson, then the administrator of economic development for the city, was largely responsible for putting together the strategy and phasing plan for the redevelopment of downtown, staging a series of development projects on city-owned land, and cooperating with King County Metro Transit in the building of the bus terminal.

In Plano, Texas, Frank Turner, executive director of the city's Development Business Center, had long been a champion of planning and improvement programs focused on preserving downtown's historic character and encouraging high-quality infill development when DART advanced its schedule for building a light-rail station in downtown. He was in a position to seize the opportunity to package a transit-oriented redevelopment program that has helped transform downtown into a lively urban center.

The early initiatives to spur transit-focused development at the BART Pleasant Hill rapid-rail station in Contra Costa County, California, were led by the county's proactive redevelopment authority; and its aggressive push for the implementation of the specific plan for station area development was energetically supported by then–County Supervisor Sunne McPeak.

Another lesson demonstrated by this chapter's examples of development around suburban transit is that
the planning for transit districts and the provision
of development assistance requires a high degree of
cooperation between the local governments and transit agency involved. Close working relationships are
an absolute necessity in promoting development on
land owned by a transit agency. The funding for joint
development projects on land owned by a transit
agency may involve local governments—and may
also involve state and federal agencies. The developers chosen by transit agencies for joint development
projects must obtain approvals and permits from local
governments. They may also have to deal with state
and federal permitting processes if wetlands issues
or brownfields issues are involved. The cooperative
relationship between local governments and transit
agencies may extend as well to transit agency involvement in winning the support of neighbors and
other local interests potentially affected by joint
development projects.

In North Dallas, the cities of Plano and Richardson
worked cooperatively with DART in its planning for
light-rail stations in those cities. The city governments were given a say in determining the specific
location and design of the stations. And even as
station designs were being formalized, station area
development was getting underway.

In the Chicago region, Metra worked closely with the
cities of Palatine and Arlington Heights in planning
the rebuilding of its commuter-rail stations in those
cities. In Palatine, rebuilding involved moving the
station about 200 feet from its original location.

In all four of the Dallas and Chicago jurisdictions
used as examples here—Plano, Richardson, Palatine,
and Arlington Heights—city agencies took the lead
in presenting the station plans to the public through
public meetings in order to secure citizen consensus.
The design of station area development at the Metra
commuter-rail station in Palatine and at the Pleasant
Hill BART station in Contra Costa County was based
in part on citizen input by means of intensive charrettes organized by local government. For the planning of the Pleasant Hill BART station area, Contra

Bob Dunphy

Costa County organized a series of design charrettes
in 2001 in which more than 500 people participated.
These turned the tide of local opposition to proposed
development on station parking-lot land by setting
conditions that required it to be less dense, more
walkable, and more sensitive to local needs.

Making transit-supportive development happen is a
process full of pitfalls. Planning for the 194-unit
affordable multifamily housing development at the
Ohlone/Chynoweth VTA light-rail station in San Jose
took almost seven years. The long length of the process can be ascribed mostly to the involvement of
multiple agencies, the inexperience of the Santa Clara
Valley Transit Authority in managing joint development, and the variety of issues raised by residents
of the surrounding neighborhoods, a predominantly
middle-class, single-family community. The neighbors
were concerned about the impacts of this and an adjacent 135-unit affordable housing project on school
capacity and traffic, and about the proposed loss of
taxpayer-built parking at the station. Numerous meetings were held to work out design changes to reduce
the visual impact of the project. Ohlone/Chynoweth
Commons was finally approved with strong support
from the city council and mayor.

The development of the BART Pleasant Hill station
area in unincorporated Contra Costa County, California, was fraught with difficulties. The real estate recession of the early 1990s hit California especially
hard and killed several planned projects. The nearby
cities of Walnut Creek and Pleasant Hill fought development that might divert businesses from locating in
their downtowns. In the 1980s, Walnut Creek took
legal action to block a major shopping center proposed for a BART parking-lot site.[3] A neighborhood
association was concerned with the potential traffic
effects of any dense development around the station.

Targeting a Transit Station in San Jose for Housing Development

In Santa Clara County, California, local governments and the light-rail transit agency, Santa Clara Valley Transportation Authority (VTA), have acted proactively to bring transit-oriented development—especially housing—to VTA station areas and they have had some success. As was noted in Chapter Two, between 1997 and 1999, about 4,500 housing units and 9 million square feet of office space were built within walking distance of the 7.6-mile Tasman West VTA light-rail corridor that was completed in 2000 through Sunnyvale and Mountain View. Ohlone/Chynoweth Commons, a joint development housing project at the Ohlone/Chynoweth station on the 21-mile Guadalupe VTA line that goes through San Jose, illustrates the kinds of public programs that have stimulated transit-supportive development.

The development of Ohlone/Chynoweth Commons evolved from two planning efforts, one by the city of San Jose and another by VTA, that coincided to produce transit-related, affordable housing.

Initiated in 1989 and approved by the city council in 1991, the city's Housing Initiative Program and Intensification Corridors Special Strategy proposed to expand the stock of affordable housing in this job-rich community by targeting light-rail station areas for high-density housing development. To implement this initiative, the city amended its general plan in 1995 and added two zoning categories to its zoning ordinance to allow retail uses in residential developments and higher-density housing in transit corridors.

For its part, VTA undertook a program to promote transit-oriented development that included the publication in 1993 of a manual by Calthorpe and Associates entitled *TOD Design Concepts for Santa Clara County* and the preparation of concept plans for many station areas along the Tasman West line. The transit agency also initiated three ambitious joint development projects to take advantage of underused park-and-ride lots as sites for housing development. One of these projects involved the Ohlone/Chynoweth station.

The station's park-and-ride lot contained 1,100 spaces. The number of spaces was pared to 366 in order to create a site on which Eden Housing, a nonprofit housing developer chosen through an RFP process, developed Ohlone/Chynoweth Commons—194 units of affordable housing for low-income families, 4,400 square feet of retail space, and a 4,000-square-foot community center incorporating a child-care center and recreational facilities. Eden Housing manages the project.

The Ohlone/Chynoweth Commons affordable housing development (left photo) was built on a site created by the VTA from an underused park-and-ride lot serving the station. For its part, the city of San Jose facilitates the development of high-density housing development in light-rail station areas.

Public Financial Participation in a Station Area Development: Richardson, Texas

The Galatyn Park DART light-rail station in Richardson, Texas, is developing into a major regional center in North Dallas. (See "Varieties of Station Area Development" sidebar on pages 124–126.) City officials and the transit agency have worked to make this happen, as demonstrated by their participation in a deal to site a large development—including the 330-room Renaissance Dallas-Richardson Hotel, the 30,000-square-foot Galatyn Park Conference Center, and the Charles W. Eisemann Center for Performing Arts and Corporate Presentations—adjacent to the station.

When the Galatyn Park Station was still only proposed, the city of Richardson undertook to improve the development market for sites around the station by constructing a new access to U.S. 75—an $11 million project that was partially funded by DART under its local assistance program, the North Central Texas Council of Governments under its congestion management air quality (CMAQ) program, and the city.

The city's agreement with DART not only established the location and design of the station, but also set forth the process for coordinating the design and construction of a proposed two-acre plaza and water feature, which was intended to provide the public setting for development in the station area. Galatyn Park Corporation, which owns the hotel/conference center site, donated the land for the plaza and the city of Richardson paid for its development. Galatyn Park Corporation also donated eight acres to establish a woodland preserve as a wetlands mitigation measure—the value of which was used as an in-kind match for a state grant to fund trail improvements along the rail corridor.

The Galatyn Park station (in the mid-distance) opens onto an expansive plaza bordered by a performing-arts center (foreground), a hotel (behind station), and a site for mixed-use development (left).

City officials and the transit agency worked with landowners and developers to attract transit-focused development to the new light-rail station.

The city provided initial funding—above a $1 million contribution by the Galatyn Park Corporation—for a 750-space parking facility to provide shared parking for the hotel, conference center, and performing-arts center. In order to obtain a high-quality conference hotel, the city agreed to provide 380 parking spaces for hotel guests at no charge for a 20-year period, after which the hotel owner would make annual lease payments. (The city reserved the right to charge parking fees to users of the conference center, performing-arts center patrons, and the general public.)

The city purchased the conference center parcel and holds the ownership of the conference center for 20 years. The hotel owner is responsible for annual payments to retire the $8.5 million of financing debt. The Galatyn Park Corporation donated the 1.9-acre performing-arts center site and construction of the $35 million facility is being funded through dedicated hotel/motel tax revenues (estimated to be about $650,000 annually).

Altogether, the city's investment in the Galatyn Park project has totaled about $76 million, only $15 million of which is drawn from property tax revenues. That $15 million ultimately will be repaid by lease payments. The city estimates that Richardson will receive $11 in direct and indirect benefits for each $1 of its investment.

In 1995, BART accepted a proposal from Millennium Partners to develop a destination entertainment complex on 11.4 acres of land used for parking at the Pleasant Hill station. The proposal soon ran into fierce opposition. (See "Development Difficulties" sidebar on pages 138–139.) The neighboring cities objected to the potential competition with their downtown development efforts. A commuters alliance fought the idea of turning 581 parking spaces along the railroad right-of-way into green space. After two years, the proposal was dropped and the county amended the station area plan to reduce allowable densities of development. The new Pleasant Hill station area plan, which is allowing development to proceed at last, emerged courtesy of the steady leadership exercised by the county and the transit agency. The long-term process of developing around transit needs such leadership in order to navigate through the political and economic cycles that it encounters.

The value of steady leadership is demonstrated as well by the completion of the Metro Center joint development project—a mixed-use complex on 5.5 acres—at the Bethesda, Maryland, Metrorail rapid-rail station in the Washington metropolitan area. The project was two-thirds complete when the early 1990s real estate recession stopped its development. Six years later, the economy recovered and continued support from the Montgomery County planning office and WMATA, the transit agency, allowed the project to be completed according to the original plan.

Suburban jurisdictions and transit agencies routinely issue RFQs (requests for qualifications) and RFPs (requests for proposals) to select developers for properties owned by a municipality, a redevelopment agency, or a transit agency. An RFQ or RFP typically spells out the desired uses and densities of development, sketches design goals for the relationships among the proposed uses and the project's relationship with surrounding development, suggests priorities for the timing and phasing of development, and describes the contributions that the city or transit agency plans to make to the project. It also lays out the proposal selection process. The difference between an RFQ and an RFP is that RFQs commonly require evidence of the responding developers' expertise in

Metropolitan Place in downtown Renton, a Seattle suburb, offers retail uses and mixed-income apartments, as well as park-and-ride spaces serving the adjacent bus terminal. It is a key project in the city's plan to create a modern urban village.

Gretchen Flickinger/Ink Plus

the type of development planned for the site and of the resources they can contribute to the development, while RFPs require a detailed design proposal. A developer selected in an RFQ process works with the issuer to prepare a specific design, and then receives formal approval to initiate the project.

It is good practice for RFP issuers to consult informally with local developers and builders in order to examine and refine their development ideas before formalizing them in RFP documents. Once the RFP issuer selects a proposal, it initiates discussions with the developer to further refine the proposal in light of specific development opportunities or interests of the developer. Such discussions can lead to innovative tradeoffs of funding and value between the public and private partners. The understandings reached in the public/private negotiations eventually are spelled out in an agreement that lays out public and private responsibilities, a timetable, and a financial plan.

CONCLUSIONS

Experience with development around suburban transit stations reveals that relating development to transit can be beneficial. The dramatic changes that transit-oriented development has wrought in terms of invigorating town centers and historic neighborhoods and strengthening the identity of communities as distinctive places in such suburban jurisdictions as Arlington Heights (Illinois), Plano (Texas), and Renton (Washington) have been welcomed by all concerned—the residents of these communities, businesses, local public official, and transit agencies.

The benefits derived from development around transit as described in this chapter can be summed up for the principal beneficiaries—developers, transit agencies, and suburban communities—as follows.

Developers frequently—though not always—

• accrue some increase in property value for locations near transit because of the accessibility of the location and its heightened visibility as a transit destination;

• find that public/private partnerships established to generate development near transit reduce project risks and costs as well as improve the civic status of the developer; and

• gain from reductions in parking requirements with the shift of some trips to transit and the greater feasibility of shared parking.

Transit agencies usually

• benefit from increased ridership generated by development near transit;

• gain visibility for transit as a convenient travel option within the region; and

• gain an understanding that the community beyond the transit system's immediate station areas is dynamic, that it responds to and can be changed by transit.

Suburban communities probably

• find that transit service is an amenity that can enhance a locality's market attractiveness and perhaps

---

How Strong a Ridership Generator Can Suburban Development Be?

The suburban jurisdictions in which this chapter's examples of development around transit are located all expect substantial increases in transit ridership from their support for transit-related development. In some cases, substantial office and retail development is expected to generate ridership. In other cases, substantial residential development is expected to do the same (although some of the people who move into housing close to stations may already commute to jobs by transit). Planners typically estimate that between 35 and 50 percent of people relocating to housing near stations will become transit users. However, because transit service and related station area development are relatively recent phenomena in most of the suburban jurisdictions where they occur, there are few actual ridership counts to confirm these estimates.

Certainly a latent demand for transit exists in at least some suburbs, as was revealed by a strong early response to the opening, on July 1, 2002, of seven new Dallas Area Rapid Transit (DART) Red Line stations terminating in Richardson. The *Dallas Morning News* reported on July 18, 2002, that this extension of transit service "created some challenges for the city, for Dallas Area Rapid Transit, and for its new riders." According to this report, the new service had added about 10,000 daily light-rail commuters and filled morning-rush-hour, southbound trains to standing room only by the time they leave Richardson. According to the *Dallas Morning News,* Richardson's transportation director, Walter Ragsdale, said that "the end of the line is always the problem station" and that he expected that the crunch would be alleviated by the opening of three more stations, two with large parking areas, later in the year.

Some of the Red Line's success in attracting riders can be attributed to the fact that it offers many long-distance commuters—to downtown Dallas, for example—a convenient alternative to driving. And some can be attributed to the transit-supportive development that is occurring around stations in Richardson and Plano. But how much credit each source of ridership deserves has yet to be determined.

become the key to jump-starting its development or redevelopment;

• receive economic benefits from station area development;

• benefit from the place-making qualities of compact, mixed-use development around transit; and

• with the shift of some trips to transit, experience a smaller increase in the volume of road traffic than would otherwise occur, although an increase in total trips made is likely to lessen this effect.

As this chapter has shown, many kinds of suburban jurisdictions have recognized these potential benefits and taken actions to shape development in ways that enhance transit service. Suburban public officials have gained confidence and expertise in collaborating with transit agencies, federal and state agencies, and the private sector. Based on the examples discussed here, it is clear that suburbs need not take a back seat to cities in promoting transit use and in attracting development to transit locations. In fact, suburban jurisdictions frequently have a competitive advantage over their urban counterparts in terms of the strength of their development markets and in terms of the quality of their public sector involvement in development around transit as measured by the skills, dexterity, and willingness to learn of suburban public officials.

Notes

1. Michael Bernick and Robert Cervero, *Transit Villages in the 21st Century* (New York: McGraw-Hill, 1996), p. 189.

2. Ibid., p. 72.

3. Ibid., p. 195.

CHAPTER SIX

FREDERICK C. DOCK

ACCOMMODATING THE TERMINAL FUNCTION

THE DEVELOPMENT OF AN EFFECTIVE TRANSIT DISTRICT around any transit station with a terminal function—that is, any station that serves an end-of-the-line function or where a significant number of riders transfer at the station from one transit mode to another—is complicated by the fact that such stations require space for the operation of transfer services. Extensive parking and transfer facilities at stations can isolate the stations from nearby land uses and also make pedestrian (and bicycle) access difficult and unappealing. A sufficiency of parking and transfer services at end-of-the-line (terminal) stations and transfer stations can both crowd the amount of land available for nearby development and bring a large number of people to these locations— enhancing their market potential for development. The way in which the terminal function is incorporated into stations will influence the potential for development nearby.

How transit riders (will) access a station determines the kinds and size of access facilities—car parking, bus arrival and departure areas, car and taxi drop-off and

Figure 6-1

COMPARISON OF HOURLY CAPACITY OF LIGHT RAIL VS. COMMUTER RAIL

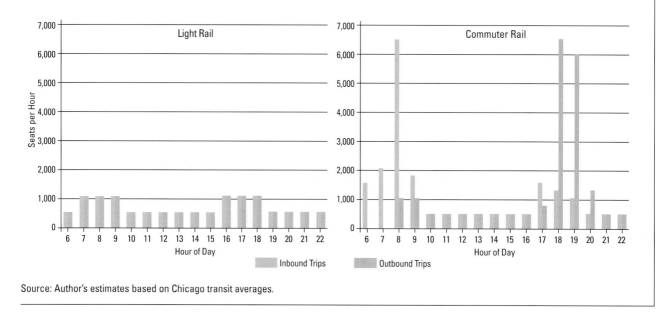

Source: Author's estimates based on Chicago transit averages.

pickup areas, bicycle parking and storage, pedestrian amenities—that should be provided. Access mode and the design of the access facilities, in turn, are a factor in the potential viability of convenience retail and service establishments within station areas.

If a terminal station's dominant access modes are car or bus, the station can become the hole in a doughnut of auxiliary land uses—parking, rider drop-off/pick-up areas, and bus layover/boarding bays. A doughnut devoted to such terminal functions separates the station from potential development areas and limits its access to pedestrian traffic. If the station attracts a sufficient level of activity, these functions can be stacked to minimize the footprint of the station area. The added costs of a stacked structure may be offset by reduced land costs and by returns from the joint development of station area land taken out of parking or other use.

If a terminal station's dominant access mode is walking, particularly in downtown areas, its bus and car/taxi transfer functions can be accommodated at curbside without requiring parking lots or special boarding areas.

This chapter discusses first how the space requirements of terminal stations are influenced by transit mode, transit operations, access mode, and station layout. It then discusses the influence that terminal functions have on station area development, and ends with descriptions of a number of different types of

terminal stations that indicate how station design, transit operations, and development market issues affect development potential around such stations.

FACTORS IN THE SPACE REQUIREMENTS OF TERMINAL STATIONS

The space requirements of transit stations are strongly influenced by transit mode(s), transit operating philosophy, mode(s) of access to the station, and station layout.

Transit Mode

The physical layout of stations must accommodate the transit vehicles using them. Transit vehicles come in many sizes and shapes and a variety of boarding characteristics. Buses, commuter-rail cars, and some light-rail transit vehicles can be boarded at street level. Most rapid-rail trains require raised boarding platforms. The more capacious the transit system's largest vehicle or consist (the set of vehicles forming a complete train), the larger the boarding area needs to be. Some rail-transit systems operate lines side by side, which requires space for horizontal separation. Rail operations also need space outside the passenger areas of stations for tail tracks and crossovers that allow trains to change tracks and reverse operating directions. Buses, of course, can reverse directions within the normal street system.

How the station layout requirements of different transit modes may vary is discussed in the following sections.

Commuter Rail

Commuter-rail service involves passenger cars that are upward of 85 feet long and often bi-level to accommodate more riders. The train consists, which can be as short as one car plus a locomotive, also can be very long—up to ten cars. Platforms must be sufficiently long to serve most or all of the cars in the longest consist. Fares are often collected on the vehicle.

Rapid Rail

The vehicles used in rapid-rail systems, which usually operate on an exclusive right-of-way with an external electrified power source, range in size from around 50 feet to more than 70 feet. Consists range from two to ten cars. Platforms are designed to accommodate the longest consist in the system, and they are typically elevated and equipped with external fare collection systems. Thus, rapid-rail stations need a considerable amount of space for accommodating passenger-related functions. Train boarding areas typically are located above or below street level.

Light Rail

Light-rail vehicles usually operate at street level in mixed traffic or on exclusive rights-of-way. Vehicles in service in the United States are typically 90 feet long, and consists range from one to three cars. Ticket machines are usually located on boarding platforms, adding to the size requirements of platforms. Usually tickets are not collected, although passengers may be required to display proof of fare purchase.

Bus

Buses typically operate as single-unit vehicles. They average about 40 feet in length. Articulated vehicles are about 50 percent longer than standard buses. Fares are usually collected on board the vehicle. Compared with other transit modes, buses require only small boarding areas, although stops on routes with frequent service must be designed to accommodate more than one bus at a time. Bus terminals can require as much space as train stations.

Operating Philosophy

Different operating procedures work to maximize the capacity of each transit mode. In general, transit systems increase peak capacity by adding vehicles (longer trains or more buses in service) and by shortening vehicle headways (the interval between trains or buses). Each transit mode's operating philosophy has its own implications for station area space needs.

Scheduling dictates if more than one vehicle or consist will be in an end-of-the-line terminal station at one time. If the route headways are shorter than the round-trip time, more than one vehicle or consist will be at the terminal, either boarding or stored, waiting to move to the boarding position.

If off-site crossover or tail tracks near the station are available for vehicle reversing and storage, the space requirements for end-of-line terminal stations serving a single rail transit route are comparable to the requirements for in-line stations, except that twice the amount of platform space is generally required. When multiple concurrently operated routes converge at a terminal station, one or two parallel platforms will be needed for each route, and vehicle storage requirements are correspondingly increased (see drawing on the next page).

Rapid Rail and Light Rail

Rapid-rail transit and light-rail transit generally operate on two reverse-direction tracks with uniform headways systemwide. Service is thus relatively equal in both directions and proportionally more frequent in peak periods and less frequent at other times. The number of trains that will be in a terminal station simultaneously is limited to one or two.

Commuter Rail

Commuter rail generally observes railroad operating rules. In some cases, it shares tracks with freight and long-distance passenger rail operations. Commuter service typically is clustered into morning and evening peak periods and has a peak-period directional bias.

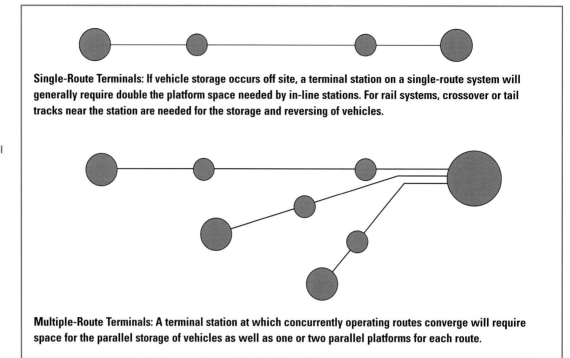

Single-Route Terminals: If vehicle storage occurs off site, a terminal station on a single-route system will generally require double the platform space needed by in-line stations. For rail systems, crossover or tail tracks near the station are needed for the storage and reversing of vehicles.

Multiple-Route Terminals: A terminal station at which concurrently operating routes converge will require space for the parallel storage of vehicles as well as one or two parallel platforms for each route.

Space requirements for terminal stations.

A large number of trains need to be stored near the terminal station at one end of the line or the other in order to meet peak-period service requirements.

Bus

For bus terminal stations, adding buses to routes and shortening headways impose additional space requirements for accommodating a larger number of vehicles in peak hours. Additionally, pulsed in/out or timed transfer scheduling (which aims at the concurrent arrival/departure of buses on all the routes serving a hub station, in order to make transferring convenient) requires more space to the degree that it precludes the sharing of boarding bays. On the other hand, space requirements are lessened by virtue of the fact that buses often can be parked on the street for layovers during the day.

Station Access Mode

The amount of space allocated for station area uses and the layout of station areas should reflect the ways in which passengers arrive at or exit from the station. The specific amenities and facilities that will have to be provided to facilitate access will vary, depending on whether the access mode is by foot, by bicycle, by bus or other transit service, or by car.

Some terminal stations—predominantly those in downtown locations—are accessed primarily by walking. They require little space for the storage of auto-

mobiles. They may be designed to accommodate transfers to other transit services, which are likely to be on another level of the station or at the curb.

Some terminal stations are accessed primarily by automobile. These basically park-and-ride facilities are oriented to the street and parking is a large component of station area design. The parking may be provided in surface lots or parking structures. And it may be located adjacent to the station or in a remote location that is accessible by shuttle services or by walking.

Terminal stations that are accessed by bus may be in suburban or downtown locations. The number of bus routes serving the station and the types of bus service provided determine, in large part, station area space requirements. The large turning radii of buses require ample roadways. The space needed for bus boarding areas varies widely depending on their basic layout—which can be in a sawtooth, herringbone, or in-line pattern. The design of pedestrian connections from bus boarding areas to the terminal is important.

Station Layout

Terminal station layouts are, in general, either horizontal or vertical, with functions either arranged alongside each other or stacked. When the primary mode of access is walking, a horizontal station area can have a small footprint. But when access is primarily by driving or by bus, a horizontal layout typically requires a large surface area for parking or bus boarding—and these functions usually are sited between the station and developed (or potentially developed) neighborhoods. A vertical station area layout will minimize a station's footprint, although the ramps that are needed to bring access vehicles above or below grade will add to total space requirements for the station area.

TERMINAL FUNCTIONS AND STATION AREA DEVELOPMENT

The generally larger space requirements of terminal stations make it difficult to achieve a pattern of compact, walkable development adjacent to the station. Many of these stations pose adjacency issues—in other words, their access functions are essentially incompatible with other desired station area land uses. They must be carefully planned and designed in order to accommodate pedestrians within station areas and also in order to not overwhelm adjacent development with the car or bus traffic generated by the station. Not all terminal stations will be suitable for transit-oriented development.

Basic approaches to optimizing the development potential at terminal stations vary depending on the type of station:

- *Stations Primarily Accessed by Walking.* The catchment area for transit riders who walk to the station extends generally one-quarter to one-half mile from the station (the distance that can be walked in five to ten minutes). In order to minimize the separation between the station and nearby residential and employment land uses and thus put more people within walking distance of the station, the footprint of the station and its functions should be minimized. This approach involves stacking station functions rather than arraying them side by side.

- *Stations Primarily Accessed by Driving and Parking.* At terminal stations that have a large park-and-ride function, the terminal footprint can be minimized by using parking structures instead of surface lots or by sharing parking with adjacent land uses. The added cost of structured parking may be offset by the savings in land costs. Another technique is to cluster parking on one side of the station, which leaves space adjacent to the station available for development. Another technique is to locate the parking in remote areas; however, this requires shuttling riders to the station, making transit trips less convenient. For terminal stations at which surface parking remains a fixture, its impact can be softened by making station area space available for community events at times when transit demand is low and by programming parking lots for farmers' markets or other suitable activities on weekends.

- *Primarily Multimodal Stations.* Stacking functions at terminals with multimodal functions can achieve smaller station footprints. It is a terminal station's concentration of activity that makes stacking an option, and, in many cases where land is sufficiently valuable, this also provides an opportunity for the joint development of complementary land uses on air rights above or on land adjacent to the terminal station.

The key components of terminal stations can be arranged horizontally or vertically.

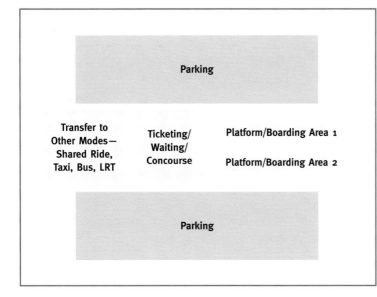

| Parking |
| Transfer to Other Modes— Shared Ride, Taxi, Bus, LRT | Ticketing/ Waiting/ Concourse | Platform/Boarding Area 1 |
| | | Platform/Boarding Area 2 |
| Parking |

Dallas Area Rapid Transit

Large parking lots, like these at the LBJ/Skillman DART light-rail station in Dallas, provide excellent transit access for people arriving by car, but limit station area development options.

The market for development around terminal transit stations depends to some extent not only on the design of the station area, but also on the reasons that people walk to transit and the nature of their transit use. For example, while a station's proximity to adjacent development is a key element in encouraging people to walk to transit, it is not the only reason why they choose to walk to a station. Walking tends to be the primary mode of access to downtown terminals because parking costs and traffic congestion persuade people to commute to work by transit. Similarly, factors in addition to the availability of shopping and service opportunities influence when transit passengers are in a terminal station area and how much time they spend there. For example:

• Transit-related activity in station areas occurs mostly during the morning and evening peak-commuting hours, and ordinarily little transit-related activity takes place outside those time periods.

• Transit passengers tend to arrive at a station to board at scheduled departure times, which minimizes the amount of time they spend in the station area.

• Multimodal transfers and timed transfers are designed to minimize the amount of time that transfer passengers spend in the station area.

The amount of time that transit riders spend in a station area affects the ability of retailers to capture sales from them. Decisions about what kinds of retail services to include in a terminal station area should be made on the basis of the likely travel behavior patterns of the transit riders who will be using the station as well as on the basis of more typical retail location factors.

For example, people departing a station on transit usually are most often focused on minimizing the time they spend in the station, although some may be induced to arrive early by the availability of opportunities in the station area to take care of daily business— such as leaving a child at daycare, buying breakfast, or dropping off dry cleaning—in a single trip. People arriving by transit at a station from which they will drive or walk to their next destination often feel less time-constrained, because they control the means of exiting the station area. The potential for station area retailers to capture sales from these passengers is good. However, people arriving at a station from which they will make another transit connection do not represent an important potential market for station area retail, because making the transit connection is their main concern.

Given the episodic nature of transit rider arrivals and departures in a station area, station area retail rarely can thrive on transit demand alone, except in the heaviest volume stations. The introduction of a transit station can bolster an already strong retail market, but it cannot be relied upon as a primary generator of retail activity. More retail activity in station areas can be encouraged by the development of retail-supporting land uses—especially housing and offices —within walking distance of stations.

TERMINAL STATION EXAMPLES

Some examples of developing around terminal stations follow that illustrate both the issues associated with terminal stations and approaches for developing around them. Two bus terminals—an end-of-the-line station in suburban Minneapolis-St. Paul (Apple Valley station) and a station in downtown Denver (Civic Center station)—are included. Three additional downtown stations are discussed next—a commuter-rail station in Chicago (Ogilvie Transportation Center), a rapid-rail station in Cleveland (Tower City Center station), and a multimodal station in San Francisco (Transbay Terminal). Finally, two rapid-rail stations located at Chicago airports (Midway station and O'Hare station) are discussed as examples, essentially, of multimodal terminals.

Apple Valley Station

The Minnesota Valley Transit Authority (MVTA) bus terminal in Apple Valley (Minnesota), a rapidly developing suburb in Dakota County in the Twin Cities metropolitan area, is near the southern edge of the city's downtown commercial area, which is at the intersection of County Highways 23 and 42. The Apple Valley station is the southern anchor for three express-bus corridors serving downtown Minneapolis, downtown St. Paul, and the Mall of America in Bloomington. The station also is a hub for MVTA local routes that connect to other hubs and park-and-ride facilities serving the portion of the metropolitan area that lies south of the Minnesota River.

Situated in the southeast quadrant of the intersection of Cedar Avenue (County Highway 23) and 155th Street, the 5,000-square-foot Apple Valley station with its 420 park-and-ride spaces is typical of suburban bus transit stations. However, the process by which it was developed and the way it has been integrated into the surrounding community make it unlike many suburban transit stations.

The 13-acre station site was developed in 1999 by a partnership of public agencies and private developers as a mixed-use, planned unit development. The master plan places the station in the center of the site, bookended by retail uses along 155th and 157th Streets and connected to residential areas to the east by a one-acre greenway. The station is set back from the street to accommodate bus boarding on its street side, thus minimizing on-site space requirements for bus circulation.

A 16-screen movie theater on the station site shares parking with the bus station and with a service station and miscellaneous convenience retail located on the high-visibility corner at 155th Street. A pedestrian plaza that was developed as part of the master plan connects the station with existing multifamily residential areas to the east and south.

The station's parking is similar in appearance to the parking provided elsewhere within the auto-oriented commercial areas north of the station. Its potential for separating the station from residential and commercial land uses has been minimized in several ways. The parking area is rectangular with the long side running north/south, which minimizes the width of the station site and facilitates pedestrian connections to the residential areas on the east. A pedestrian greenway across the narrow part of the site enhances these connections. And sharing parking with on-site retail and entertainment uses, particularly the movie theater, minimizes overall parking requirements for the station.

A coalition of agencies put together the development program for the Apple Valley station site, a program that exceeded the transit agency's space needs. The transportation providers—MVTA, the Dakota County Transportation Department, and the Metropolitan Council—were joined in this project by the city of Apple Valley and the Dakota County Housing and Redevelopment Authority. The city acted as an economic development authority for the project and

The Apple Valley express-bus terminal in suburban Minneapolis is designed with materials that help it blend into the adjacent neighborhood.

Minnesota Valley Transit Authority

created a special services district for implementing maintenance activities that would otherwise have been borne by MVTA.

Based partly on the success of the station project, the city of Apple Valley is pursuing mixed-use development for the remaining vacant sites in its downtown commercial core. The city recently approved conceptual plans for a mixed-use development called Central Village that envisions a much more intense vertical retail/office/residential mix than was achieved in the station area project. A linear greenway connection into the station area along 155th Street is planned.

Denver Civic Center station, exterior (top photo) and interior. An office building occupies the air rights over the state-of-the-art bus terminal.

Meyer, Mohaddes Associates

Civic Center Station, Denver

The Regional Transit District's (RTD) Civic Center station in downtown Denver is one of two bus terminals on the edge of downtown feeding customers to a high-frequency shuttle service through downtown—the 16th Street Transit Mall—that is in the process of adding a loop that will connect to a new light-rail line. The Civic Center station stacks joint development atop a state-of-the-art terminal.

Express buses enter and depart the terminal area below grade. Their passengers either walk to their destinations or transfer to the mall shuttle. The terminal's location adjacent to downtown Denver's high-rise core not only supports walking as a primary mode of access, but also provided a joint development opportunity. The RTD capitalized on this opportunity by developing an office tower on air rights over the bus terminal.

The Civic Center station resembles a downtown commuter-rail or rapid-rail station more than a typical downtown bus operation that uses the street system to distribute passengers. RTD's express-bus system supported by downtown shuttle services concentrates its boarding and off-loading functions in two terminals on opposite ends of downtown. By expediting bus movement in and out of the downtown core, this approach not only enhances the RTD's operations, but also provides potential for a greater return on transit investment and provides a transit interface with the downtown that, in terms of development potential, resembles a downtown rail station.

The essential elements of the Denver RTD approach are to terminate express-bus service adjacent to the downtown core and provide dedicated downtown circulator routes with sufficient capacity and frequency of service to distribute express-bus passengers to destinations beyond walking distance of the terminal station. Development of a transit mall is not required. Transit agencies wanting to replicate this approach will have to use operating savings to help fund added capital costs—a difficult but not impossible task in the current funding climate. The centralization of boarding and off-loading functions moves the primary cost for passenger waiting areas from the city

(for provision and maintenance of adequate sidewalk space) to the transit agency (for construction and maintenance of the terminal station). The capital costs thus incurred by the transit agency would be offset by operational cost savings in the form of reduced delays on individual express routes. If joint development is a possibility at the terminals, the revenue stream from that development can also help offset the added capital costs.

Ogilvie Transportation Center, Chicago

The Ogilvie Transportation Center is one of four downtown terminals operated by the Metra commuter-rail system that serves the Chicago metropolitan area. It is located in the Citicorp Center, a 42-story, 1.7-million-square-foot office tower and retail development.

Primarily serving the west, northwest, and north sectors of the metropolitan area (including southern Wisconsin) on Union Pacific tracks, the terminal is located on the western edge of downtown Chicago. The Chicago River separates it from the Loop. The terminal's location a half block west of the river makes possible a fairly unique bit of multimodalism: Between April and October, water taxis take people from the rail terminal's dock to a landing at North Michigan Avenue.

Citicorp Center occupies a full block bounded by Madison (south), Clinton (west), Washington (north), and Canal (east) Streets with its main entrance on Madison. The rail tracks terminate at elevated boarding platforms on the Washington Street side of the block that are adjacent to the lobby area of the office tower. Platforms are long enough to accommodate the ten-car trains that operate during peak periods. Eight parallel, two-sided platforms essentially fill the block between Clinton and Canal and the platform area extends above street grade another block north to Randolph Street.

A retail concourse on the same level as the elevated train platforms extends from Citicorp Center into and through Riverside Plaza, an office building across Canal Street, via an elevated walkway over the street. This route connects Metra passengers to the bridge across the river at Madison. Access is also provided to

Washington Street. The water taxi landing is accessible by stairs from a plaza that runs along the river between Washington and Madison.

Most Metra commuter destinations from this terminal are to the east or north. The strongest directional flow is to/from the river crossings at Madison and Washington. Peak-hour pedestrian volumes of more than 10,000 persons per hour are experienced at the station entrances on Madison and Washington Streets. The Ogilvie station illustrates how efficient walking can be as a mode of access. The terminal also achieves an excellent pedestrian-scale, multimodal interface involving walking, buses, taxis, and water taxis—with no park-and-ride option. The majority of rail passengers access the station by walking; the remainder use, in order of popularity, buses (which are operated by the Chicago Transit Authority), water taxis, and taxis. Bus loading, which occurs mostly along Canal and Washington, is entirely curbside, with no off-street storage or loading areas provided. Taxi operations are also strictly curbside.

Citicorp Center exemplifies the efficient integration of a rail terminal into an office tower. The terminal design deserves much of the credit. The integration of the terminal function into the north side of the block above grade left three of the four faces of the block available for development or public space use. The platforms were designed to fit within a single

The 42-story Citicorp Center successfully integrates the Ogilvie Transportation Center, a downtown Chicago commuter-rail terminal, with office uses as well as destination retail, convenience retail, and a food court.

Tower City Center —an office/retail/ hotel complex— was constructed over a rapid-rail terminal station in downtown Cleveland. Station planners designed circulation systems and waiting areas that facilitate the integration of transit and retail functions.

Forest City

block width to minimize the footprint of the terminal where it interfaces with the city. The ticket-sale windows—an adjunct function here because tickets are available on the trains and monthly and other multiple-ride passes are sold elsewhere—are located at the western side of the upper level away from the main flow of passengers to and from the train platforms. Escalators provide high-capacity access from street-level entrances to the platform level. The traffic flow into the train platform area, which is outside the climate-controlled building area, is reasonably free.

The design of the office and retail components deserves an equal amount of credit. The vertical office tower provides the necessary mass to anchor the complex's atrium and grand public entrance. The office lobby is on the podium level in the western portion of the building, outside the primary flow patterns for rail commuters but visible from the street and podium levels. The retail component consists of destination retail on the ground level; service and convenience retail that wraps the atrium at the podium level; and a food court located in a less visible space behind the escalators on the street-level concourse. Designed to

accommodate the directional nature of pedestrian movement to and from the complex, the two-level retail concourse allows for the efficient movement of very many pedestrians while providing retail services that support the rail terminal, the office tower, and the surrounding west Loop community.

Tower City Center Station, Cleveland

The historic Terminal Tower complex in the lakefront district of Cleveland's downtown dates from the 1920s and occupies a 34-acre triangle formed by Superior Avenue, Ontario Street, and Huron Road. It once contained a passenger-rail terminal as well as a rapid-rail station. In the late 1980s and early 1990s, a joint public/private redevelopment of about half of the historic complex resulted in Tower City Center, a 6.5 million-square-foot office/retail/hotel mixed-use development constructed over a relocated central rapid-rail terminal station operated by the Greater Cleveland Regional Transit Authority (GCRTA).

The rail terminal was relocated nearer to the center of the complex, with the platforms sited under Station Court, which is one of three grand spaces in the complex. Along with two other historic grand spaces—

Tower Court and Second Concourse—Tower City Center contains several office buildings, a Ritz-Carlton hotel, a cinema complex, and three floors of retail space. Some of the below-grade space that had been used by the passenger-rail operation was converted to parking for approximately 3,000 cars.

Tower City Center successfully integrates the GCRTA transit terminal functions into the retail complex. Because the station was rebuilt as part of Tower City Center, the station planners were able to design vertical circulation systems and waiting areas that facilitate this integration. Tower City Center offers an excellent example of the appropriate sizing of circulation and waiting-area facilities within both the transit and the retail realms. It also offers proof that siting a transit terminal in a central location—in this case in a location that provides direct connections to the retail and public spaces throughout Tower City Center—can make a significant contribution to the success of a mixed-use center.

The retail component of Tower City Center has attracted a strong daytime market of downtown employees, many of whom are transit users. And from the GCRTA perspective, the rebuilding of the transit station and redevelopment of the original retail concourse as a mixed-use complex have enhanced transit ridership.

Transbay Terminal, San Francisco

Construction of a new Transbay Terminal—a five-level regional, multimodal transportation hub—to replace a busy bus terminal on Mission Street in San Francisco just south of the downtown financial district has been in planning for a long time and may soon get underway. The redesign has been proposed mainly to accommodate a proposed underground extension of Caltrain commuter-rail service into downtown. (Caltrain service, which operates between San Jose and San Francisco, currently terminates on the southern periphery of downtown.)

The existing Transbay Terminal was originally constructed to serve the Key Line interurban electric streetcars that ran from the East Bay across the Bay Bridge on the lower level. Direct ramps to and from the Bay Bridge continue to provide access for the AC Transit buses that replaced the Key Line streetcars. The terminal includes a bus/streetcar boarding area used by San Francisco Municipal Railway (Muni) buses and streetcars and operational space for Greyhound intercity buses. SamTrans buses serving San Mateo County and Golden Gate Transit buses serving Marin and Sonoma Counties in the North Bay operate on-street adjacent to the terminal.

A multiyear and multiagency design process that aimed at consolidating the space-intensive terminal

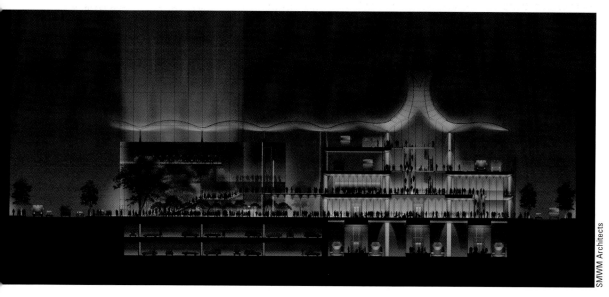

The redesigned multimodal Transbay Terminal in San Francisco will provide an uninterrupted elevated concourse that allows pedestrians to easily traverse its entire length. A substantial amount of retail, residential, and office development is programmed for locations within and adjacent to the terminal.

SMWM Architects

The CTA's Orange Line rapid-rail terminal (right foreground) is connected to Chicago's Midway Airport by a quarter-mile elevated, enclosed pedestrian walkway.

functions of commuter-rail, intercity-bus, and commuter-bus services has proposed to integrate these functions into a vertically stacked building that essentially uses the southern half of the existing Transbay Terminal site and extends it by an equivalent distance east and west into the adjacent blocks—for a total building coverage of 600,000 square feet. Five levels are proposed—below-grade platforms for Caltrain and (possible future) high-speed rail service; a street-level lobby that facilitates transfers to Muni, SamTrans, and Golden Gate Transit buses; an elevated concourse for pedestrian circulation; and two elevated levels serving AC Transit and intercity bus operations.

The proposed new terminal offers an excellent example of the vertical stacking of transit functions. The design pays close attention to pedestrian circulation issues—how to move large numbers of people among modes and to/from their destinations in downtown San Francisco. The key to free-flowing circulation is the pedestrian concourse on the first level above street grade. While three north/south streets segment the building's street level, the uninterrupted elevated concourse will allow pedestrians to easily traverse the entire length of the site. Taking advantage of the long linear nature of the building, the design distributes access between levels along the long axis of the building. These multiple points for vertical circulation between levels will help avoid people jams. The design envisages retail uses along both sides of the long concourse.

The proposed design also pays attention to issues related to development around transit. For example, the Muni bus and trolley bus loading area is moved from Mission Street at the front of the existing building to a midblock pass-through location between

Fremont and Beale Streets, which not only locates the Muni transfer directly below the second-level pedestrian concourse, but also opens up the front half of the existing Transbay Terminal block for the development of a continuous Mission Street frontage. Furthermore, the expansion of the terminal building means that several off-site parcels in the neighborhood that currently are used for bus storage can be redeveloped. And the bus loading areas on the elevated levels of the terminal will continue to use the Bay Bridge ramps to separate commuter buses from street traffic near the terminal.

The proposed terminal reconstruction calls for a substantial amount of mixed-use joint development. The proposed development program for locations within and adjacent to the terminal includes a 1,000-room hotel; 300,000 square feet of destination, entertainment, and convenience retail; 3,000 residential units; and 2 million square feet of office and educational uses.

O'Hare and Midway Airport Stations

In that they serve airline travelers, transit stations at airports are essentially multimodal. The relationship of the transit station to the airport influences the volume of transit/plane transfers and the potential for transit-oriented development. Chicago Transit Authority (CTA) rapid-rail transit stations at O'Hare International Airport and at Midway Airport are cases in point.

CTA's Blue Line terminal at O'Hare resembles rapid-transit stations at airports in other cities in that it is located within the airport grounds. The integration of a transit station into an airport terminal complex precludes the mixed-use development opportunities that the transit-station operations might otherwise offer. Furthermore, the station's multimodal function is limited to airline transfers.

CTA's Orange Line terminal at Cicero Avenue and 59th Street, on the other hand, is connected to the Midway

Airport terminal by a quarter-mile elevated, enclosed pedestrian walkway. As an end-of-the-line station, Midway station includes platform space for four trains, a bus transfer facility with multiple parallel boarding islands, and a park-and-ride facility. It is thus a more robust multimodal operation than the O'Hare station. The various transfer functions—airport, bus, and parking—require a large station and the station's proximity to the airport limits the amount of developable area around it. Thus, the Midway station area is focused mainly on transportation.

CONCLUSIONS

In summary, the additional space needed for car or bus access and mode transfers at terminal stations—whether they are at the end of the transit line or at an in-line hub—can separate the station from adjacent neighborhoods, while the access and transfer operations potentially conflict with pedestrian access. On the other hand, bus and auto access is required to get people to transit stations located in relatively low density suburban areas. Station area planning needs to resolve the tension between accommodating access (by car and bus) from a large tributary area and accommodating access (by walking and bicycling) from the area within a half mile of the station—and how planning resolves this tension will have a major influence on the potential amount and character of nearby development.

The judicious allocation of space and careful design of station areas—with special attention paid to stacked terminal functions and shared uses—can resolve many access conflicts. The development of multimodal terminal stations that generate significant trip-making activity can catalyze transit-oriented development, if they are well planned. As the examples given in this chapter show, the design of successful terminal stations requires paying attention to the effects of building form and station area land use patterns on the travel patterns of transit patrons within and near the station area.

As a general rule, all-day parking lots should be moved from the prime development area around transit stations to peripheral sites that are still convenient enough to not discourage people who drive from using transit. Ways by which parking for transit and adjacent land uses can be shared should be found. Within transit districts, all parking should be planned and managed to serve the whole district and to foster a park-once mentality on the part of visitors to the district for whatever purpose(s).

Finally, planning for terminal functions should first and foremost foster an environment that encourages walking, because pedestrians enliven the immediate neighborhood and create a market for development. Convenient bus connections and convenient parking are important but secondary to convenient pedestrian access to and circulation within the station area.

CHAPTER SEVEN

ROBERT DUNPHY, DEBORAH MYERSON,
AND MICHAEL PAWLUKIEWICZ

TEN PRINCIPLES FOR DEVELOPING AROUND TRANSIT

DEVELOPMENT AROUND TRANSIT, once the norm in urban settings, became the exception when people, jobs, and retailing moved out of cities into suburbs well removed from transit. The basic principles for developing around transit were eventually forgotten in many places. Changing demographics, traffic congestion, and public policy initiatives are once again making clear the importance of the transit/development connection. A growing number of people have reached a stage in life when access to transit is appealing—and driving is appalling. Public policy increasingly supports the goals of more mobility choices and greater sustainability in development. And many new transit projects are in operation or planned.

What does it take to make developments around transit work? The principles presented in this chapter can serve as reminders for communities, designers, and developers who may have forgotten them. For people living in newer, automobile-oriented communities who have experienced nothing else, these principles can serve as a checklist for the development of pedestrian-scale communities that will be suitable for public transportation, either now or in the future. For transit agencies and others engaged

San Diego Convention & Visitors Bureau

discussed a number of questions and issues, and devised ten principles for successful development around transit.

1. MAKE IT BETTER WITH A VISION

Transit is a tool to help achieve a community vision—a way of helping to create the kind of place in which people want to live, work, play, and raise their children. Ideally, the desired development pattern for a region should be agreed on before transit and road plans are developed. In practice, however, development plans based on a clearly articulated vision for the community are the exception, which means that private land markets and public policy are left to battle out their differences. A transit station in an attractive location for businesses and housing may encourage developers to implement their own individual visions on a parcel-by-parcel basis. But the creation of a broader vision

Introduction of light rail to the San Diego region has resulted in creation of nodes of high-value real estate around transit stations and has assisted in the revitalization of the city center.

in the planning of transit projects, these principles can help them design transit in ways that will generate transit-supportive development and thus justify transit investments.

The three most commonly desired outcomes of development around transit are: successful development, growing transit ridership, and livable communities. For suburban and city developers alike, development around transit requires the same careful attention as any other project, with some minor adaptations. If real estate development is to support transit, the single most important requirement is that it be *near* transit. Proximity is not enough, however. Examples abound of development that is close to transit, but is also out of scale and out of touch with it.

Development around transit promotes compact development, multiple rather than single uses, a pedestrian orientation, and attention to civic uses. Successful development around transit also demands a new form of community building that not only supports and encourages transit use but also transforms the surrounding area into a place that is special and irresistible for residents, visitors, and investors.

In June 2002, the Urban Land Institute convened a task force of 17 planning, development, and transit experts under the chairmanship of Marilyn J. Taylor, partner of Skidmore, Owings & Merrill. The task force visited three communities served by transit in the Washington, D.C., area, reviewed briefing books and presentations from local planners and developers,

---

Ten Principles for Successful Development around Transit

1. **Make it better with a vision.**

2. **Apply the power of partnerships.**

3. **Think development when thinking about transit.**

4. **Get the parking right.**

5. **Build a place, not a project.**

6. **Make retail development market-driven, not transit-driven.**

7. **Mix uses, but not necessarily in the same place.**

8. **Make buses a great idea.**

9. **Encourage every price point to live around transit.**

10. **Engage corporate attention.**

can help ensure that all developers pursue compatible strategies that reinforce the transit vision—and that those strategies will be supported, rather than opposed, by the residents of the surrounding community.

Shaping a vision means imagining a development future that recognizes both the community's potential and the operative economic, political, and environmental constraints. Thus, the organization leading the visioning effort should understand the community's strengths and limitations. It should foster a vision that challenges, but does not exceed, the community's capabilities, and should ensure that the implementation schedule is realistic.

To succeed, a vision should be

• oriented toward the future but based in reality,

• stakeholder centered,

• collaborative and educational,

• focused on implementation, and

• flexible.

All those who have a stake in the community's future, as well as those who have the wherewithal to shape it, must be identified and brought into the process. The list of stakeholders typically includes citizens, landowners, developers, local businesses, the transit agency, local elected officials, and local government departments (especially planning, transportation, and public works). Interactions between stakeholders may yield disagreement and contention, but these are the very qualities that render the process collaborative and ensure that critical stakeholders will support the results. Tools such as visual preference surveys, charrettes, and focus groups can help stakeholders from disparate groups learn that they have more in common than they realize.

Grounding the vision in reality will help ensure that it is not so grand or impractical that it cannot possibly succeed. Financial considerations should be addressed early, ideally with the participation of the development community, to ensure that everyone

understands the true cost of building the anticipated types of development and the marketability of the product. It is essential to test the financial feasibility of the development proposals that grow out of the visioning process and to coordinate that analysis with the financial analysis of the transit plan.

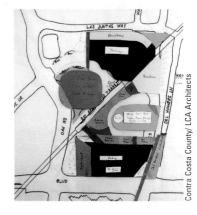

Community visioning exercise in the San Francisco Bay Area.

The levels of development assumed in the transit forecasts should be checked against the vision to see if they are realistic; if not, it may be necessary to revise the transit project. All the stakeholders must understand what actions will be needed in order to realize the vision, including supportive planning and zoning actions and public and private investments. Being ready for implementation means having in place a land use plan and zoning ordinance that support the vision; it also means identifying the necessary financing tools.

Once the vision has been developed it needs to be communicated. Over time, it will need to be adapted to reflect changes in market dynamics, land ownership, community goals, economic prospects, or consumer preferences. The lead planning agency should identify advocates, preferably civic and business leaders, who can speak persuasively on behalf of the effort and use their influence to advance the project.

Arlington County, Virginia, is a close-in suburban community that has supported a vision of concentrated development near Metrorail transit through four decades (see Chapter Three). Contra Costa County, California, is a more conventionally suburban jurisdiction that has evolved a vision for the development of the area around a BART rapid-rail station; a major business district has developed there and residential and retail uses are now being filled in. (See the discussion of the Pleasant Hill station in Chapter Five.)

Applying the Power of Partnership:
El Cerrito Del Norte Transit Village

El Cerrito Del Norte, a mixed-use transit village recently developed at the Del Norte BART rail station in the city of El Cerrito, California, provides a model for an effective public/private partnership. It contains 348 multi-family units—20 percent of which are affordable—and 170,000 square feet of commercial space.

The El Cerrito Redevelopment Agency acquired the site for $3 million through the issuance of qualified redevelopment bonds, and leased it to the Ibex Group, the project owner/developer, for a period of 65 years. The redevelopment agency in return will receive 20 percent of the net project cash flow (after the fifth year) and a 20 percent share of the sales proceeds.

Construction and permanent financing of approximately $11 million was provided through 40-year, fixed-rate, tax-exempt mortgage revenue bonds (multifamily housing bonds) issued by Contra Costa County. The loan proceeds were insured through the FHA coinsurance program, 221(d)(4), which gives the bonds a GNMA guarantee, and consequently a superior bond rating.

The principal source of the remaining funds was equity provided by the Del Norte Place Limited Partnership. The Ibex Group contributed approximately $3.2 million. Low-income housing tax credits were syndicated to 30 individual limited partners for a further $1.8 million in equity contributions. In addition, the Contra Costa County department of community development provided $200,000 through the community development block grant program. The transit agency, Bay Area Rapid Transit, participated in the partnership by selling an easement under the elevated track at Del Norte to be used for parking.

El Cerrito Del Norte.

2. APPLY THE POWER OF PARTNERSHIPS

Creating a development project around a planned or existing transit line is one of the best ways to increase ridership. And development, unlike the expansion of transit routes or the addition of more vehicles, comes at little cost to the transit agency. In addition to encouraging and supporting private development, transit agencies and local governments may take a more active role, by entering into partnerships with the development community. To be effective, however, these partnerships must be carefully crafted to benefit each of the partners.

A successful partnership relies on the strengths of each partner. The public sector has the power to resolve land assembly problems, ensure that the site is development-ready, ease the entitlement process, contribute land, and fund infrastructure costs. Private developers bring the real estate savvy, the contacts with end users, and the understanding of financial resources. Smoothing the entitlement process keeps private sector developers confident, on track, and on schedule—and helps make it possible for them to assume the risks and to produce an outcome that reflects both the community vision and the market reality.

Public/private and public/public partnerships provide opportunities to set mutual expectations and to share risks, costs, and rewards; they also provide a framework for conflict resolution. To help ensure a successful outcome, partners work together, obtaining financial leverage through tools such as tax-increment financing, state and federal financing, and foundation grants.

Because the return on investment is the first indication of success in developing or redeveloping communities around transit, it is critical for the partnership to focus on meeting investment goals. Other indicators of success are the profitability of the businesses that locate in the development, increases in transit ridership, increases in tax revenues, and the satisfaction of the community and other stakeholders.

A growing body of literature, discussed in Chapter Two, shows the financial benefits of being near transit. The challenge is to create partnerships that allow those benefits to translate into profitability not only for the landowner, but also for the developer.

3. THINK DEVELOPMENT WHEN THINKING ABOUT TRANSIT

Real estate opportunities should always take priority over low-cost transit solutions. For example, running transit along the median of an interstate may save the transit agency right-of-way costs, but it will preclude development options. Opportunities for creating higher densities and a mix of housing types to market to a broad spectrum of incomes, should be sought out during transit project development. New transit projects should be aggressive about density. Good design and a high level of amenities are vital and can make a high-density urban setting seem much less dense.

Most new development near transit will be built on private property by private developers. To help these projects succeed, public sector entities must be attuned to the needs of the private sector. This may involve a difficult adjustment in communities that have historically had adversarial relations with developers. Being sensitive to the needs of the private

sector does not mean compromising public goals, however; it simply means recognizing that those goals need to work for the developer as well.

Requirements for project amenities and exactions should be agreed upon up-front so that they can be incorporated into project cost estimates. Two factors are critical to the developer's schedule: certainty and timeliness. To ensure both, the agencies responsible for project review should agree with the developer on a timeline for project entitlement and buildout. Delays cost the project money and damage the bottom line. Facilitating the process with quick turnarounds and on-time approvals helps to hold down the cost of borrowing money. For projects that are important to the community, the developer should be able to count on attentive staff and the support of top management.

Additional development does not benefit only real estate businesses. Because growth can increase real estate value, generate jobs, and increase tax revenues, planning for areas around transit should be linked with economic development.

During the early stages of planning for new development around transit, a market-wise transit agency would collaborate with local developers to create a fiscal analysis estimating building costs and investment returns for the private development of nearby

Portland, Oregon's regulatory and financial tools to promote transit-oriented development have attracted significant development around nearly every light-rail station in the region.

This parking structure in Glendale, California, is set back from the street in order to minimize the towering effects of its six levels. A pedestrian arcade leading to the Market Place shopping plaza is enhanced by an overhead metal trellis, a waterfall, seating areas, and architectural light features.

Walker Parking Consultants

properties. This approach would ensure that developers are active participants in the process and that the outcome will be realistic. Even though the planning horizon for transit may be 20 years or more, and the planning horizon for a development project may be only two or three years, design and buildout for the development project should anticipate the eventual transit facility so that when both are in place they work together.

4. GET THE PARKING RIGHT

As Goldilocks might say, parking around transit must be "not too much, not too little, but just right." Too much parking makes the area less pedestrian friendly and wastes space that could be used for the types of development that increase ridership. Too little parking—or the perception that there is too little parking—can undermine the economic viability of projects built to take advantage of transit, making leasing or sales difficult. Insufficient parking at the station itself can force transit patrons to park in the surrounding neighborhoods, creating problems for nearby residents and businesses.

Parking is a big factor in determining the layout of the station area. How a transit station is connected with, or separated from, the surrounding community will largely determine the station's footprint and parking requirements. Terminal stations often serve as the primary location for parking lots, as discussed in Chapter Six. At closer-in stations, a greater share of transit riders arrive on foot, by bus, or by bicycle. The transit agency must find the balance between providing parking and allocating sufficient adjacent land for the types of development that will generate riders who will walk to the station.

Structured parking at Mockingbird Station, a 600,000-square-foot transit village in Dallas, Texas, is wrapped by retail and architecturally integrated into the community.

The focus on parking in the transit district extends to meeting the needs of surrounding land uses. Flexible parking standards provide some latitude in providing the optimal number of parking spaces. Of the many techniques available for reducing the impact of parking, the four principal ones are as follows:

• *Move It.* Although it is common practice to locate parking immediately adjacent to the station, broader community goals are best served when parking is moved away from the platform. The land nearest the station is the best land for development, so using it for parking means a lost opportunity. Placing parking

a five- to seven-minute walk from the station opens prime real estate for development.

• *Share It.* Sharing the parking among patrons who make use of it at different times of the day or week is an excellent way to minimize the amount of space devoted to parking. The San Diego transit system, for example, shares one of its commuter lots with a multiplex theater. Transit riders use the parking on weekdays, and movie patrons use it on evenings and weekends. Shared parking can be operated privately or by a local parking authority. Parking fees offer an opportunity for additional revenue.

• *Deck It.* Structured parking is expensive. Parking industry estimates for 2004 suggest that construction can run $15,000 per space excluding land costs, compared to about $3,000 for surface parking. For transit agencies, the option of charging for parking tends to be controversial because fees are perceived as a deterrent to riders. But parking fees may be essential to finance needed facilities.

• *Wrap It.* Creative designers can wrap a parking structure with retail and service shops, restaurants, and residences. This mixed-use approach makes the parking structure more attractive as an urban place and adds interest to the walk to the transit station. It also creates a built-in clientele for the businesses.

Under Federal Transit Administration regulations for joint development, transit agencies may sell off surface-parking lots without having to pay back the federal treasury (which typically covered 80 percent of the cost of building parking for rail systems), as long as the lots are transformed into transit-supportive developments. In some markets, such as the Washington, D.C., and San Francisco Bay regions, land values are high enough to make it economically feasible to replace surface parking with decked parking, freeing up half or more of the original parking lot for infill urban development. In growing markets, starting out with surface parking can be considered a form of land banking. See "Targeting a Transit Station in San Jose" sidebar in Chapter Five for an example of residential development on a portion of a transit agency's surface parking lot.

5. BUILD A PLACE, NOT A PROJECT

A major new transit station in a community should bring more than the trains. It represents an opportunity not only for the development of a project at the station, but for the development of a full-fledged transit-centered place, with all the attendant economic and cultural benefits.

Although transit agencies often feel that their responsibility ends at the fare gates, the creation of a genuinely transit-centered community requires attention to the scale and design of surrounding development. It is essential to engage all the principals (the transit agency, the local government, the citizens, and the participating developers), to employ highly skilled and experienced designers, and to use design principles that support the creation of a genuine sense of place, among which are the following:

Locating a new transit station in a community should be an opportunity to enhance the quality of the total place, such as the Santana Row development in San Jose.

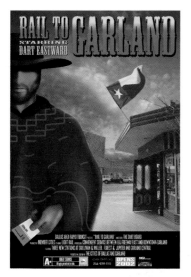

• Design and position the station to foster the creation of an activity center that surrounds the station on all sides.

• Ensure that the design of the station is of high quality and reflects the character of the surrounding community.

• Include engaging public spaces, attractive street furniture, and public art. Public space is important in the creation of place; among other functions, it allows for events such as concerts, markets, exhibits, and celebrations—events that bring people and vitality to the area and stimulate economic activity.

• Promote pedestrian connections by creating compact blocks, pleasant walkways, and comfortable, well-marked, and continuous streetfront experiences. An appealing pedestrian environment strengthens the sense of place and supports retail spending.

• Create attractive landmarks and gateways to the development.

• Incorporate a variety of residential uses to ensure round-the-clock activity.

Traffic standards designed to limit density and congestion should not be applied in transit districts that could benefit from higher density. Typical suburban standards for parking and road access are inappropriate for development around transit and can undermine the transit district's pedestrian orientation and sense of place. Local governments should apply more appropriate standards that can preserve pedestrian amenities and enhance place-making opportunities.

The goals and benefits of compact, transit-oriented development should be reflected in the impact fees applied to transit-oriented development projects. For example, fee schedules could be set on a sliding scale that allows offsets for development within walking distance of a train station or for mixed-use development.

6. MAKE RETAIL DEVELOPMENT MARKET-DRIVEN, NOT TRANSIT-DRIVEN

Although the retail component of development around transit may be viewed as a generator of excitement, it cannot be the justification for the development. The most important considerations for retail development are location, market, and design; in most mar-

Patterned after other transit-served neighborhoods like Boston's Back Bay and New York City's upper east side, Denver's Commons neighborhood is a 21-square-block district of homes, businesses, shops, and entertainment venues adjacent to the Lower Downtown historic district.

Design Workshop

kets, proximity to transit is not a prime consideration. Transit access can strengthen the retail market, but the market must be viable without the transit component. Retail is the land use that is least likely to succeed where it lacks strong market support. Retail follows rooftops and cannot be expected to drive development around transit.

Planning for the area surrounding a transit station must keep in mind retail market realities; shoppers will travel only a certain distance to patronize particular kinds of stores. High-density office or residential uses cannot be counted upon to support a large retail component. If there is an existing market for retail, the development of the retail component first, followed by the development of the residential or office component, can help reinforce the retail demand.

Public agencies must resist the temptation to require retail as part of a transit district project in the absence of adequate market support. If stores remain dark and businesses fail, the whole transit village will suffer the stigma of failure. Far better to have a few busy, successful stores than many dark and empty ones.

7. MIX USES, BUT NOT NECESSARILY IN THE SAME PLACE

A good mix of uses attracts an assortment of people going about their business at many hours of the day. But the creation of an attractive, vibrant community does not require that uses be mixed on the same site, or even at each station. Integrated mixed-use projects are difficult to finance and complex to build.

The Pepsi Center and Waterside Lofts along the C Line in Denver.

Mixing It Up on the C Line

End of the C Line at Union Station.

The light-rail C Line in Denver offers an excellent example of mixing uses along a transit corridor. Starting at Mineral Station, a 300,000-square-foot lifestyle shopping center, Aspen Grove, provides retail choices. Three stops up the line at the Englewood Station is a mixed-use area that includes a library and the Museum of Outdoor Arts. Farther on at the Auraria Station is a 33,000-student college campus shared by the Community College of Denver, the Metropolitan State College of Denver, and the University of Colorado at Denver.

Sports and entertainment uses predominate at the next two stops—first Invesco Field, home of the NFL Denver Broncos, and second the Pepsi Center, home of the NHL Colorado Avalanche and the NBA Denver Nuggets as well as a venue for arena football, professional lacrosse, and concerts. An amusement park, Six Flags Elitch's, is located adjacent to the Pepsi Center. The line ends at Denver's Union Station near the LoDo district and Coors Field, home of the Colorado Rockies baseball team.

This linear mix of uses facilitates bidirectional and off-peak travel on the C Line. Events held at Invesco Field, the Pepsi Center, and Coors Field account for a significant percentage of the off-peak use of the C Line.

A transit corridor can successfully integrate a number of activity nodes devoted to different land uses, particularly when they are close together, easily accessible, and mutually supportive. It is possible, for example, for people to live near one station, work near another, and shop near a third—with transit making the connections convenient. The accessibility of a mix of uses along the corridor will render the corridor itself attractive as a community. And the diverse kinds of trips generated by the activity nodes can help smooth out the typical peak-demand patterns that are common to transit.

Retail and entertainment uses that encourage transit trips to downtown at lunchtime, after work, or on weekends help take advantage of excess transit capacity at those times. Similarly, locating jobs at suburban stations creates demand for reverse commuting. Other uses that foster two-way travel include schools and universities, airports, hospitals, and destination retail.

8. MAKE BUSES A GREAT IDEA

The bus is the mode of choice for most transit users. Buses carry the most transit passengers in all major regional markets except Atlanta, Boston, New York, and Washington. In many metropolitan areas, they represent the only transit choice. But bus transit generally offers no frills, and buses are often perceived as crowded, dirty, and bad smelling. How can buses be made more appealing to businesses, developers, and potential riders? The answer can be found in the vehicles themselves, the quality of service, the attractiveness of bus stops, and, finally, in the characteristics of fellow riders.

While rail transit is often associated with white-collar commuters, bus transit is often associated with poor people, students, and others with few transportation choices. If buses are to generate development in transit corridors, they need to serve a strong cross section of the community—including middle-class riders. Overall service improvements are needed to attract middle-class riders. Success in diversifying the bus-rider market can encourage developers to build around bus stops.

Buses need to appeal to middle-class riders, such as this couple who left behind their car for a night on the town in Reno, Nevada.

Boulder, Colorado, has implemented a successful transit system using buses designed to fit within the local context.

Metro Magazine

Metro Rapid, a high-speed bus rapid transit system, connects Santa Monica with downtown Los Angeles.

To diversify and expand ridership, buses need to be attractive, clean, fast, and fun. Boulder's Community Transit Network, for example, strives to design services from the ground up to meet customer needs. Its sleek, brightly painted buses are appealing and easy to use. Bus routes are named the Hop, Skip, Jump, Leap, Bound, Dash, and Stampede. Powered by natural gas, the vehicles appeal to people concerned about the environment.

Buses should offer regular, reliable, and convenient service. Bus stops should be attractive, comfortable, and sheltering in bad weather. They should have clearly posted schedules and maps showing both individual and system routes that enable passengers to determine without difficulty how to get where they want to go.

Luxury apartments at the Mission Valley East station in San Diego.

Denver's 16th Street Transit Mall has helped transform a decaying downtown street into a vibrant, modern shopping and entertainment center. The one-mile-long pedestrian and transit mall provides a car-free environment with transit centers at either end, offering express and regional bus service as well as connections to the region's light-rail system. An extension of the mall built in 2001 links to Union Station, which is in the process of becoming a major multimodal transportation center.

Buses run about once a minute during peak hours and every few minutes the rest of the day, giving downtown workers, residents, and visitors convenient access to many of the city's attractions, including Tabor Center, the Denver Pavilions shopping center, and Coors Field. The mall shuttle carries 59,000 passengers on an average weekday, more than most new light-rail systems.

Developers typically fail to think of bus stops as potential hubs for development. In many transit corridors, however, bus service supports downtown businesses and higher-density residential neighborhoods. Zoning that allowed higher densities and re-

McLarand Vasquez Emsiek & Partners, Inc.

Townhouses in the Uptown District of San Diego.

quired less parking along well-served bus corridors could create opportunities for development that supports transit, even if developers did not consider such development transit-oriented. Examples of development at suburban bus terminals in Redmond, Washington, and Eden Prairie, Minnesota, are discussed in Chapter Five. Upgrading the image of bus transit can expand such opportunities.

9. ENCOURAGE EVERY PRICE POINT TO LIVE AROUND TRANSIT

Some of the more successful new transit cities have discovered what Boston, New York, and Washington have known for years: Just as people from every part of the economic spectrum ride transit, people from

every part of the economic spectrum like to live near transit. After all, some of the toniest neighborhoods developed at the dawn of the 20th century—including Chevy Chase, Maryland, and Philadelphia's suburban Main Line—were linked to transit. Urban living has undergone a resurgence in recent years, and the quest for diversity is one of the drivers of that resurgence.

Even many traditionally suburban, auto-oriented regions like Atlanta and Dallas have discovered that important market segments are seeking out residential locations characterized by a mix of incomes; such cities are expanding their transit systems to address these market needs. Young workers often choose to live in urban neighborhoods, even if their jobs are in the suburbs. Living near transit can satisfy a desire for community, independence, opportunity, and con-

---

A Hot Housing Market in San Diego

The San Diego Trolley, one of the most successful new transit projects in the United States, has become a magnet for new housing across a range of price points. In the downtown alone, where regional trolley, bus, and commuter-rail lines converge, a housing construction boom is expected to add 10,000 units by 2008. Affordable housing has been developed both in downtown and in outlying transit districts.

Planning is underway for City Heights Urban Village, a major mixed-use urban redevelopment north of downtown to be accompanied by a new high-quality, rubber-tired transit service, the Transit First Showcase Project, that will offer the speed, comfort, and amenities of a trolley connection to downtown San Diego. The project is being developed by a partnership of the city of San Diego, the San Diego Redevelopment Agency, the San Diego Foundation, CityLink Investment Corp., and Price Charities. It will include civic, employment, retail, and education uses, as well as affordable housing, a library, and a park.

The trolley station area at San Diego State University.

**BellSouth's Lind-
bergh project in
Atlanta, Georgia.**

• people who are tired of fighting traffic and are willing to give up their second car;

• people within a wide range of ages who are looking for opportunities to move up or down in housing size, depending on where they are in their lives; and

• seniors seeking an independent lifestyle and reduced dependence on the automobile.

Preserving and expanding affordable housing in newly trendy neighborhoods is a special concern for development around transit, because lower-income people often represent the core of transit ridership. Local agencies should link transit funding with the provision of affordable housing so that transit and housing can reinforce each other.

10. ENGAGE CORPORATE ATTENTION

Major employers can play an influential role in stimulating development around transit. If the executives in charge of location decisions see transit as a slow and unreliable means of getting to work, they will pay scant attention to transit access. If, however, they view transit access as a valuable tool for recruiting scarce talent, they will include "good transit

venience. Creating new communities around intown transit development offers the opportunity to put forward a mix of upscale, market, and assisted housing.

It is important for developers and their market consultants to know the demographic profiles of people who are seeking to live close to transit. They include

Workplace Culture: What's Out and What's In	
Out	**In**
Suburban/exurban campus locations	Locations close to transit
Corporate campuses	Mixed-use developments
Kiss-and-ride	Live, work, play, and ride
Location near the chief executive's home	Location convenient for workers
Free parking	Transit passes
Driving to lunch	Walking to lunch
Errands on the way home	Errands at lunchtime
Commuting car	Fuel-efficient station car
Quality of the workplace	Quality of life

access" on their checklists of considerations for site selection. An increasing number of companies are focusing on transit access for workers, even if management does not plan to use it. Some companies that had moved to remote sites accessible only by car found it so difficult to recruit workers that they have relocated again to closer-in sites.

Asked to name the most serious impediment to business in the metropolitan area, corporate leaders in Atlanta overwhelmingly responded: "traffic congestion." The BellSouth Corporation is reacting to the congestion problem by consolidating its suburban offices into three central locations accessible from the MARTA rapid-rail system. When the company's consolidation plan is completed, almost 15,000 BellSouth employees will be able to access their jobs by transit, and 30 percent are expected to use transit for commuting.